Muslim Societies
in African History

Examining a series of processes (e.g., islamization, arabization, and african-ization) and case studies from North, West, and East Africa, this book gives snapshots of Muslim societies in Africa over the past 1,000+ years. In contrast to traditions that suggest that Africa is not Muslim or that Islam did not take root in Africa, author David Robinson shows the complex struggles of Mus-lims in the Muslim state of Morocco and in the Hausaland region of Nigeria. He portrays the ways in which Islam was practiced in the "pagan" societies of Ashanti (Ghana) and Buganda (Uganda) and in the ostensibly Christian state of Ethiopia – beginning with the first emigration of Muslims from Mecca in 615 C.E., well before the foundational *hijra* to Medina in 622. He concludes with chapters on the Mahdi and Khalifa of the Sudan and the Murid Sufi movement that originated in Senegal. Finally, Robinson offers reflections in the wake of the events of September 11, 2001. The Further Reading sections suggest how undergraduate readers may follow up on the themes of this vol-ume, and illustrations and maps make the processes and case studies concrete.

David Robinson has conducted research on Islamic and francophone West Africa for thirty years, at Yale University, and since 1978 at Michigan State University, where he was named University Distinguished Professor of His-tory in 1992. His notable books include *The Holy War of Umar Tal* (Oxford University Press, 1985) and *Paths of Accommodation: Muslim Societies and French Colonial Authorities in Senegal and Mauritania, 1880 to 1920* (Ohio Uni-versity Press and James Currey, 2000).

New Approaches to African History

Series Editor
Martin Klein, *University of Toronto*

New Approaches to African History is designed to introduce students to current findings and new ideas in African history. Although each book treats a particular case, and is able to stand alone, the format allows the studies to be used as modules in general courses on African history and world history. The cases represent a wide range of topics. Each volume summarizes the state of knowledge on a particular subject for a student who is new to the field. However, the aim is not simply to present reviews of the literature, it is also to introduce debates on historiographical or substantive issues and may argue for particular points of view. The aim of the series is to stimulate debate, to challenge students and general readers. The series is not committed to any particular school of thought.

Other books in the series:

Africa Since 1940, by Frederick Cooper

Muslim Societies
in African History

David Robinson
Michigan State University

CAMBRIDGE UNIVERSITY PRESS
Cambridge, New York, Melbourne, Madrid, Cape Town,
Singapore, São Paulo, Delhi, Tokyo, Mexico City

Cambridge University Press
32 Avenue of the Americas, New York, NY 10013-2473, USA

www.cambridge.org
Information on this title: www.cambridge.org/9780521533669

First published 2004
9th printing 2011

A catalog record for this publication is available from the British Library.

Library of Congress Cataloging in Publication Data

Robinson, David, 1938–
Muslim societies in African history / David Robinson.
   p. cm. – (New approaches to African history.)
Includes bibliographical references (p.) and index.
ISBN 0-521-82627-6 – ISBN 0-521-53366-X (pbk.)
1. Islam – Africa – History. 2. Muslims – Africa – History.
I. Title. II. Series.
BP64.A1R63 2004   2003055137

ISBN 978-0-521-82627-3 Hardback
ISBN 978-0-521-53366-9 Paperback

For Rudite and Dudleigh

Acknowledgments

This book is the result of a request by Martin Klein to deal with the subject of Islam in Africa for college undergraduates. He has made it a challenge and a pleasure all along the way. I hope to say something old and something new, or something known in a new way. The process has made me think differently about materials that I research and teach. I benefited from working on an older project organized by Nehemia Levtzion and Randall Pouwels, which they edited as *A History of Islam in Africa* (Ohio University Press, 2000). Nehemia was a Visiting Hannah Professor at Michigan State at the time the book came out. During one of our sessions, he said that they should perhaps have entitled their book *Muslim Societies in African History*. I was already thinking along these lines at the time and had adopted that title in my conversations with Martin. It represents a useful and dynamic way to understand the history of a faith and its practitioners in the enormous confines of the African continent.

I profited from a number of critiques of the initial prospectus and a variety of drafts. I thank, in addition to Martin, the following friends and colleagues: Kevin Brown, Tim Carmichael, Mamadou Diouf, Alan Fisher, Bill Freund, Alaine Hutson, my deeply missed colleague Harold Marcus, Jonathan and Marie Miran, Ahmed Sikainga, Ray Silverman, Charles Stewart, Ehud Toledano, and Brian Yates. I owe special thanks to Tim's students at a Smith College Seminar in the winter of 2003: Autumn Barr, Sasha Berkoff, Emmi Felker-Quinn, Jessica Keating, Jessica Quinn, Maya Ramos, and Kavita Venkatesan, for taking the time to read through the draft and give me the benefit of their reactions. Ray Silverman has guided me through the process of selecting illustrations and made excellent suggestions. Suzanne Miers, Al and Polly Roberts, Doran Ross, and the Fowler Museum of Cultural History at UCLA have kindly granted me permission to use images from their collections. I also express my gratitude to Ellen White of the MSU Geography Department for the preparation of the maps and to Alia Winters of the press for her sustained interest in seeing the book to publication.

DAVID ROBINSON
East Lansing, Michigan
March 2003

Contents

Maps and Figures

Maps

Figures

Introduction

Europeans and North Americans have had difficulty understanding Islam, even greater difficulty understanding Muslim societies and individual Muslims, and even more comprehending Muslim societies in Africa and in African history. The task is just as great for non-Western people educated in Western traditions, including many Muslims themselves. And all of these difficulties are compounded in light of the events of September 11, 2001, their revelations and repercussions.

The difficulties may seem ironic in the light of the close relationship between Islam and the Judeo-Christian tradition, on which so much of European and world history is built. It would not be inappropriate to call that tradition by the cumbersome name of Judeo-Christian-Islamic, or Abrahamic, the name I adopt in this book. Islam honors Abraham (Ibrahim), the other prophetic figures of the Old Testament, and Jesus, and it envisions Muhammad as the last of a long tradition. Islam's emphasis on a transcendent and moral God owes much to these precedents. Jewish and Christian communities were present in Mecca and the other parts of the Arabian peninsula when Muhammad was growing up. Proximity and common tradition have encouraged understanding, but they have also led to conflict.

Conflict constitutes the first part of my answer to the difficulties of comprehension, or, to put it more usefully, the conflicts among Muslim, Christian, and Jewish societies and within each community of faith. The conflicts began in the seventh century C.E., when Muslim armies conquered a great deal of the Mediterranean world that Europe considered its original cultural home. On the western side the armies took the Iberian peninsula, moved across the Pyrenees into the area we call France, and laid the foundations for the Andalusian or Spanish Muslim culture, which flourished for several centuries.

Muslims pressed into Europe from two other directions. Forces based in what we could call Tunisia occupied Sicily and parts of the southern Italian peninsula. The third advance was from the southeast against the Byzantine Empire, culminating after many centuries in the capture of Constantinople in 1453. This advance was led by the Ottoman Turks and resulted in the creation of the Ottoman Empire, about which I have much to say throughout the book.

Western textbooks have often portrayed these three military and cultural offensives as invasions – and threats to European culture. This portrayal comes in large part from the confrontations we call the Crusades. Beginning in the late eleventh century, Europeans, encouraged by the Pope and the rulers of the Western European courts, organized expeditions to the Middle East. Their goal was to "recover" the Holy Lands of the Old and New Testaments, particularly Jerusalem, from the Arab and Turkish Muslims who dominated those areas. The European armies used their religious motivations to amass material wealth, achieve military distinction, and subject not only Muslims but also Eastern Orthodox Christians to the control of the "Franks," as the conquerors were known. All of this was done in the name of faith. The Western Christians also aroused a strong Muslim resistance, expressed most brilliantly by Saladin, lionized for his liberation of Jerusalem from Frankish control in the late twelfth century.

The enduring legacy of the Crusades was hostility and stereotype. For many Europeans Muhammad became an imposter and Islam a heresy. Muslims were the enemy. When the courts of Castile and Aragon began to push south in the eleventh century to create modern Spain, they mimicked the language of the Crusades by calling their campaign a "reconquest" for Christianity. They expelled Muslims and Jews, and these groups fled to the shores of North Africa and the Ottoman Empire. The Spanish and Portuguese sustained the crusader mentality as they expanded around the globe in the fifteenth and sixteenth centuries. The court of Muscovite Russia adopted the same attitude as it expanded by land into Muslim societies at the same time. Most Europeans shared the notion that Islam was a threat and distortion of the Judeo-Christian tradition.

Muslims were not immune to these stereotypes. They saw the Crusades and the European expansion of the past 500 years as something

achieved at their expense. They took pleasure not only in Saladin's victory but also in the capture of Constantinople and the emergence of the
Ottoman Empire as a counter to Western hegemony. Napoleon's brief
invasion of Egypt 200 years ago insulted their pride just as it revealed
their weaknesses – military and cultural. The nineteenth century witnessed an intensification of the European presence, ending in Western
occupation of most of the "lands of Islam." Much of the anger that
some Muslims express at the West has its origins in that expansion and
domination.

The second part of the answer to my original question is this Western domination in the form of colonial rule, technological superiority, and other forms of hegemony over the "lands of Islam." After
World War I, the Western European powers and Russia controlled
almost all of the Muslim world with the exceptions of Turkey, Iran,
Afghanistan, and parts of China, the Arabian peninsula, and Ethiopia.
The British, French, Russians, Dutch, Italians, and Spanish began
to portray themselves as "Muslim powers," which meant imperial authorities with Muslim subjects. The colonial governments accepted the
Muslim identity of those subjects, but they treated them with condescension and created parallel institutions of law, education, and commerce for non-Muslims or resident Europeans. The memory of the
condescension outlasted colonial rule and fuels the anger so strikingly
expressed on September 11, 2001.

The final part of the answer has to do with Africa. From the perspective of the West and the Mediterranean, Africa is "black" and
coincides with the part of the continent below the Sahara Desert –
Sub-Saharan Africa. Outside of the continent most scholars, students,
and otherwise-informed people do not think of Africa and Africans,
under these definitions, as being Muslim or, if Muslim, as only recently
converted to the faith, not very orthodox, and not very important to
the history of Islam.

All of these misconceptions are still widely held, often in very prestigious places. Samuel Huntington, the noted social scientist at Harvard, serves as a telling example of the reflexive and unreflected ways
in which many well-educated Western-educated people think. In *The
Clash of Civilizations and the Remaking of the World Order*, published in
1996, he sees Africa as a set of weaker civilizations. At the same time
he sees "the Islamic tradition" as powerful, assertive, and potentially
dangerous to the West. In the wake of the Cold War, he writes that
"the overwhelming majority of fault line conflicts . . . have taken place

along the boundary looping across Eurasia and Africa that separates Muslims from non-Muslims." Although he might not ascribe the destruction of the World Trade Center towers to mainstream Muslims, he and many influential writers and officials are predisposed to think of Islam as oppositional and Africa as irrelevant.

In this book I hope to challenge these assumptions. Islam is almost 1,400 years old. It is "ancient" in Sub-Saharan as well as North Africa. It has been expressed in all sorts of forms. Most of its African practitioners have always thought of themselves as pious and correct in their practice. They have fashioned "orthodoxies" of their own. Their stories are critical to an understanding of the variety as well as the aspiration for unity of the Islamic world and serve as an antidote to many of the interpretations of September 11. They constitute cultural traditions that have much in common with, as well as much that is distinct from, the trajectories of Western societies. As a generally educated person prepared to function in the twenty-first century, you should understand this.

More than one billion people across the whole world call themselves Muslim. Islam has become the second most important religion, in terms of numbers, in Europe and the United States. Those numbers include not just persons who have migrated from Africa, the Middle East, and Asia and their descendants, but also people of Western origin. In Africa the best estimates show that Muslims are as numerous as Christians. Roughly half of the continent is Muslim, and half of those express their faith in languages other than Arabic. African Muslims as a whole constitute close to 25 percent of the world's Islamic population. In this book I write a great deal about the variety and "pluralism" of Islamic practice in Africa. I do not express that in the plural form "Islams" because of the aspiration of unity and the common practice that characterizes the faith and the faithful.

The book starts with the beginnings of Islam, with the life of Muhammad and the vision God transmitted through him, and then the institutions that he and his successors created in the early generations of the new religion. I move then to general explorations of Muslim societies in Africa in four chapters. In Chapters 3 and 4 I am interested in how Islam spreads and how Africans make it their own. Chapter 5 looks at the relations of Muslim societies and the slave trades that have afflicted Africa, whereas Chapter 6 examines how Westerners have framed views of both Islam and Africa. I then examine two of the older "nations" of Africa, Morocco and Ethiopia, and how Muslims fared in both places. One was an ostensibly Muslim state and society, the other an ostensibly Christian one. After that I move to two chapters set in the precolonial period in Sub-Saharan Africa (precolonial means before the late nineteenth century). Finally I examine three situations of colonial rule by Europeans and others, and forms of resistance to it, before bringing the strands together in a conclusion.

Further Reading

As I indicated earlier, it is rare to find books that treat Africa and Islam or their histories together. The most complete history of Muslim societies is Ira Lapidus' *A History of Islamic Societies* (Cambridge University Press, 1988). It competes with works such as Marshall Hodgson's *The Venture of Islam* (three volumes, University of Chicago Press, 1974), which gives more attention to religious and literature questions, and the *Cambridge History of Islam* (several volumes). A shorter more synthetic recent account is Karen Armstrong's *Islam* (Random House, Modern Library Chronicles, 2000). One can also approach Islam from the standpoint of religious studies. A good example of this is Richard Martin's *Islamic Studies: A History of Religions Approach* (Prentice Hall, 1982, second edition, 1996).

All of these volumes, and other attempts, treat African Islam as something marginal to the "Islamic heartlands." Some decades ago Sub-Saharan Africa would have been ignored altogether; in more recent times it is treated in later chapters of works, alongside other zones such as Indonesia. These zones are peripheral only in the sense that they are far from the places where Islam began. The boldest attempt to treat Africa and Islam together is (editors) Nehemia Levtzion and Randall Pouwels' *The History of Islam in Africa* (Ohio University Press, 2000). The writers in this extensive volume are very competent in their various areas of expertise, give a good picture of the most recent understanding of Muslim societies, mainly in Sub-Saharan Africa, and provide up-to-date bibliographies. Ken Harrow has edited two very useful volumes on Islamic themes in African literature: *Faces of Islam in African Literature* (Heinemann and James Currey, 1991) and *The Marabout and the Muse* (Heinemann and James Currey, 1996).

For the history of Africa see Philip Curtin, Steven Feierman, Leonard Thompson, and Jan Vansina's *African History: From Earliest Times to Independence* (Longman, 1978, second edition, 1995) and John Iliffe's *Africans: The History of a Continent* (Cambridge University Press, 1995). These volumes make a concerted effort to include North Africa, although both concentrate on Sub-Saharan portions of the continent.

You can pursue a wide range of interests through several encyclopedias. *The Encyclopedia of Islam* (Brill), revised beginning in 1960, is now complete and available in paper (nine volumes) and on CD-ROM. *The Oxford Encyclopedia of the Modern Islamic World* [John Esposito (ed.), Oxford University Press, 1995] is available in four volumes. *The Encyclopedia of Africa South of the Sahara* [John Middleton (ed.), Charles Scribner's Sons, 1997] is also available in four volumes. *The Encyclopedia of Religion* [sixteen volumes, Mircea Eliade (ed.), Macmillan, 1987] deals extensively with Islam, Islam in Africa, and African religions.

I

The Historical and
Institutional Background

CHAPTER 1

Muhammad and the Birth of Islam

There are several ways to understand Islam and its emergence and development. In this book I employ two of those ways: an institutional approach and a historical approach. Chapter 2 deals with the institutional perspective, whereas this chapter features the key human figure in the emergence of the faith, Muhammad, and the context in which that faith emerged. I find it useful to understand the doctrine in light of the history to see how the beliefs and practices of Islam came to be.

The Setting of Muhammad's Life

Muhammad lived from 570 until 632 C.E. He did not become a public figure until relatively late in his life, much later than Jesus of Nazareth. His arena of activity was an area called the Hijaz, the western side of the Arabian peninsula (Saudi Arabia today) just across the Red Sea from Africa. The Hijaz had some connections to the two dominant powers of the day: the Byzantine or East Roman Empire, controlling the eastern Mediterranean, and the Sasanian Empire, centered in Iran. The Hijaz was off to the south, a periphery in relation to both of these states. In religious terms it was very diverse. It contained Jewish, Christian, and other monotheistic communities as well as practitioners of local cults – those whom Muslims later would call "pagans." Muhammad came to associate himself with the monotheistic orientation, but he did not emerge from a particular tradition in the way that one could say that Jesus was rooted in, and then went beyond, Jewish practice.

Most of the people in the Hijaz were Bedouin, nomads living in the desert. They were organized in clan or kinship groups with relatively little difference in wealth or status. Men dominated the public life of these groups, raised the camels on which they depended, and engaged in raids and competition for the key resources – the mounts, the oases, and trade routes. The clans were often in conflict, resolved temporarily when one group asserted its dominance, usually without great loss of life.

Sometimes the nomadic clans resolved their disputes through mediators, and a number of these were found in and around the religious shrines in the leading urban center of the Hijaz, Mecca. Mecca and the Hijaz were pluralistic in their religious practice; Muhammad later pinned the label of polytheism on them. The city was at the midway point for caravans that plied the routes between the Mediterranean and Yemen. It offered a major market, refreshment station, mediation services, and pilgrimage organized around the Kaba, a huge black stone in the middle of the city. Its merchant community was deeply engaged in the trade along the western side of the Arabian peninsula and promoted the town's shrines and services, like a chamber of commerce. A number of merchant families grew quite wealthy. Some of them belonged to the Quraysh clan into which Muhammad was born.

Muhammad thus grew up in two overlapping societies. One was nomadic, accustomed to the vast desert environment, living in tents, constantly moving, and caring for and raising camels. Their fundamental problem, at least from the later Islamic perspective, was division. The other environment was urban, organized around trade, festivals, and the reception of caravans guided and protected by the nomadic clans. Their fundamental problem was class division, in particular the exploitation of the poor by the wealthy.

Muhammad was not a particularly prominent member of the Quraysh. He became more successful as a merchant under the sponsorship of an older woman, Khadija, who had commercial experience and capital. She invested these resources in her young protegé and permitted him to ply the routes between the Mediterranean markets and Yemen. She saw the great sensitivity and ability of her charge, married him, and gave him four daughters, including Fatima (the only child who had surviving children of her own). Khadija also counseled him at a very critical juncture in his life. When he was in his late thirties he began to go each year to a mountainous area outside of Mecca for meditation and fasting. During these periods he received revelations from

God related to the problems of division and social justice mentioned earlier. Khadija confirmed the validity of his revelations. She encouraged him to develop a new career as a preacher and leader of reform.

This public career began in 610 C.E., when Muhammad was 40 years old. Muhammad probably did not write Arabic, which was mainly a spoken language in those days, but he was an eloquent preacher. He often recited poetry as beautiful as any of the local bards, and he presented it as something he had received from God. A small community of followers gathered around him and constituted the first community of *Islam*, which means "submission." Their submission was not to Muhammad but to God, and they expressed that in the prostration of prayer, which became the fundamental symbol of the new community. Public prayer is still the most visible symbol of Muslims across the world today – whether it is performed out of doors or in the mosque, which is simply a place of prayer.

Muhammad was a private, sensitive individual, but as he gained confidence about his mission of promoting unity and social justice he took his message into the streets and assemblies of Mecca. In a few short years he won more followers and even more opposition, often from his kinsmen. They were not prepared to accept a critique of their exploitation of the nomadic clans and the poor, a reduction of the multiple shrines that attracted pilgrims to the city, and the affirmation of a transcendent God who called for submission. By 615 C.E. some Meccans were threatening his community. Muhammad sent some disciples across the Red Sea to Aksum, a leading state in the region that offered them protection. Aksum had adopted Christianity as the religion of the court, and its king treated the refugees as practitioners of the common Abrahamic tradition. We look at Aksum, and the Abyssinia or Ethiopia of which it was part, in Chapter 8.

Expansion and the Early Islamic State

By 620 C.E. the situation in Mecca had become quite dangerous for the new religious leader. His chief protectors, Khadija and his uncle Abu Talib, had passed away. Muhammad began to seek refuge for himself and the rest of his community and started negotiations with the leaders of Yathrib, a town and oasis 200 miles to the north. Within two years he and his people moved to the site, gave it the name of Medina ("city" in Arabic), and called their movement the *hijra*, the emigration. The emigrants from Mecca were the *muhajirun*, and their hosts in Medina were the *ansar*, the companions. The emigrants included two women who would come to wield a great deal of influence. One was Fatima, Muhammad's daughter by Khadija. The other was Aisha, who became his favorite wife. Together with Khadija, they have had enormous influence on Muslim women over the centuries.

In Medina Muhammad became the leader of the community, the *umma*, and the head of a fledgling state. He and his followers committed their lives to the survival of their vision of a single, transcendent God who sought unity and justice for His people. They began to work out the basic obligations of the Muslim faithful, something I discuss in the next chapter, and had their first experience in what might be called "Islamic" government.

They also began to think in terms of a new calendar. Muhammad and the early Muslims were so persuaded of their mission that they saw themselves as living in a "time of Islam." Over the next decades this became the Islamic calendar, the Anno Hegira, in which the *hijra* was year one; what we call 622 C.E. became 1 A.H. The Arabs had a lunar calendar, like the Jews and other groups in the Middle East. Because of this the length of the Islamic year is about ten days shorter than the solar or Gregorian calendar that has become standard in the West and most of the world. This means that at the beginning of the twenty-first century Muslims are living in the 1420s A.H.

The early Muslims faced an awesome task: how to secure the loyalty of the nomadic clans, persuade them of the validity of the new vision, and use them to coerce a recalcitrant Mecca. Muhammad made temporary alliances with groups in the central Hijaz, including several Jewish clans that he hoped – incorrectly, as it turned out – would share the new faith. With the help of his allies and the commitment of his community, he was able to win some victories. The most celebrated came at Badr in 624 C.E. against his Meccan foes. By 630 C.E. he was able to persuade the city of his birth to welcome and swear allegiance to him. He transformed the pilgrimage into a fundamental event for the Muslim community and spent the last two years of his life securing the loyalty of the Arab nomads who ranged across the Arabian peninsula.

Muhammad's death two years later (in 632 C.E.) produced consternation among his followers. Everyone agreed that the vision had to be sustained, but not about who should become the leader of the community and how the new faith should be consolidated. The initial competition focused on the successor or *khalifa* (caliph) of Muhammad. Four groups vied for precedence: first, Muhammad's own family; second, those who had followed the Prophet since the early days in Mecca and migrated to Medina (the *muhajirun* or migrants); third, the Medinans (*ansar* or helpers) who had sworn allegiance in 622 C.E.; and finally the Meccans who enlisted at the last hour. Was long, demonstrated loyalty to Muhammad the key value? Was it knowledge of his vision and the emerging Islamic faith? Was kinship or marriage the key ingredient, or was it Meccan sophistication and political savvy? Should it be leadership and charisma or military distinction? These were the questions that were debated – and fought over – in the years after the Prophet's death.

Expansion and Dissension

Most of the qualities of attachment and commitment were expressed in the choices of the four caliphs who ruled over the emerging and expanding world of Islam in the first thirty years after the Prophet's death. Collectively they are known as the "rightly guided" leaders. Their names, along with that of Muhammad (and the variant Ahmad), have become some of the most frequent male names for Muslims over the past 1400 years: Abu Bakr (or Abubacar), Umar, Uthman, and Ali. Abu Bakr was the father of Aisha, Muhammad's "favorite" wife. Umar ruled for ten years from Medina and sent armies into the area from Egypt to Iran at the expense of the Byzantine and Sasanian Empires. Uthman ruled for another ten years and presided over further expansion. By the time Ali took charge in 656 C.E. the new religion and politics controlled a huge territory.

But the Islamic community was about to burst at the seams. Uthman and Ali died violent deaths at the hands of other Arab Muslims. Ali was the cousin and son-in-law of Muhammad and had a strong following among many of the military and civilians. His principal rival was Muawiyya, the son of a Meccan who had joined the community just before the Prophet's death. Muawiyya operated out of Damascus, one of the emerging centers of the movement. Another group rejected both Ali and Muawiyya and became known as the *kharijites*, the "seceders." Aisha, competing army leaders, and companions got involved in the competition. This period, from 656 to 661 C.E., is remembered in Muslim annals as the first *fitna* ("discord") or civil war. *Fitna* has been repeatedly used in Islamic history to refer to a time of trouble.

After 661 C.E. Muawiyya maintained a fragile hold on the new territories from Damascus. His dynasty acquired the title of Umayyad, after the name of his Quraysh ancestor. When he tried to pass the succession to his son, the latent conflicts among the new ruling classes erupted. Ali's son Husayn was killed by Umayyad forces at Karbala in Iraq, while a revolt of an important general in the Hijaz threatened the very birthplace of Islam. This period of the 680s C.E. was called the second civil war. The Umayyads were able to reassert their control, but at great cost.

The Kharijites moved away from the centers of Arab power, and they can be found today on the edges of the main Islamic centers in areas such as Oman at the bottom of the Arabian peninsula or Zanzibar, just off the coast of East Africa, as is discussed in Chapter 3. The Shia or Shiites, "followers" of Ali and then of his son Husayn, were much more numerous. After what they called the "martyrdom" of Karbala in 681 C.E. they participated in the overthrow of the Umayyads in the middle of the eighth century. They did not fare better under the rule of the Abbasids, however, and soon went "underground" by organizing their opposition in secret cells. But they emerged from time to time to take charge of particular regions of the Islamic world. The Fatimids, named after Muhammad's daughter, controlled Egypt in the tenth and eleventh centuries, whereas other Shia have dominated the area of Iran for the past 500 years. Their most prominent recent leader was the Ayatollah Khomeini, known not just for his Shia identity but also for his radical critiques of the practice of power in the world.

The Umayyad and Abbasid Caliphates

The majority of Muslims in the first century of Islam submitted to the Umayyad regime under its caliph in Damascus. They began to take for themselves the name of Sunni, those who followed the *Sunna* or "way" of God and Muhammad, and they conflated Sunni with Islamic orthodoxy. Muslim leaders and scholars began to interpret key passages of the Quran and to collect traditions about the Prophet and in general to strengthen the institutional bases of the new faith (see Chapter 2). They regularized the pilgrimage to the birthplace of Muhammad, locating it in the twelfth month of the lunar calendar; the pilgrimage was often accompanied by a journey to Medina.

The Umayyads also established a third holy city of Islam, Jerusalem, by building the Dome of the Rock, one of the most intensely disputed areas of the Old City today. By this time the tradition that Muhammad had ascended to heaven from the Dome on the wings of Jibril (Gabriel) had developed (see the Swahili version of this in Chapter 3). Since that time Jerusalem has been an important shrine and center of pilgrimage for all three religious communities attached to the Abrahamic heritage. Except for the period of the Crusades (see Chapter 6) and the twentieth century, these distinct but related communities have usually been able to cooperate.

Under the Umayyads the Arab Muslims tended to live separately from the indigenous communities they conquered. Most of their subjects were Christian, Jewish, or Zoroastrian in belief, and the Arabs made no effort to convert them. The processes of *islamization* and *arabization* developed slowly and often separately. Only gradually did the practice of Islam and the preference for the Arabic language spread to the majority population. Only gradually did the separation between Arab and non-Arab diminish. To put it differently, only slowly did people of non-Arab origin become Arab by the adoption of the Arabic language and Islamic culture. Millions more embraced Islam without adopting Arabic, except as a language of worship and learning.

The processes of islamization and arabization were more rapid under the Abbasids, who took their name from another Meccan relative of Muhammad. The Abbasid regime took over in the 750s c.e. and maintained a relatively unified control of the Muslim world for the next 200 years from a new capital, in Baghdad. It was under the Abbasids that the arts and sciences flourished under "royal" – that is to say, "caliphal" – patronage. Muslim, Christian, and Jewish scholars and artists, using the medium of the Arabic language primarily, developed calligraphy, architecture, mathematics, medicine, philosophy, literature, linguistics, and other spheres of knowledge. They took the heritage of ancient civilizations of the Mediterranean and the Middle East, added their own contributions, and created the dominant systems of knowledge of the Middle Ages. Baghdad, the Abbasid capital, was the leading intellectual center in the world in the ninth century.

These early centuries of Islam, the first 300 years, are often known as the Glorious Age. Some Muslims invoke this period as the "reign" of "pure" Islam, usually without recognizing the great diversity, tolerance, and intellectual richness that marked the worlds of Damascus, Baghdad, and other leading capitals. It was during this period that most of the Muslim world was under one ruler, the caliph. It was during this period that most of the institutions that we associate with Islam and that form the burden of the next chapter were developed. In the same period of time Islam spread into Africa, in two directions: to the west, across Egypt, North Africa, and the Sahara; and to the south, down the East African coast. These two "gateways" into the continent are discussed in Chapter 3.

Further Reading

The sources mentioned in the first paragraph of the Further Reading section of the introduction have important sections devoted to Muhammad and the rise of Islam. The *Encyclopedia of Islam* has long and learned articles devoted to Muhammad, Khadija, Fatima, Aisha, and a range of other persons and subjects by the best scholars in the field. For a set of reflections by an Algerian Muslim intellectual about the foundations of the faith and other subjects, see Mohammed Arkoun's *Rethinking Islam: Common Questions, Uncommon Answers* (Westview Press, 1994).

For a more traditional Muslim account of Muhammad's life, see Ibn Hisham's *The Life of Muhammad* (translated from the Arabic by A. Guillaume; Lahore, Pakistan, 1955). For accounts by a leading Western authority with an intimate knowledge of the Arabic materials, see W. Montgomery Watt's *Muhammad at Mecca* (Oxford, The Clarendon Press, 1953) and *Muhammad at Medina* (Oxford, The Clarendon Press, 1956). For a focus on the relations of Islam to Jewish and Christian traditions, see Bernard Lewis, *The Jews of Islam* (Princeton University Press, 1984), and Peter Brown's *The Rise of Western Christendom: Triumph and Diversity, AD 200–1000* (Blackwell, 1996).

An excellent view of the transformation of Bedouin tribes into the early caliphate is Fred Donner's *The Early Islamic Conquests* (Princeton University Press, 1981). For the Umayyad and Abbasid caliphates, in addition to the general histories, see M. Shaban's *Islamic History I* (Cambridge University Press, 1971) and *The Abbasid Revolution* (Cambridge University Press, 1981).

CHAPTER 2

The Basic Institutions of Islam

The leaders of the new Islamic community worked to create justice, unite the Bedouin, and conquer new lands. They also set about to establish the meaning of the faith and its implications for individuals and society. This was not an easy process, especially after Arabs and Islam spread beyond the Arabian peninsula. But slowly, from Medina, Damascus, Baghdad, and other cities, they constructed the essentials of the faith and the history of its emergence. Cities have been the laboratories of islamization throughout the history of the faith. Muhammad began his career at Mecca and was determined to assert his domination over the key city of the Hijaz before his death. Since then cities have been critical to the fortunes of the faith, whether as political capitals, markets, or centers of institutional development.

The first task of the new Muslim community was to develop a scripture. More quickly than the early Christians, they established the text of the Quran, within the first generation after the Prophet's death. The participants were the close associates of Muhammad, working under the direction of Caliph Uthman. A second sequence, working out rights and responsibilities that would govern Muslim conduct, took about two centuries; its product was Islamic law or Sharia. The main laboratories for this development were schools of "lawyers" who lived in the key cities and worked under the patronage of the ruling classes.

These processes of "constructing" Islam are just as important as the political and military narrative that dominated Chapter 1. It was this "constructed" Islam – a canonical scripture, a body of law, as well as a history of the founding – that became the norm that Muslims would carry, spread, and adapt in the different parts of Africa over the past millennium. The same thing happened in various parts of Asia. One can find similar processes in the elaboration of Christianity or other religions that have survived over long periods of time.

The Processes

The first task of construction was to establish the basic scripture in a language that had been primarily oral. The Quran, which means "recitation," is understood to be the revelation of God to Muhammad through the angel Jibril (Gabriel) in Arabic. It began as statements by the Prophet to his scribes. The third caliph, Uthman, mobilized the early Muslims to collect the statements, create the sequence of chapters, and establish a final version that has been authoritative for Muslims ever since. The effect of writing down and creating a scripture sped the development of Arabic as a written language as well as schools and books for the teaching of the Arabic humanities.

The verses and chapters of the Quran exhort the faithful, give legal maxims, and tell stories. The stories are similar to Old Testament accounts and feature the familiar patriarchs and prophets, most especially Ibrahim (Abraham). This is why Islam is often called one of the Abrahamic religions, along with Judaism and Christianity; I use that term, rather than the more cumbersome formulation Judeo-Christian-Islamic, in this book. In the Quran everything is expressed as God speaking to Muhammad. This means that the Muslim scripture does not occupy the same theological space as the Bible, which is much more a series of stories of people who engaged and reengaged with God, stories written by members of the community and transmitted in different languages across many centuries.

The Quran is entirely in Arabic and has a much shorter span of oral transmission. Since it is understood as the language of God's revelation to Muhammad, Muslims have been reluctant to translate it into other languages or to take translations as authoritative. They have, however, in the many places and cultures of the world, developed pedagogical systems for teaching the Quran in local languages. This process occurred all over Africa – for example, in the Swahili, Mandinka, and Berber languages mentioned in the next two chapters.

The early Muslims used another source to shape Islamic culture and obligation. This was the *hadith*, the traditions about the Prophet's life (see Figure 1). These accounts were collected over a longer period

FIGURE 1 Calligraphy. Illuminated page from a biography of Muhammad, from the Centre Ahmed Baba, Timbuktu, Mali. Author's photo, 1979.

of time and placed in several collections by the ninth century C.E. Specialists in authenticating and interpreting these traditions developed in the major centers of Islamic thought. For many Muslims the *hadith* provided crucial guidance to the moral life, because they dealt with the human instrument who founded the faith. Some of them have elevated Muhammad to a very important status, as someone who ascends to heaven (see the selection in Chapter 3), appears in dreams bearing the messages of God (see the references to the Tijaniyya Sufi order in Chapter 4), or inspires reformers to take courageous action (see Chapter 10). The *hadith* that tell the story of the Prophet are often called *Sira*. Several of these biographies have circulated in the Islamic world for centuries and inspired Muslims to emulate his example (see Figure 1).

The legal scholars applied two major principles in working with the Quran and Hadith. One was called "consensus," which meant the prevailing learned opinion, namely the views of the main doctors of law. The other was called "analogy" and referred to links made to other traditions as the Arab Muslims confronted situations that they had not faced before. "Analogy" allowed the scholars to bring in precedents from other practices, including Jewish, Christian, Zoroastrian, Roman, and Sasanian. In using these principles the "doctors of law" were interested in stabilizing the new faith and applying it to the regulation of behavior and governance of the complex societies under Muslim rule. They sought deliberately to be inclusive of the practitioners of other faiths.

Using the two sources and the two principles, scholars gradually built up a body of doctrine to guide individual and collective behavior. This code was called the *Sharia*, divinely ordained law, and was contained in the works of four schools of law that developed in different cities of the Middle East. The Maliki school became dominant in North and West Africa, whereas the Hanafite and Shafiite interpretations were used in the eastern part of the continent. The differences among them were not very great, nor were the differences with the interpretations developed by Shia and Kharijite authorities. When Muslims today urge the application, or more complete application, of Islamic law, they are talking about the Sharia.

Alongside the Quran and Sharia, Muslim scholars developed historical and theological guidelines. By the end of the first century A.H. (622–719 C.E.) they established a rough consensus about the history of Muhammad, the "rightly guided" caliphs, the civil wars, and the Umayyad reign. Umayyads, Shia, and Kharijites might disagree strongly about the interpretation of these events, but not about the events themselves. Scholars also developed a basic theology common across the divisions. For them Islam built upon Christian and especially Jewish traditions, but it corrected the errors that had crept into the interpretations of those faiths. Muhammad was the last and greatest of the prophets; he was the Prophet and Messenger of God, and the Quran was the revelation that had come through him. He was human; his death in 10 A.H. or 632 C.E. was commonly acknowledged. At the same time his life, especially after he began receiving revelation at the age of forty, was worthy of imitation; some thought he was pure and sinless. With Muhammad and the establishment of the Quran, the revelation of God was fulfilled. From then on innovation (under the term *bida*) was condemned, but independent interpretation (*ijtihad*) allowed theologians, judges, and other authorities to adapt the faith to new situations over the times and spaces of the Islamic world.

The Fundamental Obligations and Institutions

The Sharia was a "portable" version of Islam that could be carried into the various times and situations of Africa and other parts of the world. It could be referred to in courts of law, palaces, or private settings to remind people of their obligations or adjudicate disputes. It is in the Sharia as well as the Quran that we find the five fundamental obligations that Muslims follow.

The first obligation is the witness or profession of faith: "There is no god but God and Muhammad is His Prophet." This profession expresses monotheism and the signal role of Muhammad and is the essential affirmation of the Muslim. It is expressed in each prayer, which is the second obligation. Prayer is performed at five very specific moments of the day. The second prayer on Friday, which occurs about 2 P.M., is a time of gathering at the main mosque in the community; the *imam*, the "one who stands in front of" and leads people in prayer, gives a sermon on that occasion. Giving alms to the community, and particularly its poorer members, is the third obligation; it is an expression of the mission of social justice in Islam. The fourth commitment is fasting, concentrated in the ninth month of the year (or Ramadan), when Muslims seek to remember their blessings, confess their sins, and recommit their lives to God.

The fifth obligation is the *hajj* or pilgrimage, the journey to Mecca
during the twelfth month of the calendar. It has the same basic purposes as the remembrance and recommitment involved in Ramadan,
but it also demonstrates the potential unity and equality of Islam by
bringing together people from all over the world – millions today, thousands in earlier times. It represents a transformation of the old "poly-
theistic" pilgrimages that Muhammad preached against, and it involves
visits to many of the sites made famous by his life. Each Muslim is
supposed to perform the pilgrimage at least once in his or her life, if
conditions permit. Until recent times this obligation was difficult to
fulfill from most parts of the African continent. Those who performed
it were often distinguished scholars or heads of state with considerable
means to put to the task or very pious young men who were willing to
undertake an arduous journey of several years.

The Sharia contains a great deal more than the five individual obligations. It treats the rights and responsibilities of persons, including
slaves, and the subjects of property and inheritance. It deals with justice, wealth, communal obligation, contracts, marriage and divorce,
punishments, the situation of non-Muslims, obedience to the state,
and a host of other subjects. Many judges throughout the Islamic world
have applied the law through reference to shortened or condensed versions prepared for wider dissemination.

To communicate these obligations and the law Muslims developed
a set of physical spaces and institutions. One was a place of worship,
the mosque. This could be very simple – a place to pray on the ground,
for example – in which the worshipers were pointed in the direction
of Mecca. But mosques could become very elaborate buildings, constructed by well-known architects and artisans working with mosaic
and other techniques. These buildings often became places of assem-
bly, discussion, and teaching. Another public institution was a place
of judgement, a court of law. Here a *qadi* or judge would apply his
training in the Sharia to cases of divorce, property, compensation, and
a range of other issues affecting Muslim societies.

These doctors of law were trained in a third kind of institution, the
school. The schools ranged from the most simple, where boys and girls
learned to recite and understand the Quran (hence the name "Koranic
school"), to the most complex, where scholars would teach law, theology, philosophy, calligraphy, and other subjects to the next generation.
The latter were often called *madrasa*, "place of study." Some deserve
the name of university, an institution of higher education. The most

famous in the whole Islamic world was and is al-Azhar, founded in Cairo in the tenth century. In West Africa the most famous one was Sankore (see Figure 4), which served as both a mosque and a school in Timbuktu in the fourteenth to the sixteenth centuries and attracted students from North and West Africa.

These key institutions – mosque, court, and school – have marked the lives of Muslims for over 1,400 years. They can be found in Africa in all times and stations, including those where the majority of the inhabitants were not practitioners of Islam at all. In those instances Muslims typically lived in one neighborhood in a town where, with the permission and often the encouragement of the local chief, they created the structures which allowed them to practice and transmit the faith. We examine this more closely in Chapters 4 and 9.

The Quran and the Sharia contained the basic theological under-standing of Islam. The world was divided into two times and spaces. The first period was the *jahiliyya*, the time of "ignorance" before the *hijra* and creation of the Muslim community. The second period was "Islam," the time when the revelation of God through Muhammad was available to human beings and they had the opportunity to live a life of morality, unity, and social justice. In the Hijaz this occurred in 622 C.E. or 1 A.H., that is, with the *hijra* from Mecca to Medina. Outside of the Hijaz, the shift from Jahiliyya to Islam came later, at various times.

The two spaces of the world were similar to the two periods. The "good" or central space was the *Dar al-Islam*, the "abode of Islam," where Muslims practiced the faith, fulfilled its obligations, and lived its law. The "bad" or exterior space was the *Dar al-Kufr*, the "abode of unbelief," sometimes called the *Dar al-Harb*, the "abode of war." In theory Muslims were obligated to keep extending the first space at the expense of the second. This obligation could be expressed in a variety of ways: by preaching, persuading, example, and ultimately force. All of these ways were *jihad*, which means "effort." In recent times jihad has become stereotyped, by some Muslims and non-Muslims, as re-ferring mainly to the forceful option, the "*jihad* of the sword." The name has been adopted by a variety of radical groups to symbolize their determination to change the status quo, combat secularism, and strike back at Western domination.

Muslims had to be more pragmatic than these divisions of time and space suggest. When the early Arab Muslims took possession of the Mediterranean and Iranian worlds, they recognized quickly the knowledge and skills of the non-Muslim majorities over whom they ruled. They made little effort to convert them; indeed, they often encouraged the continuing separation of the different religious communities. They developed the concept of *dhimmi*, "protected communities," to describe the other "people of the book," those with scriptural traditions not unlike the Quran – Jews, Christians, and the Zoroastrians of old Persia. Most scholars who shaped the culture of Islam indicated that the obligation to wage the "jihad of the sword" should not be followed if a Muslim victory was unlikely and that any government, even a non-Muslim or "not very Muslim" one, was preferable to none at all. Chaos was worse than order, even a repressive one. In these and other ways, Muslim authorities adjusted to the complexities of the worlds in which they lived. African Muslims, as we shall see, adopted these formulas and adapted them to the realities they faced.

As one might well imagine, Muslims were not as united as Muhammad wanted them to be. We have seen the divisions between Kharijites, Shia, and those who accepted the Umayyad and Abbasid caliphates and took the name of Sunni or "mainstream" Muslims. There were also conflicts within each of those traditions. Muslims fought against other Muslims. Within a given dynasty members fought for power, and new dynasties threw out old ones. Reform movements, seeking to recapture the early vision of Muhammad and the preaching about unity and social justice, were a constant of Islamic history. The reformers often adopted a kind of "imitation of Muhammad" that we shall see with Uthman dan Fodio in Chapter 10; it was not unlike the "imitation of Christ" encouraged by the medieval Christian Church.

Sufism and Sufi Orders

A critique of Sunni Islamic practice that took a somewhat different form was Sufism or mysticism. Beginning in the early centuries some reform-minded Muslims, concerned that the community was forgetting the core vision of Muhammad and God, began to stress the internal dimensions of the faith as distinguished from the external obligations. These Sufis accepted the transmission of the tradition through mosque, court, and school, but worried that the faithful were going through the motions rather than believing and searching in the faith. They drew a great deal of inspiration from the life of Muhammad as reflected in the Quran and Hadith. Sufi scholars and saints began to emerge in different parts of the Islamic world and to attract disciples; often they kept a certain distance from the courts of caliphs and sultans. Some were hermits with small followings; some were warriors on the frontiers of the *Dar al-Islam*; some were preachers in the cities. Others wrote important treatises in law and theology. But all were engaged in the search for wisdom, piety, and closeness to God and developed particular rituals and litanies to encourage this search.

In time some Sufis formed orders, often bearing their own names. The Qadiriyya order, named for Abd al-Qadir al-Jilani of twelfth century Baghdad, was one of the oldest and most widespread. The orders were essential to the spread of Islam in many times and places. In North and Sub-Saharan Africa, they helped extend the faith from town to countryside and from those born in the faith to new converts.

In the past three centuries Sufi orders have become widespread throughout the Islamic world. Each order or suborder has its founder, its "mother" lodge, a set of rituals and practices, and a chain of transmission for those authorized to provide initiation into the order. Each order made particular claims to *baraka* or spiritual blessing and sought to complement the basic Muslim institutions and practices in a particular way. Some Sufi orders thrived in the cities, some in the countryside, and still others in particular areas of the world or under particular regimes. Some acquired a reputation for being relatively quiescent and "orthodox" and others for being demonstrative and perhaps even marginal to the faith. Sometimes Sufi orders cut across the fundamental doctrinal divisions of the faith – among Sunnis, Shia, and Kharijites. Muslim rulers have favored some orders and penalized others. In Chapter 13 we discuss the emergence of a new Sufi order, the Muridiyya, in the difficult conditions of French colonial rule.

In more recent times reformers have often leveled critiques at Sufi affiliation in general. This is the position, for example, of the Salafiyya reformers that we see in Morocco in Chapter 7 and of the Wahhabi, whose doctrines became dominant in today's Saudi Arabia. Saudi opinions, because of the wealth and prestige of the country and the control of the Holy Places of Islam, carry considerable weight.

In Africa, Sufism and Sufi orders have been instrumental in the spread of the faith and are still widely current. In Sub-Saharan Africa, where conquest from outside was not an option, the Sufi order provided a visible place of gathering and a key demonstration of the practice and power of Islam. To illustrate, I cite the Muslim teacher and writer whom we meet again in Chapter 10, Uthman dan Fodio. Born in the middle of the eighteenth century, Uthman developed much of his understanding of Islam through Sufism and in particular the Qadiriyya way. He often described his experience in the language of mysticism:

> When I reached the age of 36, God stripped the veil from my sight, the imperfection from my hearing and sense of smell, the flatness from my taste, the knots from my hands, and the heaviness from my feet and body. I saw things far away like near things and heard distant sounds like close ones. I smelt the good smell of the worshiper of God, sweeter than any sweetness, and the bad odor of the sinful man, more repugnant than any putrefaction.

A few years later he expressed a particular connection to Muhammad, whose revelations began at the age of forty, and to the founder of his own Sufi order, the Qadiriyya:

> When I reached the age of 40 years, 5 months and some days, God drew me to Him. I found there Our Master Muhammad . . . with the companions and prophets and the saints . . . . Then came the Intermediary, the Lord of Men and Spirits, Abd al-Qadir al-Jilani, bringing a green robe embroidered with the phrase, "There is no god but God and Muhammad is His Messenger."

A few years later Uthman used his understanding of Qadiriyya Sufism and Muhammad's mission to construct his own vocation as a Muslim reformer. Eventually he declared the *jihad* "of the sword" on the frontiers of the *Dar al-Islam*. Throughout all of this development he consistently saw himself as a Sufi Muslim.

Islam and Women

Islam is often described as misogynous, "women-hating." This image is reinforced by reports of measures taken by the Taliban in Afghanistan, the clerics in Iran, the Islamic Salvation Front in Algeria, or by descriptions of the scarves and other "conservative" dress that Muslim women wear the world over.

The image of misogyny is obviously wrong. Equal numbers of women and men across the world practice Islam. Millions of families have been raised in and have shaped the faith over the past 1,400 years, and women have been active in that process. But it is true that the institutions and practice have been dominated by men and have reinforced the patriarchal dimensions of society. The principal actors of Muhammad's time were men, notwithstanding the importance of Khadija, Aisha, and Fatima. The principal doctors of law as well as warriors in the military were men. The Sharia decreed that women should pray in a different part of the mosque. They inherited less and had more difficulty initiating proceedings for divorce. Their testimony in court proceedings is not as highly regarded as that of men.

The historical record and the case studies of this book reveal the same bias. The principal records are by and about men. The principal actors, such as Uthman dan Fodio of Chapter 10, are men. But this should not obscure important realities that may not always be apparent. First, Muhammad, the Quran, and the Sharia show great concern about the welfare of women. The Islamic revelation represented a considerable improvement over conditions in Bedouin and Meccan society. Second, women in Muhammad's lifetime, and especially in his family, played critical roles in the emergence of the faith. Three women in particular stand out. Khadija saw the wisdom and conviction of the Prophet and gave him the courage to assert his role; it is difficult to imagine the birth of Islam without her sustained engagement. Aisha, who married Muhammad at a very young age, became an important player in the inner councils after her husband's death, from the first civil war and beyond. Fatima played a much less important historical role, but a more important symbolic one. As daughter of Muhammad, wife of Ali, and the sole channel of descent from the Prophet, she has become an object of great veneration, especially for Sufis and Shia, and she gave her name to a powerful dynasty in Egypt – the Fatimids. Some commentators would say that she has played a role similar to that of the Virgin Mary in Christianity.

All three of these figures have provided inspiration for the roles that women have played in the transmission of the faith and nurturing of new generations of Muslims over 1,400 years. Across the *Dar al-Islam* women have conscientiously learned the faith and demonstrated piety, practice, and learning to their children, whether they spoke in Arabic or other languages of the faithful. They have also played vital parts as educators on a larger canvas. Uthman's daughter, Nana Asmau, was the principal pedagogue in the new society launched by her father, as is discussed in Chapter 10.

Finally, we should note the strong role that educated and pious women have played in recent decades against the patriarchal orientations of their faith. These activists have often diverged from the path of Western feminists, developing their own perspective rooted in the faith and values of Islam, and they have been more effective precisely because of that. One of the strongest women's voices is that of Fatima Mernissi, an author from Fez, the intellectual capital of Morocco. We meet her again in Chapter 7.

Further Reading

The works of Lapidus and Martin, cited after the introduction, are useful sources for the institutionalization of Islam. Another important resource, by an anthropologist, is Dale Eickelman's *The Middle East: An Anthropological Approach* (Prentice Hall, 1981; the third edition includes sections on Central Asia and appeared in 1998). The *Encyclopedia of Islam* is an invaluable source; the article "Fatima," for example, tells us what is known about Muhammad's daughter in history and in legend. The journal *Islam and Christian–Muslim Relations* has thoughtful articles about the institutions and deeper meanings of Islam in comparative perspective.

There are numerous editions of the Quran in English and other languages. A trustworthy translation is (translator) A. J. Arberry's *The Koran Interpreted* (Macmillan, 1955). On the Internet one can find numerous commentaries as well as recitations, including the call to prayer. These give the non-Muslim a sense of the beauty and power of the original Arabic message and how it must have sounded as Muhammad repeated and preached it and as subsequent generations have been inspired by it. For a fascinating essay on the question of translating scripture, written from within the Christian tradition and with African situations in mind, see Lamin Sanneh's *Translating the Message: The Missionary Impact on Culture* (Orbis Books, 1989).

For the general process of institutionalizing Islam, see Fred Donner's *Narratives of Islamic Origins: The Beginnings of Islamic Historical Writing* (Princeton University Press, 1998). For an introduction to the Hadith, see G. H. A. Juynboll's *Muslim Tradition: Studies in Chronology, Provenance and Authority of Early Hadith* (Cambridge University Press, 1983). For the development of the Sharia, a good beginning is J. Schacht's *An Introduction to Islamic Law* (Oxford University Press, 1964), whereas N. Anderson applies this to Africa in *Islamic Law in Africa* (Cass, 1955, 1970). For an exploration of the pilgrimage and other forms of travel, see (editors) Dale Eickelman and James Piscatori's *Muslim Travellers: Pilgrimage, Migration and the Religious Imagination* (Routledge, 1990); compare this Muslim practice with Christian traditions through Victor and Edith Turner's *Image and Pilgrimage in Christian Culture: Anthropological Perspectives* (Columbia University Press, 1978).

For an approach to Sufism and its orders, try Hodgson's *Venture*, vols 1 and 2; Annemarie Schimmel's *The Mystical Dimensions of Islam* (University of

North Carolina Press, 1975); and J. Spencer Trimingham's *The Sufi Orders in Islam* (Oxford University Press, 1971). For Sufism in Egypt, see Michael Gilsenan's *Saint and Sufi in Modern Egypt* (Oxford University Press, 1973). The selection cited for Uthman dan Fodio comes from Brad G Martin's *Muslim Brotherhoods in 19th Century Africa* (Cambridge University Press, 1976).

For excellent syntheses on the development of Muslim society and thought, see Lapidus' *Islamic Societies*. In Chapters 11 and 12 he discusses "normative Islam" and "alternative Islam," categories that are especially interesting in light of the debates in the Islamic world of today. Ibn Khaldun, a fourteenth-century Muslim scholar in North Africa, wrote interpretations of the history and sociology of the Muslim world. Some of this material is available in a translation published by Franz Rosenthal, *The Muqaddimah* (three volumes, Pantheon, 1958).

For the role of women, start with Asma Barlas' *Believing Women in Islam: Unreading Patriarchal Interpretations of the Qur'an* (University of Texas Press, 2002) and consult (editors) Herbert Bodman and Nayereh Tohidi's *Women in Muslim Societies: Diversity within Unity* (Lynne Rienner, 1998), Leila Ahmed's *Women and Gender in Islam: Historical Roots in Modern Debate* (Yale University Press, 1992), Kaukab Siddique's *The Struggle of Muslim Women* (American Society for Education and Religion, 1986), and (editor) Jane Smith's *Women in Contemporary Muslim Societies* (Bucknell University Press, 1980). For the institution of the harem, start with Leslie Penn Peirce's *The Imperial Harem: Women and Sovereignty in the Ottoman Empire* (Oxford University Press, 1993). The Moroccan author Fatima Mernissi has written a number of important works about women and Islam, especially in her native Morocco; three that have been translated into English are *Beyond the Veil* (Schenkman Publishing Company and Halsted Press, 1975), *Doing Daily Battle* (London: Women's Press, 1986), and *The Veil and the Male Elite* (Addison-Wesley Publishing Co., 1991).

II

General Themes

CHAPTER 3

The Islamization of Africa

Obviously Islam was born outside of the continent. Its key institutions developed in the early centuries in areas that we call the Near or Middle East. But the faith spread into Africa – quickly into some regions and societies and more slowly into others. Today about half of the people living in the continent profess Islam, and almost 25 percent of the Muslims of the world live on the continent. This chapter deals with the spread and profession of faith in Africa, whereas the next chapter deals with the ways in which African societies have appropriated Islam.

I talk about **islamization** and **africanization** to suggest that at least two processes were at work: first, the extension of something that Africans and outsiders would recognize as Islam, and second, the "rooting" of that faith in Africa. In fact, as this book shows the processes were much more complex than that, because we are dealing with a 1,400-year period, a huge continent, and millions of people. For most of that time most of those people have not identified themselves as African, but by smaller names for regions or ethnic groups, such as Swahili, Mandinka, or Berber, or indeed entities much smaller than that.

Note that I use the term *islamization*, not *arabization*. Arabic was the language of revelation of God to Muhammad and consequently the language of the sacred book, the law, and prayer. After several centuries it became dominant in North Africa and much of the Sahara. Arabic words spread into the languages of many more African societies, especially to describe religion, government, warfare, and trade. But most African Muslims continued to speak their own languages, the

Swahili, Mandinka, and various Berber tongues, for example, that had long been native to their regions. Male and female teachers in these societies soon developed ways of transmitting the faith, the Quran, and the prayers into their vernaculars.

The main commentators about the islamization process have cast it as "penetration" that advanced by regions and stages (see Map 1). In North Africa, from Egypt to Morocco, the initial process was conquest, when Arab or Arab-led armies took over the main cities and agricultural areas that stretched along the Mediterranean. But these forces neither moved into the mountains above the plain, nor attempted to go south into the Sahara desert.

In looking at the south, or Sub-Saharan Africa, the commentators have postulated a process in three stages. The first presence came from merchants involved in the Transsaharan trade. These entrepreneurs and their families lived principally in the towns, often in quarters that were labeled "Muslim." They lived as minorities within "pagan" or non-Muslim majorities. This phase is often called "minority" or "quarantine" Islam. The second phase often goes by the name "court" Islam, because it features the adoption of Islam by the rulers and members of the ruling classes of states, in addition to the merchants. No significant effort was made to change local religious practices, especially outside of the towns. The third phase can be called "majority" Islam, whereby the faith spread beyond the merchants and ruling classes to the countryside where most people were living (see Map 2).

The three phases are thus associated with a growth of Islam in quantity and quality. The numbers grow – from minority to majority status. The quality "improves" with an advance in "orthodoxy," which is to say conformity to the main norms of Sunni Islam as outlined in Chapter 2. The third phase, the movement to the countryside and majority status, is often associated with two phenomena: Sufi orders and military revolution, specifically, Islamic revolutions labeled *jihads* in which the "privileged" practices of urban merchants and ruling classes were called into question by reformers. These reformers became increasingly radical, seeing themselves as following the example of Muhammad and declaring the *"jihad* of the sword" as he did upon his arrival in Medina. We examine celebrated cases in Chapters 10 and 12.

These frameworks have merit in many situations. They conform to what a number of African Muslims, especially reformers like Uthman dan Fodio, saw as the pattern of spread of Islam. But they do not begin to capture the complexity of Islamic practice in African history. They

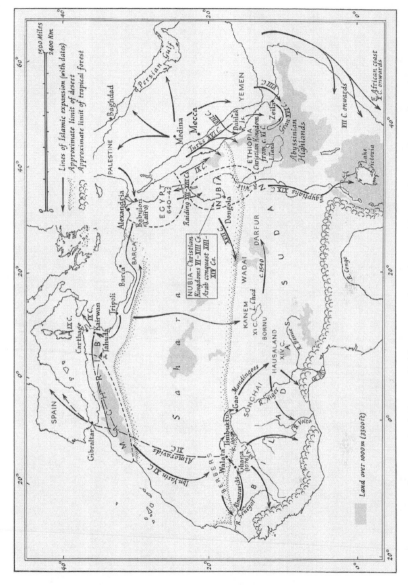

MAP 1 A typical portrayal of the spread of Islam in Africa. Adapted from John D. Fage and Maureen Verity, *An Atlas of African History*, New York, 1978.

29

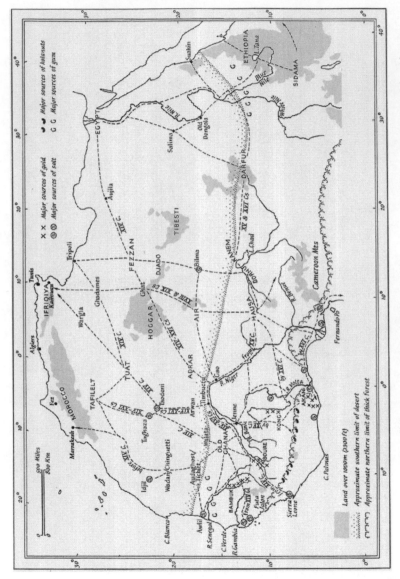

MAP 2 Trade routes of Northern Africa. Adapted from John D. Fage and Maureen Verity, *An Atlas of African History*, New York, 1978.

FIGURE 2 The secret to ocean trade. The East African dhow that permitted travel around the Indian Ocean. Peter S. Garlake, *The Kingdoms of Africa.* Elsevier-Phaidon, Oxford, 1978, p. 93.

do not get at the ways in which Islamic practice was useful and used, nor the particular classes and vocations with which it was associated, nor the different Sufi orders in which it was communicated. They do not illuminate the many patterns of conversion – fast and slow, individual and group – to the faith. Nor do they show the "africanization" of Islam: the ways in which African societies made Islam their own, as is shown in the next chapter.

In the rest of this chapter I take two "gateways" and two sets of people to suggest the complexity of islamization and prepare for the discussion of the africanization of Islam. The two gateways are the Sahara desert and the Indian Ocean. The similarity between dry sand and wet ocean may not seem obvious at first glance, but a little imagination shows the comparability of these two environments. The Arabic word for coast, *sahil*, is applied to both. *Sahil* can be used for the coast of an ocean, what you might term the "normal" sense. The East African littoral is an example, and the people who live there came to be called Swahili, which literally means "those of the coast." But because the desert is likened to a sea, the same word can be applied to its shores. Consequently the northern and southern edges of the Sahara are also *sahil*. Since the early 1970s, the whole southern edge, afflicted by drought and running across Africa from the Atlantic Ocean to the Red Sea, has been called the Sahel. Drought and famine have driven that word into dictionaries of the English language.

The East African and Swahili Gateway

I deal with the "normal" ocean gateway first. The first Muslims on the East African coast followed in the wake of a lot of other maritime travelers from the Middle East and South Asia. They used an old, well-tested technology of sailing in dhows (see Figure 2) close to the coast, down the Red Sea or the Persian Gulf, and along the Indian Ocean. Primarily Arab, they were interested in acquiring ivory, gold, other metals, leather goods, and some slaves. They interacted with the local fishing and agricultural peoples who spoke the language we call Swahili. Over time the Swahili language evolved to include a considerable Arabic vocabulary, in addition to some Malay and other infusions, within a basic Bantu language structure.

The language was the basis for a culture, and both were built around small towns along the ocean, running about 2,000 miles from

Mogadiscio in the north (in today's Somalia) to Sofala in the south (in today's Mozambique). Most of the towns were autonomous. We can call them city-states, confined essentially to islands or the coast, with very small hinterlands devoted to farming. The inhabitants of these city-states were committed to the vocations of agriculture, fishing, ship building, and trade. They practiced Islam, but in combination with earlier gods and customs, and they lived in the cosmopolitan world built around the Indian Ocean. The more wealthy Swahili began to use Islamic forms in the architecture of their homes, as well as for mosques and other public buildings, and to travel and trade alongside the Muslims of Arab origin. Many of them fulfilled the pilgrimage obligation, which was much easier to perform than from other parts of the African continent.

The most prosperous period for the Swahili city-states ran roughly from 1250 to 1500 C.E. We are fortunate to have an eyewitness account from that period by a Moroccan who spent a great portion of his life traveling around the vast Islamic world of the fourteenth century. In 1355 he visited the Mali Empire of West Africa. Some years earlier, in 1331, he came to the East African coast. Muhammad ibn Abdullah ibn Battuta, or Ibn Battuta as he is usually called, visited Mogadiscio and then set out for the south. He had this to say about the towns he visited:

> Then I set off by sea ... for the land of the Swahili and the town of Kilwa, which is in the land of Zanj. We arrived at Mombasa, a large island ... quite separate from the mainland. It grows bananas, lemons, and oranges. The people also gather a fruit ... which looks like an olive. It has a nut like an olive, but its taste is very sweet. The people do not engage in agriculture, but import grain from the Swahili [in the interior]. The greater part of their diet is bananas and fish. They follow the Shafiite rite [one of the four schools of law], and are devout, chaste, and virtuous.
>
> Their mosques are very strongly constructed of wood. Beside the door of each mosque are one or two wells, one or two cubits deep. They draw water from them with a wooden vessel which is fixed on to the end of a thin stick, a cubit long. The earth round the mosque and the well is stamped flat. Anyone who wishes to enter the mosque first washes his feet; beside the door is a piece of heavy material for drying them. Anyone who wishes to perform the ritual ablutions takes the vessel between his thighs, pours water on his hands, and so makes his ablutions. Everyone here goes barefoot.

> We spent a night on the island and then set sail for Kilwa, the principal
> town on the coast, the greater part of whose inhabitants are Zanj of very
> black complexion. Their faces are scarred.... A merchant told me that
> Sofala is half a month's march from Kilwa, and that between Sofala and
> Yufi in the country of the Limin is a month's march. Powdered gold is
> brought from Yufi to Sofala.
>
> Kilwa is one of the most beautiful and well-constructed towns in the
> world. The whole of it is elegantly built....

Kilwa, like Mombasa, was an island, and it enjoyed the reputation as
the most wealthy city-state during the period of prosperity (see Figure
3).

The main location of the Swahili language, culture, and people,
and of the practice of Islam, was concentrated in the towns of the
East African littoral until very recent times. Most of the Muslims were
Sunni, but some belonged to the Kharijite persuasion through their
connections with Oman, a small state at the southeastern end of the
Arabian peninsula. The literate elite, and especially those that we could
call "professional" Muslims, understood and wrote Arabic, but Islam
was typically taught orally through Swahili explanations. Beginning
about 300 years ago some scholars and writers began to adapt the
Arabic alphabet to the language and thereby create a written literature
alongside the older oral one. The written corpus contained the same
stories, chronicles, and poetry as the one that had been transmitted
orally down the generations.

The story that follows comes from the Swahili written tradition, but
it was certainly transmitted, told, and retold much earlier in families
and public settings. It shows the appropriation of Islam and the proximity of East Africans to the Holy Cities of the faith (Jerusalem as well
as Mecca and Medina):

> [Muhammad's Ascension] One morning the Holy Prophet told his com-
> panions: "Last night the angel Jiburili [Gabriel] came to me and brought
> me greetings from the Almighty. He summoned me to come before His
> throne and receive His commission. I opened the door of the house, and
> there on the road, and also in the sky, thousands of angels were waiting
> for me. They all greeted me in chorus."
>
> ...Muhammad continued: "I was then taken to the mosque [the
> Dome of the Rock built by the Umayyads] in Jerusalem. Suddenly I saw
> the great prophets of the past appear before me: Burahimu [Ibrahim or
> Abraham], Musa [Moses] and Isa [Jesus]. We exchanged greetings and
> prayed together. After the prayer, Jiburili led me outside, and there I saw

FIGURE 3 Kilwa, the most prominent of the Swahili cities in the early period. An artist's reconstruction of the palace, Kilwa Island, Tanzania. Garlake, p. 101.

a golden ladder hanging down from the zenith of the sky to where I was standing. I could not see the top, although the whole ladder radiated like the moon in the night sky.

"As soon as I put my foot on the bottom rung, it soared up in the air with me, and before I knew what was happening we were flying through the clouds. I clung to the ladder, but Jiburili was flying beside me, keeping up with ease on his own huge wings.

"In a moment we were in Heaven, flying over a vast sea. I asked Jiburili what it was, and he told me: 'That is the blue sky which mortals like you see from the earth.'

"The name of the first level of heaven is Rafiu; its width is 500 years. Jiburili knocked on the gate, and when the voice of an angel answered, 'Who is it?' Jiburili stated our business and our names. The angel, whose name was Sumaili, together with his 70,000 angels, bade me welcome. Inside there I saw two arched gateways, and between them there was a throne on which was seated our forefather Adam. We greeted one another with a *salaam aleika* [peace be upon you], after Jiburili had introduced us. Adam said he was happy that at last Allah had sent me to mankind with His final message of salvation, for many erring souls had been condemned to the Fire since he had first fallen into sin . . . ."

The story is testimony to the strong continuities in Judaism, Christianity, and Islam – the Abrahamic tradition.

The Swahili Muslims did not strive to spread Islam by preaching, colonization, or the military *jihad*. They were generally content to practice their faith, ply their trades, and interact with the people of the interior who were largely non-Muslim. The spread of Islam inland, and of the Swahili language and culture, did not begin until the eighteenth century.

The pattern of prosperity and autonomy changed dramatically around 1500. Portuguese explorers, using their new maritime technology, rounded the Cape of Good Hope at the bottom of the African continent, in their quest to know the world and monopolize the spice trade of Asia. Alongside their commercial goals they carried a very strong "Crusader" vocation, borne out of their experience of "reconquest" when they "wrested" and "wrestled" the Iberian peninsula from Muslim control (see Chapters 6 and 7) with the encouragement of the Pope.

Ever since the First Crusade in the late eleventh century, Rome had urged European Christians to move against Muslim societies and states. In the fifteenth and sixteenth centuries, its efforts were directed particularly at the Ottoman Empire. The Ottomans had established their capital at Istanbul, on the site of the "Christian" city of Constantinople, and made significant inroads into southeastern Europe, the area called the Balkans today. They also controlled the two holiest cities of Islam, Mecca and Medina, as well as the city that was sacred to three faiths, Jerusalem. The Ottomans had some influence in the horn of Africa, but very little on the Swahili coast.

This detail was lost on the Portuguese explorers, who were animated by religious zeal as well as commercial ambition. They used their artillery and naval superiority to attack the most prosperous Swahili towns. Kilwa, in the Tanzania of today, was destroyed. Mombasa, the biggest city-state on the northern part of the coast, was captured. The period of great Swahili prosperity was over. The Muslim communities now thought of the military *jihad* as a way to defend themselves from non-Muslim attack in much the way that Muhammad began to think in Mecca before the *hijra*.

The Portuguese did not maintain control over the East African coast, but the Swahili did not regain their momentum and prosperity until the eighteenth century. At that time the Omani Arabs became more active along the coast, and in the nineteenth century actually transferred their capital to the island of Zanzibar. The Omani sultans controlled a significant portion of the Swahili region in what we today

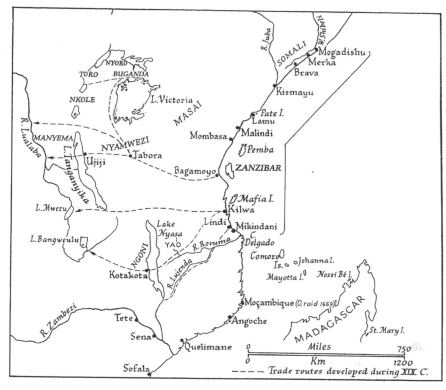

MAP 3 The Omani trading networks in East Africa. Adapted from John D. Fage and Maureen Verity, *An Atlas of African History*, New York, 1978.

call Tanzania and Kenya, primarily for commercial reasons. They continued the trade in ivory and gold, but now added a significant trade in slaves (see Chapter 5). Some were sent to the Middle East and South Asia, whereas others were used at the coast to produce cloves and grain for export. The Zanzibari system resulted in more active contact between coast and hinterland, and the spread of Islam and the Swahili culture to the towns of the interior (Map 3).

These networks laid the basis for the spread of Islam in East Africa in the nineteenth and twentieth centuries. The main agents of islamization were merchants and teachers, not the reform-minded scholars who became so prominent in West Africa. The Omanis themselves were Kharijites, but most of the older Swahili communities as well as many of the slaves were Sunni. Relations across these doctrinal lines were not difficult. The tradition of military jihad remained a minor theme, except when it came to resistance to European domination. In

His grace and to command good and forbid evil and to fight the Holy War for His sake."

They replied: "O blessed Shaikh, make what commands you will, you will find us obedient. Were you to order us to kill our parents we should do so." "Go with God's blessing," said he. "Warn your people. Make them fearful of God's punishment. Tell them of his proofs. If they repent, return to the truth, and abandon their ways, let them be. But if they refuse, continue in their error, and persist in their wrongheadedness, then we shall ask for God's help against them and wage Holy War on them till God shall judge between us, for He is the Best of Judges."

Both the merchants and the militant Almoravids held on to their Berber languages long after they became Muslim. The process of arabization was slow, and its vehicle was not the early armies who conquered the Mediterranean zones. It came later from Bedouins, desert nomads, who spread from the Arabian peninsula across North Africa and filtered down into the desert from the fourteenth to the sixteenth centuries. In fact these nomads did not succeed in the central zones (the Saharan portions of today's Algeria, Mali, and Niger), where the Tuareg people, their Berber language (*tamasheq*), and its ancient script (*tifinagh*) remain dominant.

Berber and Swahili Muslims lived at the two principal gateways into Sub-Saharan Africa and played critical roles in demonstrating the practice of Islam and making it available to other groups of people. The faith did not spread automatically, easily, or without significant adaptations. Africans might appropriate Islam in the more inclusive way of the Swahili tradition or in the more radical and exclusive form of the Almoravids. In the next chapter I look more closely at a whole range of appropriations.

Further Reading

The general histories of Islam mentioned in the introduction all deal with the conquest of North Africa and the drive into the Iberian peninsula to create the "Andalusian" or Spanish Muslim civilization; to a lesser degree they deal with the spread of Islam south of the Sahara. For an imaginative construction of what it might have meant to be Berber in the western extreme of North Africa at the time of the Arab conquests, see the novel of the Moroccan writer Driss Chraibi, *Mother Spring* (Three Continents Press, 1989, translation from the French version of 1982). The best synthesis on the Berbers of North Africa, including their resistance to and appropriation of Islam, is Michael Brett and Elizabeth Fentress' *The Berbers* (Blackwell, 1996).

The three "phases" of Sub-Saharan islamization can be found in most books on Islam in Africa, including Levtzion and Pouwels' *History of Islam*. They are especially prominent in the understanding of islamization in West Africa, beginning with the leading commentator on African Islam for many decades, J. Spencer Trimingham (see his *History of Islam in West Africa* and a variety of other works). They continue in two relatively recent syntheses, Mervyn Hiskett's *The Development of Islam in West Africa* (Longman, 1984) and Peter Clarke's *West Africa and Islam* (Edward Arnold, 1982).

To explore the Swahili, begin with the chapters of Pearson, Pouwels, and Sperling in Levtzion and Pouwels' *History of Islam*. For a fuller synthesis of Swahili culture, see Pouwels' *Horn and Crescent: Cultural Change and Traditional Islam on the East African Coast (800–1900)* (Cambridge University Press, 1987) and Ali Mazrui and Ibrahim Shariff's *The Swahili: Idiom of an African People* (Africa World History, 1994). The selection from Ibn Battuta comes from G. S. P. Freeman-Grenville's *East African Coast, Select Documents* (Oxford University Press, 1962), whereas the passage on Muhammad's ascent is taken from Jan Knappert's *Myths and Legends of the Swahili* (Heinemann, 1970). A good collection of translation and commentary on Ibn Battuta in Africa is (editors and translators) Said Hamdun and Noel King's *Ibn Battuta in Black Africa* (Marcus Wiener, 1988).

For the concept of oral literature and oral tradition in Africa, see Jan Vansina's *Oral Tradition: A Study in Historical Methodology* (Aldine Press, 1965), (editor) Joseph Miller's *The African Past Speaks: Essays on Oral Tradition and History* (Dawson, 1980), and the comprehensive treatment in Ruth Finnegan's *Oral Literature in Africa* (Oxford University Press, 1970).

The Almoravid movement can be pursued in Lapidus and in Levtzion's article in the *History of Islam*. The passage comes from a work of translation by Levtzion and J. F. P. Hopkins' *Corpus of Early Arabic Sources for West African History* (Cambridge University Press, 1981), which is an invaluable source for the "medieval" history of West Africa and the processes of islamization. For a novel written by a Senegalese Muslim in the 1950s that reflects the strong reform tradition and is set in an area not far from the Almoravid domain, see Cheikh Hamidou Kane's *Ambiguous Adventure* (Heinemann, 1971, translation from the French edition of 1962).

Ken Harrow has edited two very useful volumes on Islamic themes in African literature that I cited at the end of the introduction: *Faces of Islam in African Literature* and *The Marabout and the Muse*.

CHAPTER 4

The Africanization of Islam

The companion process to the islamization of Africa was the africanization of Islam. By this I mean the various ways that, at different times over the past 1,400 years, Islam has been appropriated or articulated in particular societies; to put it another way, how African groups have created "Muslim" space or made Islam their own. The process is the same one that happened throughout the world that became Muslim or indeed throughout the world that became Christian or Buddhist or of any other persuasion. There is *nothing* pejorative about the africanization of Islam or, more appropriately, the "Berberization" or "Swahili-zation" or "whatever-ization" of Islam. There *is* something pejorative about the way that Europeans and many Mediterranean-based Muslims have perceived "African Islam" and the africanization of Islam. That is the subject of Chapter 6.

The question, then, for the Swahili, the various Berber groups, and many other communities in Africa is how could Islam become theirs. In what follows I discuss these "africanization" processes in terms of space and time, visual culture, and genealogical and spiritual attachment. Finally I look at one specific case study that I call "theological." We could draw many analogies from the history of Christianity as it spread and was appropriated in different parts of the world.

Appropriation in Space and Time

Islamic law and theology did not create an obvious space and time for Muslims outside of the Hijaz. For the founders of the new faith and the doctors of law and theology, the world was divided into two parts: the "good" *Dar al-Islam* and the "bad" *Dar al-Kufr*. The "good" Islamic area quickly expanded outward from Mecca and Medina to embrace a large part of the "known" world. The emergence of a third area, the *Dar al-Sulh* or "area of truce," did not fundamentally alter this dichotomy. Similarly, time was bifurcated into two: the time before, which is *jahiliyya* or ignorance, and the time after, which is *Islam*. The boundary between the two was sharp: the *hijra*, 622 in the common era calendar but the year one in the new Islamic one.

Outside the Hijaz each Muslim community had to find a way to adapt these fundamental tenets to its situation. The Swahili towns, strung like beads along the coast, seem to have adopted Islamic practice gradually and differentially, across the different vocations of their communities and classes. The relatively easy contact with the Arabian peninsula encouraged trade and settlement in several directions. The Swahili language developed simultaneously with islamization. To the oral literature was joined a literature written in the Arabic script, featuring religious as well as secular themes.

The Berbers had much greater problems of distance. In the case of the Lamtuna the whole "tribe," a group built around camel raising and the exploitation of the Saharan oases, became Muslim as a group on the basis of the decisions of their leaders. Their Islamic identity, however, did not run deep, and it was only as Ibn Yasin instructed them that their commitment to the faith, and to the cleric's interpretation of the faith, began to grow. In their instance it took the form of *jihad*, first by preaching and persuasion and then by military force. In the course of about one generation, these Lamtuna reconstructed the division formulated by Muhammad between the two worlds and the two times. In their understanding they ended "ignorance" and created the *Dar al-Islam* in the northwestern parts of Africa. But once they were masters of the desert and Morocco, they became the targets of similar critiques – by the succession of reformers who have marked the history of Islamic societies.

Outside of East Africa and the areas along the Red Sea, relatively few Africans could make the pilgrimage, at least before the twentieth century and the emergence of boat and plane travel. The Lamtuna chief was exceptional in this regard, as were the opportunities available to the wealthier Swahili. In most areas it was imperative to establish local sanctuaries to celebrate the faith, show devotion, and give Islam roots in the local society. Eventually these places and rituals might become

as important, or even substitute for, practices such as the pilgrimage to
Mecca. We encounter two of these spaces, Mawlay Idriss in Morocco
(Chapter 7) and Touba in Senegal (Chapter 13), later in the book.
Another striking appropriation of Islam comes from Hausaland, the
area of today's northern Nigeria. There Muslim clerics defined certain
groups of nonbelievers as "Magians," by analogy to the practitioners of
the Zoroastrian religion of old Persia, and thereby placed them within
the theological space of Islam as a "people of the Book." I take this up
in Chapter 10.

Time was a more transportable commodity than space. Muhammad's birthday and other events could be commemorated anywhere.
The lunar month could be calculated throughout the Muslim world,
permitting the observance of the month of fasting (the ninth month) or
the month of pilgrimage (the twelfth month). The pilgrimage month
contained the biggest festival, the Id al-Kabir, which commemorated
Ibrahim's (Abraham's) willingness to sacrifice his son, as well as a feast
to remember Fatima. But alongside these "big" dates emerged moments associated with particular movements and founders that were
relevant to the local Muslim communities.

The Murids, a Sufi order that originated in rural Senegal in the
early 1900s (see Chapter 13), developed a number of ceremonies to
celebrate particular memories of their movement. The "Great Magal"
commemorated the founder's departure into exile in 1895, whereas
the "Small Magal" marked his death in 1927. The largest celebrations
take place in Touba, a town created by the founder with the meaning
of "conversion." These ceremonies function as a pilgrimage and reen-
gagement for members of this order; they come by the hundreds of
thousands every year, from all over Senegal and now from all over the
world.

Appropriation in Visual Culture: Amulets and Architecture

Muslims in the different parts of Africa were eager to express their
faith in concrete terms, what academics often call visual culture. Often they attached particular importance to trade goods that arrived
from the Mediterranean world, which they associated with the Islamic
heartlands: beads of various kinds, glass, metal sculptures, and leather
work, for example. But they also adopted what they took to be very
specific Islamic forms for their own production. They were especially

inspired by Arabic writing, which could be used without knowing the language fully and which created a new skill, that of calligraphy. Calligraphy, or "beautiful writing," developed in many civilizations; in the Islamic one, where certain prejudices against human representation existed, the use of the Arabic script became extremely important. Muslims across Africa developed skills in calligraphy; sometimes they were primarily teachers of the Quran and the other basic texts; sometimes they were artists or artisans (see Figure 1).

One of the most concrete expressions of visual culture was the amulet or talisman. Widely found throughout Africa, the talisman was something that the individual wore on his or her body for protection for his or her person, family, and possessions. Typically the manufacture of the amulet involved at least two people: a scholar who knew Arabic and the holy texts and could write the appropriate verse for an individual's needs, and a leather worker who would place the paper verse inside of a leather pouch and construct a string or necklace to attach the amulet to the body. Parents often had talismans fabricated for their newborn children, who might be particularly vulnerable to disease and other threats. Quranic verses and calligraphic designs were also written and woven into clothing. Those wearing the clothes felt they had protection against particular dangers. The Asante chief of Figure 10 is wearing a war shirt bristling with talismans.

The talismans often ventured into numerology, the "science" of numbers. For millennia practitioners of the Abrahamic traditions and other religions have assigned attributes and numerical values to particular letters and constructed formulas of protection and divination. Some Muslim clerics became experts in the manipulation of attributes, numbers, and letters. They transmitted their knowledge orally and in small books of formulas, crossing religious "boundaries" to use the wisdom contained in Jewish, Christian, or African traditions. Figure 11 is a page from such a book of formulas.

Another very visible expression of visual culture was the place of prayer, the mosque. Mosques were sometimes constructed on Arabian or Egyptian models; this was often the case on the East African coast, given the relative ease of communication between the two worlds and the availability of stone for construction. In much of West Africa the main building material was mud or mud brick reinforced with wooden struts. This indigenous style, used for houses, was adapted to the building of mosques, often of several stories. One of the most famous is in the town of Jenne on the Niger in today's Mali. The

FIGURE 4 Mosque in the traditional mud-brick style of the West African savanna. The Sankore mosque and university in Timbuktu, Mali. Author's photo, 1979.

FIGURE 5 Another mosque in the traditional style. Friday mosque at Mopti, Mali. Author's photo, 1976.

FIGURE 6 Mosque in the Moroccan style. A minaret of the Grand Mosque of Dakar, Senegal, built by Moroccan designers and mosaic workers in the early 1960s. Author's photo, 1968.

FIGURE 7 A modern artist's rendition of the mud-brick mosque style. A painting by Boubacar Coulibaly, Senegalese painter, about 1975. Author's photo.

Jenne mosque was probably built 700 years ago and has been repaired many times since then. Even better known is the Sankore mosque of Timbuktu, which doubled as an important center of higher education (see Figure 4; see also Figure 5 for another example of a Mosque in mud-brick style). Moroccan (see Figure 6) and Saudi Arabian styles have been adopted in West Africa in recent decades. Look at a contemporary Senegalese artist's rendition of the traditional style (Figure 7 and on the cover).

Attachment and Competition

Another way to appropriate Islam came through genealogy and genealogical invention. Although the essential message of the faith was submission and performance of basic obligations (see Figures 8 and 9 for West African examples), Muslims were often prone to seek distinction by descent from the founders. The most holy level was descent from the Prophet Himself, which could only come from the one child who bore children, namely Fatima, wife of Ali. This was called the

FIGURE 8 Basic Islamic instruction. Quranic teacher and pupil, Guinea, about 1890. From Felix Dubois, *La vie au continent noir*. Paris: J. Hetzel, 1893, p. 170.

"Sharifian" or noble line, and it did not necessarily mean belonging to the Shia branch of Islam, which separated from other Muslim traditions after the death of Ali and his sons. One of the most visible Sharifians was Idriss, the founder of the first Islamic state in Morocco (see Chapter 7). He set a kind of "standard" of descent to which all subsequent rulers and dynasties of Morocco aspired. Some of the leading East African Swahili also claimed Sharifian origins.

The next levels of holiness took the form of descent from the Quraysh, the larger family of Muhammad, or the companions, those

FIGURE 9 Piety and prayer. Senegalese Muslim praying on
a boat; from a sketch of a colonial soldier made by a French
artist. From Dubois, p. 13.

who joined him during his preaching at Mecca or Medina. A final level
featured Arab Muslims of the first or second generations who distinguished themselves in war, diplomacy, or institution building. All of
these varieties of descent involved *baraka* (blessing) or charisma associated with the bloodline in the minds of Muslim societies over much
of the world.

Many of these genealogies were inventions. It was simply not possible for most of the Arabs to be descendants of Muhammad, the
Quraysh, or the early companions, and it was even less likely that

FIGURE 10 Piety and protection. Photo of an Asante chief,
Ejisuhene Nana Diko Pim III, in his great warshirt with
talismans, 1976. Collection of Doran Ross.

Persian, Turkish, Berber, Swahili, or Mandinka Muslims would have
genealogical ties to the Hijaz. But that was not the point. Those who
made the claims, and who had qualities of personal command, learning, or military leadership to reinforce the claims, came to be believed,
and their descendants in turn drew upon these genealogical credentials to build their careers. Over time the claims, usually expressed in
recitations of chains of ancestors, were accepted; critics, in any case,
could not demonstrate that they were false.

FIGURE 11 Divination and protection. Arabic text
showing magic squares to be used in talismans and for other
purposes. Claudia Zaslavsky, *Africa Counts*. Boston: Prindle,
Weber and Schmidt, 1973, p. 144.

Genealogical attachment among African Muslim communities usually became important as the faith was spreading, both in the sense
of numbers and greater depth of practice. Sometimes it took the
form of a kind of competition for spiritual ascendancy – who could
make the strongest claim and make that claim stick. We know little
of the genesis of this process, only the results. Much of the information we have comes from the late nineteenth century, when European

administrators were taking over vast stretches of Africa and trying to write down the histories – and claims – of their new subjects.

Other forms of attachment and competition often used the same formula. Scholars competed for disciples and prestige. They taught particular works of Islamic law, theology, poetry, and the other "sciences" and allowed their disciples to make their own copies. Then they certified those copies with a chain of transmission – in which they formed the last link. Similarly, the founders of Sufi orders competed for followers and gave authorization to their disciples to found branch lodges and confer initiation on others. These scholarly and Sufi chains were often "intellectual" or "spiritual," but they functioned in the same way as the biological credentials described above. Over time they became more difficult to contest.

One Sufi group that sought to trump the competition was the Tijaniyya. This order bore the name of an Algerian Muslim named Ahmad al-Tijani, who lived at the end of the eighteenth century. Al-Tijani claimed to have received his vision directly from Muhammad and God and thus had no need of the chains of transmission on which other orders had long relied. His claims led to heated debates throughout the nineteenth and twentieth centuries between Tijaniyya proponents and those who defended other ways or opposed Sufism altogether.

Perhaps the most intriguing attachment, from the standpoint of Sub-Saharan Africa, is to Bilal, the companion of Muhammad who served as *muezzin*, the one who called the faithful to prayer. Bilal was an Ethiopian or Abyssinian and probably initially a slave of a Meccan family. The early Hijaz traditions make him one of the earliest converts and trusted advisors, who continued to call to prayer in Medina and then in Mecca, after the conquest at the end of the Prophet's life. He then distinguished himself in the early military campaigns and died in the vicinity of Damascus. At some point – we will never know when – some African believers began to invoke Bilal as their ancestor, probably because of his darker color and perhaps because of the racial attitudes expressed by "white" Arab Muslims (see Chapter 5).

The most conspicuous link to Bilal comes from the old empire of Mali, whose rulers claimed a Muslim identity and descent from the *muezzin*. One version of the Malian tradition, passed down across the centuries, goes as follows:

> ...Those who are today called Mandinka, inhabitants of Mali, are not indigenous; they come from the East. Bilali Bunama, ancestor of the

Keitas, was the faithful servant of the Prophet Muhammad (may the peace of God be upon him). Bilali Bunama had seven sons of whom the eldest, Lawalo, left the Holy City and came to settle in Mali; Lawalo had Latal Kalabi for a son, Latal Kalabi had Damul Kalabi who then had Lahilatul Kalabi.

Lahilatul Kalabi was the first black prince to make the pilgrimage to Mecca. On his return he was robbed by brigands in the desert. His men were scattered and some died of thirst, but God saved Lahilatul Kalabi, for he was a righteous man. He called upon the Almighty and spirits appeared and recognized him as king. After 7 years' absence Lahilatul was able to return, by the grace of Allah the Almighty, to Mali, where none expected to see him any more.

Bilal linked the ruling dynasty to an ancient and prestigious Islamic memory.

Muslims in a Minority Posture: The Suwarian Tradition

The Malian state which laid claim to Bilal emerged in the early second millennium of our era. In the thirteenth century it became a large entity centered on the Middle Niger River, in the heart of today's Mali; in the fourteenth century it reached its apogee, acquiring a considerable reputation for the Islamic practice of its court and the pilgrimages of several emperors who followed in the tradition of Lahilatul. It was at this time that Mali began to encourage some of its merchants to establish colonies close to the gold fields of West Africa (see Map 2). Several colonies settled in the south, especially near gold mines controlled by the Akan people of today's Ghana and Ivory Coast. These Muslims went by the name of *juula*, which referred simultaneously to their language (a dialect of Mandinka), commercial vocation, and religious practice. They typically lived in demarcated neighborhoods within the main commercial towns and organized trade in gold and other products between the forest areas of the south and the Sahel to the north. They left the realm of "politics" to their local hosts (not always easily, as Chapter 9 reveals).

These *juula* constituted a Muslim minority within a non-Muslim majority, corresponding to the first "phase" of islamization mentioned in Chapter 3. They worshiped, educated their children, distributed their property, and in almost every respect conducted their lives as would Muslims anywhere in Africa or the world. They were no less

learned nor pious than believers elsewhere, and they did not compro-
mise their faith. But they could not afford to, and generally did not
want to, change the religious identities of their hosts, who welcomed
their presence and accorded them favors because of the prosperity they
brought through trade. They were not about to try transforming the
Dar al-Kufr in which they lived into a *Dar al-Islam*.

Over time these *juula* colonies developed a theological rationale for
their relations with non-Muslim ruling classes and subjects. The person who is credited with formulating this rationale is Al-Hajj Salim
Suwari, a learned cleric from the core Mali area who lived around
1500. He made the pilgrimage to Mecca several times and devoted his
intellectual career to developing an understanding of the faith that
would work for Muslim minorities in "pagan" lands. He drew on
North African and Middle Eastern jurists and theologians who had
reflected on the situations of Muslims living among non-Muslim majorities, situations that were frequent in the centuries of Islamic expansion. Suwari formulated the obligations of the faithful in West Africa
into something that we can call the "Suwarian tradition." In this understanding Muslims must nurture their own learning and piety and
thereby furnish good examples to the non-Muslims who lived around
them. They could accept the jurisdiction of non-Muslim authorities,
as long as they had the necessary protection and conditions to practice the faith. In this teaching Suwari followed a strong predilection in
Islamic thought for any government, albeit non-Muslim or tyrannical,
as opposed to none. The military *jihad* was a resort only if the faithful
were threatened. Suwari esteemed that God would bring non-Muslims
to convert in His own time; it was not the responsibility of the faithful
to decide when ignorance should give way to belief.

In practice, of course, the Muslims and non-Muslims did not function in isolation. Across the many times and places in the woodlands
and forest, they were in constant contact with each other. They conceived of their relationship in terms of estates: the merchant estate,
which was Muslim, and the ruling classes, which were "pagan" or at
least "ignorant" from the standpoint of Islam. But the ruling classes
typically esteemed the merchants and their religion and sought the
baraka or blessing that Muslims might bring to the political realm.
This esteem was reflected in a number of ways and particularly in the
demand for amulets produced by clerics for their "pagan" hosts (see
Figures 10 and 11). A British traveler in the early nineteenth century,

Joseph Dupuis, gives an account of this demand in the Kingdom of Asante (see Chapter 9):

> The talismanic charms fabricated by the Muslims, it is well known, are esteemed efficacious according to the various powers they are supposed to possess, and here is a source of great emolument, as the article is in public demand from the palace to the slave's hut; for every man (not by any means exempting the Muslims) wears them strung around the neck.... Some are accounted efficacious for the cure of gunshot wounds, others for the thrust or laceration of steel weapons, and the poisoned barbs of javelins, or arrows. Some, on the other hand, are esteemed to possess the virtue of rendering the wearer invulnerable in the field of battle, and hence are worn as a preservative against the casualties of war.
>
> Besides this class of charms, they have other cabalistic scraps for averting the evil of natural life: these may also be subdivided into separate classes; some, for instance, are specific nostrums in certain diseases of the human frame, some for their prevention, and some are calculated either to ward off any impending stroke of fortune, or to raise the proprietor to wealth, happiness and distinction.

The relationship between leading merchants and rulers in the same kingdom is captured well in another passage from the same author. Merchants, clerics, and rulers were all residents of the same city, Kumasi, the capital of Asante. The speaker here is the head of the local Muslim community, and he talks of his role within the Muslim estate, mainly through education, and his ties to the political estate:

> "When I was a young man," said the Bashaw [Pasha], "I worked for the good of my body. I traded on the face of God's earth, and traveled much. As my beard grew strong [I became older] I settled at Salgha [a trading center] and lastly removed to this city. I was still but an indifferent student [of Islam] when, God be praised, a certain teacher from the north was sent to me by a special direction, and that learned saint taught me the truth. So now that my beard is white, and I cannot travel as before, I am content to seek the good of my soul in a state of future reward. My avocations at Kumasi are several, but my chief employment is a school which I have endowed, and which I preside over myself. God has compassionated my labors [i.e. made them prosper], and I have about 70 pupils and converts at this time.
>
> Besides this, the king's heart is turned towards me, and I am a favored servant. Over the Muslims I rule as *qadi* [judge], conformably to our

law. I am also a member of the king's council in affairs relating to the believers of Sarem and Dagomba [areas to the north with significant Muslim populations].

The king, Osei Bonsu, was obviously sympathetic to the local Muslim community, who esteemed that he was infinitely preferable to the ruler of neighboring Dahomey, whom they called the "infidel of infidels" (*kafir al-kuffar*).

The Suwarian teaching was a realistic rationale for Muslims living in the woodland and forest regions of West Africa in the past five or six centuries. Thanks to several historians and Islamicists, it has been rather fully explored. It was not without tension that came in part from the missionary dimension of Islam itself; it was challenged by Muslim reformers in recent centuries. Its neat compartments were obscured by occasional intermarriage between merchants and rulers. But the Suwarian tradition was resilient and useful, and it is probably similar to the positions of many African Muslim communities who found themselves in situations of inferior numbers and force, took advantage of their networks for trade, and enjoyed good relations with their "pagan" hosts.

Further Reading

For the Murid order and its adaptation of Islam, see Chapter 13 in this volume. The most complete source is Donal Cruise O'Brien's *The Mourides of Senegal: The Political and Economic Organization of an Islamic Brotherhood* (Oxford University Press, 1971). I explore some dimensions of Murid adaptation in my book *Paths of Accommodation: Muslim Societies and French Colonial Authorities in Senegal and Mauritania, 1880 to 1920* (Ohio University Press, 2000). A recent treatment of the Murids in the context of Senegalese history is James Searing's *"God Alone is King": Islam and Emancipation in Senegal: The Wolof Kingdoms of Kajoor and Bawol, 1859–1914* (Heinemann and James Currey, 2002).

For genealogical and spiritual attachments, see an earlier book that I wrote, *The Holy War of Umar Tal* (Oxford, University Press, 1985), especially Chapter 2, and my *Paths of Accommodation*. The Tijaniyya is one Sufi order that has been extremely controversial and generated a good deal of literature as a consequence. See Jamil Abun-Nasr's *The Tijaniyya: A Sufi Order in the Modern World* (Oxford, 1965) and (editors) Jean-Louis Triaud and David Robinson's *La Tijaniyya: Une Confrérie à la Conquête de l'Afrique* (Karthala, 2000), which contains a number of articles in English. The excerpt on Bilal comes from D. T. Niane, *Sundiata: An Epic of Old Mali* (Longmans, 1965, p. 2). Look also at the selection on Bilal in *The Encyclopedia of Islam*.

For mosque architecture, see the two chapters on Africa in (editors) Martin Frishman and Hassan Uddin Khan's *The Mosque: History, Architectural Development and Regional Diversity* (Thomas and Hudson, 1994). For Islamic architecture in West Africa, see Labelle Prussin's *Hatumere: Islamic Design in West Africa* (University of California Press, 1986). For the East African coast, see Peter Garlake's *The Early Islamic Architecture of the East African Coast* (Oxford University Press, 1966). To explore the practice of producing and consuming amulets, see the article of David Owusu-Ansah in the Levtzion and Pouwels volume cited at the end of the introduction, Louis Brenner's *West African Sufi: The Religious Heritage and Spiritual Search of Cerno Bokar Saalif Taal* (Hurst, 1984), and the work by the anthropologist Edward Westermarck based on his research in Morocco: *Pagan Survivals in Mohammedan Civilisation* (Philo Press, 1973, from a 1933 edition).

The main source on the Suwarian tradition is Ivor Wilks, and the most recent formulation by him is his chapter in Levtzion and Pouwels' *History of Islam*. But he picks up the same theme in a collection of essays, *Forests of Gold: Essays on the Akan and the Kingdom of Asante* (Ohio University Press, 1993). Rene Bravmann has explored the same tradition in the Levtzion and Pouwels volume and in his earlier volume, *African Islam* (The Smithsonian Institution, 1983). The excerpts on the Suwarian tradition, as expressed in the time and space of Asante, come from Joseph Dupuis' *Journal of a Residence in Ashantee* (Henry Colborn, 1824, reprinted by Cass in 1966, p. 97 and the appendix, p. xi).

CHAPTER 5

Muslim Identity and the Slave Trades

In the chapters on islamization and africanization I have not mentioned the slave trade and slavery. That was intentional, because I wanted to present Islam as a religious practice, which is what Arab founders and African practitioners intended. But islamization and africanization occurred in very specific contexts, political, economic, and social. Sometimes the context involved transforming people into commodities – what we commonly call enslavement, the slave trade, and slavery.

For most of human history, systems of exploitation called slavery have existed and have required practices of "recruitment" or slave trade to bring new men, women, and children into bondage. Definitions based on religious identity have usually been a part of enslavement. Africa has been no exception to the practice of slavery and the slave trade, either inside the continent or by export to other areas. In fact, although the name *slave* originates from Slav and the Roman Empire's exploitation of eastern Europe, no area of the world has been more victimized by slave trade and slavery than Sub-Saharan Africa. Slaves who were Muslim used their religious identity as comfort and a rallying cry in some of those systems. In others slave traders and slave owners used Islamic identity to justify enslavement. It is this resource of Islamic identity that I explore in this chapter.

Muslims and the Atlantic Slave Trade

Most of the research on slave trade has focused on the Atlantic or trans-Atlantic system, managed by European companies, entrepreneurs, and ships from the 1400s to the late 1800s. That system brought at least ten million human beings from Africa to the Americas to work primarily in agricultural production, often in appalling conditions, with no promise of freedom. This "chattel" form has become almost synonymous with American slavery. A relatively small number of these Africans were Muslim, and scholars have focused a good deal of attention on them, in part because of their visibility among the slave population. That visibility in turn comes in great part from their literacy and religious practice.

One of the Muslim slaves who reached the Americas was a teenager named Abu Bakr, named for the first caliph after the Prophet. He fits the definition of *juula* that I set out in the previous chapter, and his case graphically demonstrates the transformations involved in the Atlantic or any other slave trade. Abu Bakr was a cosmopolitan West African, whose roots lay in the Sahelian region. The Mali Empire had long disappeared, but family trading firms continued to ply the routes that led from west to east and north to south and from the Sahelian ports at the desert edge, such as Timbuktu, to trading centers in the forest like Kumasi. Just after 1800 Abu Bakr was forced to enlist in a war between non-Muslim powers. When his patrons were defeated, he was captured and taken to Jamaica as a slave. His new name, Edward Donellan, was a symbol of this dramatic change. He still thought of himself as Abu Bakr and some 30 years later could still use his Arabic language skills to write a short autobiography.

The first portion of the autobiography provides an excellent description of the life of Muslim trading and teaching families across the Sahel and forest regions of West Africa. It reinforces the descriptions in Chapters 3 and 4:

> My name is Abu Bakr as-Siddiq, my birth place Timbuktu [in about 1790]. I was educated in the town of Jenne and fully instructed in reading and interpreting the Quran.... My father's name was Kara Musa the Sharif, a Watara [his lineage name] and a *Tafsir* [one learned in Quranic exegesis]. His brothers were named Idris, Abd al-Rahman, Mahmud and Abu Bakr.... After my grandfather's death, there was dissension between them and their families, and they separated and went into different countries of the Sudan [Sahelian West Africa]. Idris went to the country of Massina, where he dwelt in Diawara.... Abd al-Rahman traveled as far as the land of Kong. He married the daughter of the lord of that country and dwelt there. Mahmud traveled to the city of Buna and settled there. Abu Bakr remained in Timbuktu with the rest of the family.

Before all these things happened my father used to travel about. He went into the land of Katsina and Bornu. There he married my mother and then returned to Timbuktu, to which place my mother followed him. After two years had elapsed, my father thought about his brothers, whom he repented having parted with, which grieved him exceedingly. He then ordered his slaves to make ready for their departure with him to visit his brothers and see whether they were in health or not. They therefore obeyed their master's orders . . . and went to the town of Jenne, and from thence to Kong, and from there to Buna, where they stopped. There they resided and continued to serve their master [my father], collecting much gold for him there . . . . My father collected much gold in that country and sent much to his father-in-law [still in Hausaland or Northern Nigeria], together with horses, asses, mules and very valuable silk garments brought from Egypt, with much wealth, as a present to him . . . .

After this my father fell ill of a fever, and died in the city of Buna. He was buried there, and his brothers went and made a great lamentation for him. At that time I was a child [in Jenne] . . . . About 5 years after my father's death, I asked my instructor, who taught me the Quran, to go with me to the city of Buna to visit my father's grave . . . . We reached the city of Kong, and afterwards went on to the city of Buna, and resided there a long time, reckoning that country as our own. We found protection in that country . . . .

Two years after our arrival in Buna, it entered into my teacher's heart to set out on the pilgrimage . . . . My master . . . left me in the city of Buna with my uncle Mahmud.

Then the peace that marked Abu Bakr's early years was shattered. His hosts in Buna joined a coalition fighting against the western province of the Asante Empire (see Chapter 9). When his side lost, Abu Bakr was taken prisoner, shipped out, and forced into a new life in Jamaica. No longer part of a family with domestic servants, no longer respected for the credentials of learning and prosperity that marked his family, Abu Bakr became a plantation slave:

On that very day they made me a captive. They tore off my clothes, bound me with ropes, gave me a heavy load to carry, and led me to the town of Bonduku, and from there to the town of Kumasi, where the king of Asante reigned . . . . From there [I went] to the town of Lago, near the salt sea, all the way on foot, and well loaded.

There they sold me to the Christians, and I was bought by a certain captain of a ship at that time. He sent me to a boat and delivered me over to one of his sailors. The boat immediately pushed off, and I was carried on board the ship. We continued on board ship, at sea, for three months, and then came on shore in the land of Jamaica. This was the beginning of my slavery until this day. I tasted the bitterness of slavery from them, and its oppressiveness.

The brevity and poignancy of Abu Bakr's account can stand for the experience of millions of other Africans and many millions more throughout the world and world history. These human beings were torn from their clothes, torn away from a rhythm of life, torn out of a set of social institutions that provided identity, education, and career opportunities. Suddenly they found themselves in situations of nonfreedom and alienated work. Most of these people could not articulate their autobiographies in writing as well as Abu Bakr, but they experienced the same tearing, the same disjunction, as he.

Slave Trades More Directly Associated with Islam

Abu Bakr was unfortunate. He was one of a number of West African Muslims who wound up in the Americas. Because of their relatively small numbers, European surveillance, and fear of Islam, it was rare for Muslim slaves in the Americas to be able to function as a community. It was impossible to live the lives that "Suwarian" Muslim minorities in West African towns had long enjoyed and that was discussed in Chapter 4.

Some African Muslims were involved in other export systems of Africa and usually on the side of the "winners" – those capturing, transporting, or using slaves. These systems made use of Islam, just as European slavers and American slave-owners often made use of Christianity or as Roman and many Asian societies had long enlisted their ideologies to justify the exploitation of "lesser" human beings.

What do I mean by "made use of Islam"? Essentially two things: first, that most of these slave traders considered themselves to be Muslim, as did most of the owners of the slaves at the points of "consumption," and second, that most of those who were enslaved and taken away were considered to be non-Muslim. Islam recognized slavery and the legitimacy of enslavement, as long as it occurred across the basic divide discussed in Chapter 2: between the *Dar al-Islam* and the *Dar al-Kufr*, between the faithful people of Islam and the "pagans" who were still in ignorance and darkness. When a demand developed, among the ruling or wealthy classes, or when warfare conducted in the name of Islam produced prisoners, then a slave trade, complete with markets, prices, and inspectors, was likely to develop. These "recruitment" systems developed all over the Mediterranean, Middle Eastern, and South Asian worlds, and in Africa.

These patterns of exportation of Africans were older but less intense than the Atlantic slave trade. They are much less well documented. It is extremely rare to get first-hand accounts from the victim's side, as we do with Abu Bakr, but we can assume that the experience was just as heart-rending as his. One such system can be called the Transsaharan slave trade, which was part of the overall Transsaharan trade. It existed for about 1,000 years and "fed" people from the Sahel, woodlands, and forests of Africa to owners in the Sahara, North Africa, and other parts of the Mediterranean. Another can be called the Northeast African trade, which channeled people to the Arabian peninsula, the Middle East, and as far as India, and it lasted for an approximately equal period of time. Finally, we can identify an East African trade to ports and consumers around the shores of the Indian Ocean. This slave trade was not important until the eighteenth and nineteenth centuries, as I indicated in Chapter 3; at that time, however, it became quite intense and dominated much of the economic activity of the region. Taken together, these three systems involved the displacement of millions of people from Sub-Saharan Africa.

In each of these structures most of the owners used their slaves in what we can loosely term domestic service: helping to run the household, serving as wives or concubines of their masters, and raising families. Some slaves labored on farms or in mines or did other work that approximated the appalling conditions of sugar plantations in the Americas. Other slaves could acquire a modicum of power, such as those who served in the palace bureaucracy or as soldiers in the army, as is discussed in Chapter 7. Slave soldiers could become the rulers of societies, as they did in the Mamluk dynasty, which governed Egypt beginning in the thirteenth century. Indeed, the tradition of the slave as soldier and ruler was maintained in Egypt right down into the nineteenth century.

Another slave trade deserves mention here: the "Muslim-Christian" slave trade of the Mediterranean and Atlantic Ocean. In the sixteenth to the eighteenth centuries Middle Eastern, North African, and European powers raided the ships of their rivals, took prisoners, and ransomed some but subjected most to very difficult conditions of confinement and work. The spark was the struggle for supremacy around the Mediterranean between Ottoman forces, who ran the dominant Muslim state, and the emerging European nations. The two sides defined the competition in religious terms, "Islamdom" versus "Christendom," and drew to a significant degree from the enmity born during the period of the Crusades (see Chapter 6).

As discussed in Chapter 3 the anti-Islamic animus motivated the Portuguese when they came to the East African coast in the early 1500s. To a lesser extent the same could be said of other European nationalities and their Ottoman rivals. In general the Muslim raiders and powers got the "better" of the bargain, that is, they took more Christians than they lost of their fellow believers. Probably a million Christians, which is to say Europeans, were enslaved by Mediterranean Muslims between 1480 and 1800; some were ransomed, some died, and most were subjected to very harsh conditions of labor. Many of the Muslim powers and ships were based in North Africa, and they gave the name of "Barbary pirates" to the lexicon of diplomatic history. The founding fathers of the United States had to deal with the capture of American sailors by the "pirates" in the fledgling years of the American republic.

Debates on the Legitimacy of Enslavement

Some Muslim scholars and merchants involved in the slave trades became concerned about the legitimacy of the enslavement process – more than their Christian and European counterparts, at least until the eighteenth century. They raised questions about the legal and moral acceptability of enslavement – that is, whether the people taken were identifiable as non-Muslim. The greatest evidence of this concern comes from North and West Africa and the Transsaharan trade. The time was the sixteenth to early seventeenth century, when an empire named Songhay had replaced Mali and controlled the corridor formed by the Niger River, and when the Moroccan state intruded more sharply into the events of West Africa – including the only successful Transsaharan military expedition in 1591 (see Chapter 7). These processes of state formation and conflict produced great violence, large-scale capture of people, and discussions of what was legitimate and what was not – in Islamic terms.

The discussions were written in Arabic in the framework of question-and-answer essays. Someone poses a set of questions, usually in

a letter to a cleric learned in the law, and the scholar writes a set of responses, question by question. My first illustration comes from about
1500, after a new, more "islamizing" dynasty had come to power in
the Empire of Songhay. Askia Muhammad was the new ruler, from
his capital in Gao, at the point where the Niger River turns southeast to flow through today's Niger and Nigeria. He also ruled over the
city of Timbuktu, the famous African center of Muslim learning and
an important market in the Transsaharan trade. Even though Islam
was still practiced primarily in the cities, by the merchant and ruling
classes, the Askia wanted Songhay to be considered a part of the *Dar al-
Islam*. He was seriously concerned about islamization and about what
constituted legitimate "Islamic government." In 1497–8 he performed
the pilgrimage to Mecca with ceremony and publicity like those of his
Malian predecessors. On his return he greeted a well-known itiner-
ant scholar and asked him a range of questions about proper Islamic
practice.

Al-Maghili, as the scholar was known, came from North Africa
and was in the habit of commenting on issues confronting Muslim
societies from Spain to Sub-Saharan Africa. The most riveting issue
involved religious identity and enslavement, and it was framed around
the character of his predecessor as the ruler of Songhay, a man named
Sonni Ali:

The Second Question [posed by the Askia and recopied by al-Maghili].
Sonni Ali's father was the sultan of its people and his mother was from
the land of Far, and they are an unbelieving people who worship idols
of trees and stones; they make sacrifices to them and ask their needs of
them. If good befalls them they claim that it is those idols who gave it to
them and if it does not befall them they believe that those idols withheld
it from them . . . . Now Sonni Ali, from childhood to manhood, used to
frequent them a great deal to the extent that he grew up among them
and became stamped with their pattern of polytheism and with their
customs . . . .

The Reply [of al-Maghili] . . . is that Sonni Ali and all his supporters
and followers and partisans are no doubt among the most unjust op-
pressors and miscreants, who cut asunder what God has ordained to be
joined and commit mischief in the earth. So the *jihad* of the *amir* Askia
against them and his seizing of power from their hands is one of the most
worthy and important of *jihads* . . . . It will be clear to you that what you
have mentioned of the behavior of Sonni Ali is a sign of unbelief without

doubt. If, then, his behavior is as you have stated, he is an unbeliever as are all those who act like him . . . .

As for enslavement . . . the born unbeliever, his offspring and his wives are to be made captives and his property is to be divided up. There is no divergence over that among the scholars . . . .

Al-Maghili supported what Askia Muhammad wished to do against the previous dynasty and its supporters and more generally against the smaller scale societies of the Sahelian region who resisted incorporation into his Songhay state.

The second illustration was written about 100 years later, after the Songhay Empire fell to Moroccan forces and disintegrated into a number of small states and cities. The victorious army forced a number of prominent families from Timbuktu to accompany them back to Morocco. One of the exiles was Ahmad Baba, the most illustrious cleric of that illustrious city of learning. He was able to use his learning in a society that was Muslim, or at least aspired to be Muslim, and he could achieve goals that were not available to Abu Bakr. He was treated more as hostage than slave, and eventually he received his freedom and returned to Timbuktu. He was widely consulted on issues, often at the court of the Moroccan sultan.

After returning home, Baba continued his consultations and wrote a response to questions from merchants engaged in the Transsaharan trade. In his answers he went further than al-Maghili in the sense of articulating a "religious ethnography" of West African peoples that had been operating in practice for some time:

You [the merchants] write: What do you say concerning slaves imported from lands whose people have been established to be Muslims, such as Bornu, . . . Kano, Gao and Katsina, and others among whom Islam is widespread? Is it allowable to own them or not?

The reply is this. Be it known that the people of these lands are, as you have said, Muslims . . . . However, close to each of these is a land in which there are unbelievers whom the Muslim people of these lands make raids on. Some of them, as is well known, are under their protection and pay *kharaj* [a tax], according to what has come to our ears. Sometimes the sultans of these lands are at loggerheads one with the other and the sultan of one land attacks the other and takes whatever captives he can, they being Muslims. These captives, free Muslims, are then sold . . . . This is commonplace among them in their lands. The people of Katsina attack Kano, and others do likewise, though they speak one tongue and their

languages are united and their way of life similar. The only thing that
distinguishes them is that some are born Muslims and others are born
unbelievers.

You said: It is known that according to the Sharia the only reason
for being owned is unbelief. Thus whoever purchases an unbeliever is
allowed to own him. In the contrary case he is not. Conversion to Islam
after the fulfillment of the aforementioned condition has no effect on
their continued possession.

The reply is that the matter is thus [i.e. your assumptions are
correct] . . . .

You said: Similarly he whose land is unknown and whose status is
unclear in as much as it is not known whether his enslavement pre-
ceded his conversion to Islam or not. Is it allowed to sell him without
investigation? Or is investigation obligatory or recommended?

The reply is that you should be aware that the reason for enslavement
is unbelief, and the unbelievers of the Land of the Blacks [*Sudan*] are like
any other unbelievers in this regard – Jews, Christians, Persians, Berbers
or others whose continued adherence to unbelief rather than Islam has
been established. . . . Whoever is enslaved in a state of unbelief may
rightly be owned, whoever he is, as opposed to those of all groups who
converted to Islam first, such as the people of Bornu, Kano, Songhay,
Katsina, Gobir and Mali . . . . They are free Muslims who may not be enslaved under any circumstance. So also are the majority of the Fulbe . . . .

The scholars and traders were concerned that some Muslims were
being enslaved and that they might be held accountable for that fact.
In reality there was little inspection and accountability. The religious
ethnography "worked" most of the time because the Sahelian societies
that were identified as Muslim, whether city-states in Hausaland such
as Kano and Katsina or larger states such as Bornu and Songhay, usually had the power to enslave rather than be enslaved. Indeed, slavery,
including often slave soldiers and bureaucrats, added to their power
and gave them the ability to acquire new captives, whether for local
"consumption" or for sale into one of the export trades.

The use of all of these elements – religion, state, class – as markers of
who could be enslaved sharpened racial and color consciousness. The
elites of ostensibly Muslim societies hastened to clarify their Islamic
identities by adding linkages, as "ancient" and as close to Muhammad
as possible, such as the genealogical attachments described in Chapter
4. Rulers and merchants also invoked Mediterranean traditions of difference. One of the oldest was the belief that the people who inhabited
the temperate zones were civilized, whereas those who to the north

or south were barbarians who lost all traces of humanity as the temperature became colder or hotter, respectively. This "Mediterraneo-centric" tradition has been very persistent, especially with reference to the hot climes of Africa, as we shall see in the next chapter (see Map 4).

Another venerable tradition was the myth of Ham, a resilient part of the Abrahamic tradition. A common Biblical version of the story runs as follows:

> And the sons of Noah that went forth of the ark were Shem and Ham and Japheth, and Ham is the father of Canaan. These are the sons of Noah, and of them was the whole earth overspread. And Noah began to be an husbandman, and he planted a vineyard. And he drank of the wine and was drunken, and he was uncovered within his tent. And Ham, the father of Canaan, saw the nakedness there, and told his two brethren without. And Shem and Japheth took a garment, and laid it upon both their shoulders, and went backward and covered the nakedness of their father; and their faces were backward, and they saw not their father's nakedness.
>
> And Noah awoke from his wine, and knew what his younger son had done unto him. And he said, Cursed be Canaan, a servant of servants shall he be unto his brethren. And he said, Blessed be the Lord God of Shem, and Canaan shall be his servant. God shall enlarge Japheth, and he shall dwell in the tents of Shem, and Canaan shall be his servant.

Did Noah become so drunk as to leave himself uncovered? Why was he so embarrassed by the event? How did he discover that his sons behaved differently in the face of his nakedness? Did he then curse one of the sons and his progeny? Can the son Ham and the grandson Canaan be identified with darker color and the African continent? Who made that connection and when?

We will never know the answer to these questions. What we do know is that Ham and Canaan have been identified with darkness or blackness among many practitioners of the Abrahamic tradition for a long time. We can sense how this identification resonates in the story of Bilal told in the last chapter. It is not difficult to see why such a venerable account in the life of one of the great figures common to three world faiths would be useful to owners and traders engaged in the "recruitment" and "consumption" of human beings. The "Hamitic" myth strengthened the racial prejudices of Mediterranean-based societies toward Sub-Saharan Africa, the part of the continent most frequently connoted by the term "Africa." Arabs absorbed these ideas, as did Europeans. I examine this in Chapter 6.

"Arab Slave Trading"

In the nineteenth century, under the impetus of economic changes and humanitarian pressure, the managers of the Atlantic slave trade and American slavery began to lose control of the systems of exploitation that they had created. Abolitionist movements gained force in Britain, the United States, and continental Europe. They moved first against the maritime trade, then against slavery in the Americas, and finally against slave trade and slavery throughout the world. The movement's rhetoric ran far ahead of its accomplishments, but it achieved one of its goals: putting freedom, and thereby opposition to slavery and slave trade, at the center of the human rights agenda. By 1900 the Western countries routinely articulated their hostility to enslavement in any form, as well as their commitment to free expression, free association, free trade, the freedom of religion, and a host of other "basic human rights." These commitments were now understood as part of being "civilized."

As the abolitionists and their Christian missionary supporters succeeded against the slave traders and slave owners of the American system, they and their fellow Westerners identified a new enemy: "Arabs," the "Arab slave-trade," and by extension Islam. Europeans had scarcely noticed the trades dominated by Muslim entrepreneurs, except occasionally as possible competitors for slaves. Now, as they reconstructed themselves as humanitarian and civilized and moved into the African continent as explorers, missionaries, and potential colonial powers, they focused on other exportations of people from Africa, what I have called the Transsaharan, Northeast African, and East African trades. To some degree the Europeans were correct: Arabic-speaking peoples and Muslims did play a significant role in these networks. Local slavers and the Ottoman Turks were also involved.

The Transsaharan, Northeast, and East African trades were tied to configurations of slavery that differed from the American patterns. Most of the slaves ended up in something that one could call domestic service. There was always a strand of recruitment into the army. Slave soldiers could acquire considerable power as well as an *esprit de corps*. This was true of the West Africans taken into the armies of the Moroccan sultan from the seventeenth century (see Chapter 7) and of people from the Nile valley region taken into Egyptian forces from the early days of Islam (see Chapter 12).

The Europeans of the nineteenth century trumpeted their opposition to the violence of the slave trade in Africa, identified it with Arabs and Islam, and used it as a justification for their "humanitarian" occupation of Africa. The most significant anglophone voice in this effort was David Livingstone, a Scottish doctor, evangelist, and explorer who ranged through Southern, Central, and East Africa from 1841 until his death in 1873. Livingstone articulated one version of the European mantra of the "three Cs" – Christianity, commerce, and civilization. He spoke out constantly about the slave trade, particularly the system which moved people to and through East Africa, and he played a critical role in shaping European attitudes about Africa and Islam.

The French equivalent of Livingstone was Charles Lavigerie, a Catholic priest and bishop who established his base in Algiers, the capital of the oldest French colony in Africa. It was from there in 1868 that he founded a missionary society, the White Fathers, with a focus on waging a "relentless and unceasing warfare" against slavery and the slave trade in "Islamic Africa." Lavigerie's missionaries played important roles in the "Berber" zones of North Africa and the Sahara and among a variety of Sub-Saharan African societies, and they had a great impact on French attitudes toward Africa.

This "crusade" against the "Arab" and "Islamic" slave trade and slavery was an important justification for the conquest and establishment of European colonial rule. But the Europeans learned that it was much easier to rail against slave trade and slavery in Africa than to actually bring about its demise. They soon toned down their commitments without abandoning the rhetoric of freedom. It is to these complex and changing attitudes of Europeans toward Africa and Islam that we now turn.

Further Reading

For the slave trades and Africa, a good place to begin is Robin Blackburn's *The Making of New World Slavery: From the Baroque to the Modern, 1492–1800* (Verso, 1997), because he gives a lot of "Old World" background to the "New World" of the Americas. You may also wish to consult (editors) Seymour Drescher and Stanley Engerman's *A Historical Guide to World Slavery* (Oxford University Press, 1998) and the bibliographies contained in the journal *Slavery and Abolition*.

The most complete treatment of slavery in Africa is Paul Lovejoy, *Transformations in Slavery: A History of Slavery in Africa* (Cambridge University Press,

1983, 2000). For West Africa and the passages by Abu Bakr, see Ivor Wilks' article and other selections in (editor) Philip Curtin's *Africa Remembered: Narratives by West Africans from the Era of the Slave Trade* (University of Wisconsin Press, 1967). For an exploration of slavery in South Africa, where Islam often served as an identity and rallying point for slaves and ex-slaves, see Robert Shell's *Children of Bondage: A Social History of the Slave Society at the Cape of Good Hope, 1652–1838* (Wesleyan University Press, 1994). For Muslim slaves in North America, see Allan Austin's *African Muslims in Antebellum America: A Sourcebook* (Routledge, 1984), and Michael Gomez's *Exchanging Our Country Marks: The Transformation of African Identities in the Colonial and Antebellum South* (University of North Carolina Press, 1998).

For the connections of Islam to slavery, start with Bernard Lewis' *Race and Slavery in the Middle East* (Oxford University Press, 1990). For Africa, see Allan and Humphrey Fisher's *Slavery and Muslim Society in Africa* (Hurst, 1970), and (editor) John Ralph Willis' *Slaves and Slavery in Muslim Africa* (volume 1, Cass, 1985). For one of the first attempts to gauge the Transsaharan slave trade, see (editor) Elizabeth Savage's *The Human Commodity: Perspectives on the Trans-Saharan Slave Trade* (Cass, 1992); for an estimate of the numbers involved, see Ralph Austen's "The Mediterranean Slave Trade Out of Africa: A Tentative Census" in *Slavery and Abolition* (1992). Occasionally the slave trades associated with the Islamic world produced appalling working conditions. The best known example occurred in today's Iraq in the late ninth and early tenth centuries, where slaves of East African origin revolted against their owners and the Abbasid authorities. The best source on this is Alexandre Popovic's *The Revolt of African Slaves in Iraq in the 3rd/9th Century* (Marcus Wiener, 1999). For the "Barbary pirates" and the enslavement of Europeans by Muslims in North Africa, see Stephen Clissold's *The Barbary Slaves* (Rowman and Littlefield, 1977) and Ellen Friedman's *Spanish Captives in North Africa in the Early Modern Age* (University of Wisconsin Press, Wis, 1983).

On Muslim debates about the legitimacy of the slave trade and slavery, see the Willis volume cited above. The selection from the responses of al-Maghili comes from John Hunwick's *Sharia in Songhay* (Oxford University Press, 1985). The selection from the responses of Ahmad Baba comes from John Hunwick and Fatima Harrak's annotation and translation of Ahmad Baba's *Mi'raj al-Su'ud: Ahmad Baba's Replies on Slavery* (Institute of African Studies, Rabat, Morocco, 2000).

The passage about Noah, Ham, and Canaan comes from Genesis 9, verses 18–27 from the King James Version (National Bible Press, 1954). You may wish to pursue the question of Ham and the "Hamitic" theme in the Blackburn volume cited above and in Edith Sanders' "The Hamitic Hypothesis: Its Origin and Functions in Time Perspective" in *Journal of African History* (volume 10.4, 1969, pp. 521–32), Benjamin Braude's "The Sons of Noah and the Construction of Ethnic and Geographical Identities in the Medieval and Early Modern Periods" in *William & Mary Quarterly* (volume 40.1, January 1997), and John Block Friedman's *The Monstrous Races in Medieval Art and Thought* (Harvard University Press, 1981).

On the pressure to end the "Arab slave-trade" see Ehud Toledano's *The Ottoman Slave Trade and Its Suppression* (Princeton University Press, 1982). For East Africa, see (editor) William G. Clarence-Smith's *The Economics of the Indian Ocean Slave Trade in the 19th Century* (Cass, 1989). For Livingstone and Lavigerie, see Adrian Hastings' *The Church in Africa: 1450–1950* (Oxford University Press, 1994). The best sources on slave soldiers in the Islamic worlds are Daniel Pipes' *Slave Soldiers in Islam: The Genesis of a Military System* (Yale University Press, 1981) and (editors) Miura Toru and John Edward Philips' *Slaves Elites in the Middle East and Africa: A Comparative Study* (Kegan Paul International, 2000).

CHAPTER 6

Western Views of Africa and Islam

The "West" has been the dominant force in world history in the past two centuries, if not the past five. In the form of the Western European countries and North America, it has imposed on the rest of the world a calendar; a way of dividing the day; a system of mapping; an international monetary system; many agricultural, industrial, and electronic norms; a construction of education from kindergarten to professional studies; and other frameworks that we usually take for granted. These are simply the way "things" work. Along with these structures come some very important definitions and attitudes about Africa and Islam that a book such as this one cannot ignore.

The Ancient Heritage and Africa

To uncover the layers of these attitudes, we need to go back to the "beginning," which I take to be the Ptolemaic conception of the world. Ptolemy was a Greek scholar who lived in Alexandria, Egypt, in the second century C.E.; he put together much ancient wisdom and lore about the world. This view, mentioned in the previous chapter, took the Mediterranean societies of Ancient Egypt, Greece, and Rome and other areas as the "norm" – centers of civilization in a temperate climate, permitting the development of agriculture and urban life. In this framework of zones or "climes" the "Mediterraneans" occupied the middle positions (3 and 4) out of 7. The first clime was in the far south, amid intense heat, and was essentially uninhabitable. This

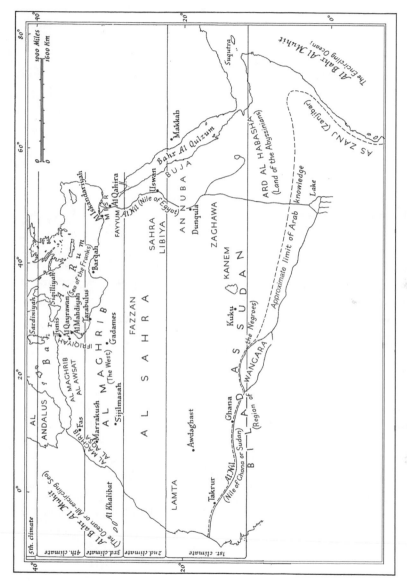

MAP 4 The Arabs' conception of Africa in the thirteenth century C.E. Adapted from John D. Fage and Maureen Verity, *An Atlas of African History*, New York, 1978.

would correspond roughly to the deeper parts of Sub-Saharan Africa, around the Equator today, about which the ancient authorities knew little or nothing. The last or seventh clime was in the far north, amid intense cold, and was likewise essentially uninhabitable. This would correspond to the northern portions of today's Europe up to the Arctic Circle; again there was very little knowledge of the area through which to modify, much less challenge, the basic schema.

This ancient heritage was appropriated by the Arabs and other Muslims as they expanded around the Mediterranean and established schools of translation, teaching, and research in Baghdad and other centers of learning. To a significant extent this "Mediterranean" perspective corresponded to what they understood as the "real" *Dar al-Islam* (see Map 4). It was also appropriated by European societies during the Middle Ages and then reaffirmed during the Renaissance, when the ancient heritage of Greece and Rome was celebrated.

Europeans themselves disproved the perceptions about the colder climes by showing that civilization could develop there. But no one challenged the perceptions of the south, that is, the area that we call Sub-Saharan Africa. This was partly because Muslims and Europeans did not have the means to obtain new information. In terms of observations by sea, navigation was limited essentially to the Indian Ocean and Swahili areas described in Chapter 3. In the fifteenth century the Portuguese developed the ability to round the Cape of Good Hope, land on both the Atlantic and Indian Ocean shores of Africa, and return to Europe. Only then did new, first-hand information about the coast of the continent begin to be accumulated. By itself these data might have altered the schema, but they were soon overwhelmed by the structure I discussed in the previous chapter, the Atlantic Slave Trade. The justification for the enslavement of other human beings needed a basis in color, climate, and civilization – or its absence. The ancient schema, with some modification, worked fine.

The information that came in by land did not alter the schema, either. The Romans did not penetrate very far into the Sahara and made no efforts to extend their control below the agricultural littoral of North Africa – in other words, they kept to the same Mediterranean orbit of the previous empires and networks. Arab and Berber Muslims did cross the Sahara and develop the systems of Transsaharan trade that I have already discussed. But their activities tended to reinforce the vision. As shown in the previous chapter, they were prepared to accept the Islamic religious identity of the Sahel, of extensive states such as Bornu, Mali, and Songhay or Hausa city-states such as Katsina and Kano, and equate them with clime 2 or 3. They continued to believe that those who lived further south, in clime 1, were pagan and uncivilized with all the marks of those conditions – hot climate, little or no dress, scarification, rudimentary housing, no state formation, and so on. The Sahelians themselves found this to be a convenient framework as well; it justified their superiority and participation in the slave trade and slavery.

The Challenge of Islam

Europeans could not dismiss or marginalize Islam as easily as Africa. From their perspective it originated in a marginal part of the world, the Hijaz portion of the Arabian peninsula, but soon occupied "recognized" centers of civilization and appropriated the ancient heritage. Islam occupied important geographical and intellectual space. It challenged Christianity on its own theological turf, as an alternative version of the Abrahamic tradition. Muslims believed in the prophets from Adam to Jesus and in their divine inspiration; indeed, they even had the audacity to call those prophets "Muslims," that is, people who oriented their lives around submission to God. Islam called its followers to a life of moral rectitude, accountability, and living by God's laws. It stressed the Day of Judgment, Hell, and Heaven. Its believers were also capable, through Arab, Berber, and Turkish armies and navies, of competing for control of the Mediterranean and pressing into Europe itself.

This intellectual, theological, and military challenge led many Europeans and Christians during the Middle Ages to create a countervision – to demonize Islam, the Quran, and the Prophet. Dimensions of that vision have persisted down to the present and can easily be invoked by commentators around bombings, conspiracies, and other acts of "Islamic" terrorism. This countervision began in the seventh century C.E. or the first century A.H., with the "incursions" of Muslims into the northern shores of the Mediterranean, what came to be called Europe. The occupation of most of the Iberian peninsula, under the name of Andalusia, was the most important of these invasions because it was the most enduring. It lasted until 1492, with the capture of Granada and the expulsion of the last Muslims and Jews from "reconquered" Spain. Muslim control of Sicily and southern Italy was not as enduring, but left a substantial impact on local culture. The movement into the southeast, the domains dominated by the Byzantine Empire, was spasmodic until the fourteenth and fifteenth centuries. But then, in the form of the Ottoman Empire, it was perceived as a major threat.

Muslim expansion shaped the European imagination in very fundamental ways. The year 732 C.E., for example, marks the defeat of the Arab and Berber armies by Charles Martel, ancestor of Charlemagne, at Poitiers. The battle has become a staple of textbooks treating the emergence of French "nationhood." Participants in the Balkan struggles of the 1990s have often invoked the 1389 battle of Kosovo, where Ottoman armies fought the "Christians." Slobodan Milosevic and other Serbian nationalists have called this a "martyrdom" as a way to justify a continuing fight against Islamic civilization – and the Muslim people who embody it in southeastern Europe. A different kind of example comes from Istanbul, which claims that the reluctance to admit the secular regime of Turkey into the European Union is based on a latent bias against Islamic culture. One could multiply almost infinitely these signposts of difference and enmity over the past 1,400 years.

But it is possible to concentrate on two sequences of events between 1100 and 1500 C.E. that solidified the negative stereotype of Islam. The first sequence is the "reconquest" of the Iberian peninsula by Christian armies and nations under the leadership of the courts of Castile and Aragon. In 1085 the Christian forces captured the famous intellectual center of Toledo, and over the next 400 years they gradually pushed the Muslim forces further and further south and finally out of the peninsula altogether. In the process they undermined a culture in which Jewish, Christian, and Islamic communities had fully cohabited and collaborated.

Rome and the Pope encouraged this reconquest and orchestrated the second and even more important sequence, the Crusades. Beginning in 1099, a series of Western European armies and clergy marched and sailed to the eastern end of the Mediterranean to "recover the cradle" of Christianity from the Arab and Turkish Muslims who controlled it. In the process they created crusader or Frankish states in the area of today's Palestine, Israel, and Lebanon and retained a presence there for several centuries. They also provoked a Muslim reaction, led by Saladin, who united Egypt and Syria, mobilized the counterattack, and took Jerusalem back in 1187. Saladin became a great hero, and Muslims sharpened their stereotypes about Christianity.

What was the vision of Islam that many Europeans shared in the Middle Ages and that has persisted in many dimensions to this day? Islam was "Muhammadanism," that is, a religious faith and practice manufactured by an ambitious but not very admirable man. Muhammad was a false prophet who added nothing to the Judeo-Christian heritage; in fact, he distorted the images of the Old Testament prophets and Jesus. In addition, he was violent, lascivious, and untrustworthy in the treatment of his contemporaries, be they Muslim, Jewish, Christian, or pagan, and these qualities were reflected in the conquests and societies created after his death. The Quran was not God's own revelation and a miracle, but a collection of statements from Muhammad and his contemporaries that compared very badly to the Bible. Islam in essence was a heresy, to be combated, and harsh treatment of Muslim prisoners or captives was legitimate. Force and violence had to be answered in kind.

At the same time that the demonization of Islam was developing, the Catholic Church and some of the Western European courts were creating the Inquisition, a procedure to identify and destroy heresy within Christianity. Beginning in the twelfth century, the Pope authorized inquisitors to investigate suspected communities, summon the accused, and render judgments upon them. Heresy was equated with treason against God, and some of those convicted were executed. The Inquisition was especially strong in southern France and parts of Italy in the thirteenth century. The procedures were adopted by Castile and Aragon in the fifteenth century in the sequence that we know as the Spanish Inquisition. In this case the investigation was turned not just against heretics but also against Muslims, Jews, and those who had converted to Christianity from the two faiths. These inquisitions sharpened the boundaries and definitions of belief and deepened the distortions about Islam.

At the time of the inquisitions Europeans gave credence to the report of a Christian king who ruled over a prosperous and powerful regime behind the domains of Islam. This Prester John, "priest John," was at times located in India and other places, but by the late medieval period he was usually placed in the Horn of Africa and Ethiopia. According to the story, the Prester John was ready to join with the Europeans in a movement against Islam and for the recovery of the holy lands of Christianity. The early Portuguese explorers and missionaries who rounded the coast of Africa and went into the Ethiopian highlands believed that they had found the monarch and the church, as is discussed in Chapter 8.

The negative vision of Islam was not operative everywhere, and it did not eliminate all cases of cooperation or instances where members of one faith lived as minorities in societies controlled by the other. But it became much more difficult, after the reconquest, the Crusades, and the inquisitions, to find situations where Christians and Muslims – and Jews – could live and work together, as they once had in Baghdad and Toledo. The negative images persist to the present day. Hilaire Belloc, a French Catholic intellectual who lived much of his life in Great Britain in the early twentieth century, had this to say in a book published in 1919:

> There remains, apart from the old Paganism of Asia and Africa, another indirect supporter of Neo-Paganism: a supporter which indeed hates all Paganism but hates the Catholic Church much more . . . . I mean Islam. Islam presents a totally different problem from that attached to any other religious body opposed to Catholicism. To understand it we must appreciate its origin, character and recent fate . . . .
>
> How did Islam arise? It was not, as our popular historical textbooks would have it, a "new religion. – It was a direct derivative from the Catholic Church. It was essentially, in its origin, a heresy . . . .
>
> When the man who produced it – and it is more the creation of one man than any other false religion we know – was young, the whole of the world which he knew, the world speaking Greek in the eastern half and Latin in the Western – the only civilized world with which he and his people had come in contact – was Catholic. It was still, though in process of transformation, the Christian Roman Empire, stretching from the English Channel to the borders of his own desert.
>
> The Arabs of whom he came and among whom he lived were Pagan; but such higher religious influence as could touch them, and as they came in contact with through commerce and raiding, was Catholic – with a certain admixture of Jewish communities. Catholicism has thus distinctly affected these few pagans living upon the fringes of the Empire.
>
> What Mahomet did was this. He took over the principal doctrines of the Catholic Church – one personal God, Creator of all things; the immortality of the soul; an eternity of misery or blessedness – and no small part of Christian morals as well. All that was the atmosphere of the only civilization which had influence upon him or his followers. But at the same time he attempted an extreme simplification . . . .

In Belloc's views one can find many of the attitudes that mark the treatment of Muslim societies in the Western media.

Images of Africa and Islam in The Modern Period

The views of Sub-Saharan Africa and Islam did not change appreciably after 1500 C.E. European observers poured the new data about the Atlantic coast of Africa into the mold of justification for American slavery. Many slave traders and slave owners claimed that they were improving the opportunities of Africans to rise to the lower levels of civilization. They invoked the myth of Ham to reinforce the "miserable" state of societies in the southern climes and legitimize their actions.

Islam posed a larger intellectual challenge, because it still occupied Mediterranean space and had two political champions. The smaller one was Morocco, an Islamic state since the eighth century C.E. It welcomed many Muslim and Jewish refugees from reconquered Spain, and I examine it in the next chapter. The larger, newer, and more dangerous foe was the Ottoman Empire, which began to occupy Anatolia and southeastern Europe in the fourteenth century.

The Ottoman Turks captured the old Byzantine capital of Constantinople in 1453 and renamed it Istanbul. They took Egypt and most of North Africa in the early sixteenth century. By their armies and navies, elaborate bureaucracy, appropriation of the ancient and medieval intellectual heritage, and placement at the "entrance" to Europe, they were worthy opponents for several centuries. They laid claim to the leadership of the Islamic world. Their strength helped to fuel the Muslim-Christian slave trade that I discussed in the previous chapter.

Despite the enslavement of Christians and Muslims, despite the distortions and demonizing of Islam, the Western European countries established diplomatic relations with Morocco and the Ottoman Empire. Their ambassadors and consuls could observe first-hand the multiethnic and multireligious situations in these "Muslim" lands. Indeed, Moroccan and Ottoman societies were relatively diverse and tolerant at the time when the Germans and British were fighting religious wars, the French regime was persecuting the Huguenots, and the Spanish were wielding the Inquisition. The sultans imposed certain restrictions of dress, residence, and vocation on non-Muslims, but made no effort to impose the creed. Indeed many Christians and Jews occupied important positions in artisan production, commerce, and the court. This was the basic orientation that Islamic governments had taken since the seventh century.

Neither Morocco nor the Ottomans controlled any significant portions of Sub-Saharan Africa. Nor did they challenge the old vision of climes: Muslim and civilized zones as far south as the Sahel, followed by paganism and barbarism at the bottom of the world. Indeed, they provided the framework in which the Transsaharan and Northeast African trades continued to supply slaves for domestic service and other niches within Mediterranean and Middle Eastern societies. Increasingly enslavement and slavery were identified with color, race, and Sub-Saharan Africa.

Western European expansion into the Islamic and African worlds intensified in the nineteenth century, fueled by the Industrial Revolution, the Enlightenment, the abolitionist movement, and a growing sense of superiority on all fronts. Along with the expansion went a growing secularization and commitment to modernization; European economies and societies became a model for others to follow. Although democracy and secularism gained ground in Europe, old stereotypes dominated outside it. Western civilization was superior, and non-Western societies should take the opportunity to modernize. Islam was still a worthy foe to be feared, but Muslim societies could now be pardoned and pitied for their backwardness. Sub-Saharan Africa still occupied the bottom of the civilization scale. It needed complete reconstruction, from outside; Catholic and Protestant missionaries were among the first to start the task.

The Western powers began to refer to the Ottoman sultan as "the sick man of Europe" and to contemplate how his empire should be dismantled. The British, French, German, and Russian courts competed in interventions against the Istanbul regime – or in efforts to prop it up. A bit later the same governments, along with Spain, took up the Moroccan case.

The most signal expression of growing Western domination came in 1798. In that year Napoleon Bonaparte took control of Egypt, center of ancient civilization as well as the heart of the Arab Middle East and North Africa. He portrayed himself as the great friend of Islam (see Figure 12). He took not just soldiers and administrators but a battery of scholars of all disciplines. They wrote the monumental, multivolume *Description de l'Egypte*, founded the Institute of Egypt, and helped create the disciplines of Egyptology and Islamic Studies in European higher education. It is this event sequence – the sudden appropriation of the culture of one country by another – that Edward Said takes as the beginning of modern Orientalism in the Occident. By "Orientalism" Said means the ways in which the West has framed, studied, and ruled the Other, and particularly the Middle Eastern Muslim Other. I come back to Said in the next section of the chapter.

Napoleon's invasion was fed by his rivalry with Great Britain and desire to challenge the route to British India, and it was the British

FIGURE 12 European intrusion. Napoleon in Egypt, investing an Arab shaikh, ca. 1800. Normal Daniel, *Islam, Europe and Empire*, Edinburgh University Press, 1966.

fleet, dominant in the Mediterranean, who put an abrupt end to the French occupation in 1801. No Saladin was available to mobilize the Arab or Muslim cause. The damage was enduring. A Western European power had invaded a central territory of the Ottoman Empire, not just militarily but also intellectually. Forced to withdraw by another European power, it nonetheless took away an immense array of artifacts for museums and libraries and left behind an indelible impression of strength.

In the wake of Napoleon's departure a new dynasty came to power in Egypt. Muhammad Ali, a former military slave of Albanian origin, became the governor and engineer of a vast program of modernization over the next four decades (1805–48). Ostensibly Egypt was still under Ottoman control, but in fact it functioned quite independently. Muhammad Ali became an example of "development" for his non-Western contemporaries.

Muhammad Ali, Napoleon, and the French Revolution of which he was beneficiary ushered in a new level of European involvement in Muslim societies. Rulers from Istanbul to Morocco felt a need to "modernize." European military strategists, engineers, accountants, and other consultants were recruited for the process and came under the observation and often the protection of the ambassadors and consuls that had been operating in the Muslim capitals for centuries. Loans were made and interest collected, if not by direct payment then through the control of customs duties. Outlets for manufactured goods as well as sources of raw materials for European industry were developed. Western schools were founded, not just for Christian and Jewish minorities but also for a "modernizing" Muslim intelligentsia.

These developments prepared the way for the next step, the establishment of various forms of colonial rule. This type of European control came to Algeria beginning in 1830; to Egypt in 1882; Sudan in 1898; Morocco in 1912; and Syria, Iraq, Palestine, and Transjordan after World War I. The only parts of the old Ottoman Empire that escaped were Turkey itself and parts of the Arabian peninsula. By 1900 the Western European countries were referring to themselves as "Muslim powers," by which they meant the custodians of Muslims. Although they still feared Islam and actively watched for signs of *jihad* and revolt, they were confident of their ability to control their subjects. In general the Western rulers employed similar structures to channel the use of Islamic courts and law, monitor education, control the pilgrimage, and "handle" other questions connected with secular authority over Muslims.

The conquest and establishment of European rule in Sub-Saharan Africa occurred in the same time frame but under different ministries with different intellectual assumptions. The Europeans assumed that they knew less about Black Africa than about North Africa and the Middle East. They appropriated the designations of medieval and early modern writers in Arabic about the religious ethnography of the region. The Sudanese and Mauritanian people who spoke Arabic were of course Muslim. The Mandinka, Songhay, Hausa, Fulbe, and Swahili

were Muslim, or at least "almost as Muslim" as the "Arabs." The people of the southernmost clime, below the Sahel and west of the Indian
Ocean littoral, were not Muslim at all. This old but crude classification
played a large role in where Christian missionaries wanted to go and
where the fledgling colonial governments gave them access.

In effect, the British, French, and Italian regimes that dominated
the African colonial landscape were ambivalent about Muslim practice
and Sub-Saharan Africa. This is not surprising given the combination
of traditions we have examined: the enduring influence of the "climes,"
the impact of the Atlantic slave trade, the association of Islam with Arab
and Arabic identity, the clashes of "Islamdom" and "Christendom,"
and the tendency to see civilization in racial terms.

Some of the first "experts" to work in Sub-Saharan Africa were
"Orientalists," because this multidisciplinary "discipline" was the
principal training for understanding the "Other" in the nineteenth
century. In the twentieth century, however, the colonial regimes of
places such as Senegal, Nigeria, or Kenya put a premium on "home-
grown" expertise, whether that of the missionary, the ethnographer,
or the administrator who produced monographic studies of particular
districts.

The regimes also sought in various ways to "quarantine" Islam,
which meant two things. First, they limited and guided the contacts
between Sub-Saharan Muslim groups and the "heartlands" of the
faith, especially around the obligation to perform the pilgrimage. This
involved health checks, political inquiries, intelligence operations by
Muslims in colonial employ, and finally "sponsoring" the pilgrimage
by chartering boats and planes. In the second place, the regimes sought
to control the contacts between Muslims and non-Muslims, fearing
that the "stronger" civilization of Islam would overwhelm the "weaker"
civilizations of African societies. The clearest example of ambivalence
and quarantine was the French West African formulation *Islam noir*.
"Black Islam" was separate from and inferior to "Arab" or "North
African Islam." The efforts of colonial administrators were not particularly successful, but they left their marks on the practices of African
Muslims.

Orientalism and African Studies

Growing European domination of Muslim societies and Africa produced the two overlapping intellectual enterprises that shape this

book. Orientalism has become the catch word for Western studies and discourses about the "East," with the emphasis on Islam. Edward Said helped fashion the term over twenty years ago in a book by the same name. From his vantage point as a Palestinian raised outside of his homeland, a resident of New York, a professor of journalism, and a writer, he has become the leading critic of the enterprises launched by the Napoleonic invasion of Egypt and other European intrusions into the "Muslim lands."

Said has this to say about Orientalism:

> My contention is that without examining Orientalism as a discourse one cannot possibly understand the enormously systematic discipline by which European culture was able to manage – and even produce – the Orient politically, sociologically, militarily, ideologically, scientifically, and imaginatively during the post-Enlightenment period. Moreover, so authoritative a position did Orientalism have that I believe no one writing, thinking or acting on the Orient could do so without taking account of the limitations on thought and action imposed by Orientalism ....
>
> Historically and culturally there is a quantitative as well as a qualitative difference between the Franco-British involvement in the Orient and – until the period of American ascendancy after World War II – the involvement of every other European and Atlantic power. To speak of Orientalism therefore is to speak mainly, although not exclusively, of a British and French cultural enterprise, a project whose dimensions take in such disparate realms as the imagination itself, the whole of India and the Levant, the Biblical texts and the Biblical lands, the spice trade, colonial armies and a long tradition of colonial administrators, a formidable scholarly corpus, innumerable Oriental "experts" and "hands," an Oriental professorate, a complex array of "Oriental" ideas (Oriental despotism, Oriental splendor, cruelty, sensuality), many Eastern sects, philosophies and wisdoms domesticated for local European use – the list can be extended more or less indefinitely. My point is that Orientalism derives from a particular closeness experienced between Britain and France and the Orient, which until the 19th century had really meant only India and the Bible lands. From the beginning of the 19th century until the end of World War II France and Britain dominated the Orient and Orientalism ....

Said is certainly correct about the leading roles that Britain and France played in the past two centuries in fashioning Oriental and particularly Islamic studies. One need only look at the School of Oriental and African Studies at the University of London, the Ecole des Langues Orientales Vivantes in Paris, or Western institutes established in the Middle East to understand the ways in which the studies of this "Other" have been framed. This process is quite different from the study of French, German, and Spanish languages and literatures or the disciplines of history, sociology, and political science. "Oriental" and "Middle Eastern" are adjectives applied to multidisciplinary studies that emphasize the study of a religion, Islam, its fundamental language, Arabic (and sometimes the two "second" languages of Islam, Turkish and Persian), and a range of supporting courses. Graduate work in these centers, and similar ones in other parts of Europe and North America, equip you for teaching, research, government, and civil society work in the Islamic "heartlands."

These centers, then, are where you would go if you had a strong interest in Egypt and North Africa. If you were interested in the Sahel and points south, you would go into the different framework of African studies. You would probably enroll in a particular discipline within a university with a range of complementary Africanists in other disciplines, and you would emerge with a competence in a more limited body of knowledge. This has to do in part with the enormous complexity of Africa – it cannot be encapsulated in three much less one language, and it has no unifying religious creed or practice. But it also has to do with the venerable biases about the southern climes, the enslavable peoples, and the descendants of Ham. Africa did not have a history, not even one of opposition to Christianity or European domination. It was only in the late 1950s, when African countries ended colonial rule and joined the United Nations, that centers of African studies and fields such as African history emerged.

This book, then, bridges an old and yawning gap. It is about Islam, and it is about Africa. It is about North and Sub-Saharan Africa. It draws from Islamic and African studies. It draws from the "Islamic history" of North Africa, recognized however grudgingly by the West as a valid subject for many centuries, and "African history," a subject that has a recognition of scarcely forty years. It draws on Arabic, which is spoken by millions of Africans in the northern part of the continent and is labeled as a language of the Middle East; it draws on Hausa, Fulani, Mandinka, Swahili, and other "Islamic" tongues of Africa, which are labeled as languages of Sub-Saharan Africa. It deals with white people and black people and every shade between. It deals with those who construct themselves or who are perceived to be "white" and "black" and other things "between." It deals with the constructions of color, race, civilization, and hierarchy.

Further Reading

In this chapter I have benefitted from a copy of a lecture, "A Region of the Mind: The Arab Invention of Africa," delivered by John Hunwick at Northwestern University in 1993. A very useful work is Bernard Lewis' *Race and Slavery*, cited at the end of Chapter 5. The medieval European background about Africa and Islam can be found in two books by Norman Daniel, *Islam and the West* (Edinburgh University Press, 1960) and *Islam, Europe and Empire* (Edinburgh University Press, 1966), and the Friedman book cited in the previous chapter. For the inquisitions, see Bernard Hamilton's *The Medieval Inquisition* (E. Arnold, 1982). There is a vast literature on the Crusades; the most comprehensive work is (editor) K. M. Setton's *A History of the Crusades* (University of Wisconsin Press, 1969–77, second edition, four volumes). The Hilaire Belloc selection comes from his *Survivals and New Arrivals*, published in 1919; for the text, provided by Catholic Resource Network, see http://www.ewtn.com/library/homelibr/hbislam.txt.

More background, and a comparison of the attitudes engendered by the slaves trades toward Muslims and Africans, can be found in Blackburn's *The Making of New World Slavery*, cited at the end of Chapter 5, and David Eltis' *The Rise of African Slavery in the Americas* (Cambridge University Press, 2000).

For a treatment of the climes and the Hamitic hypothesis, see the Friedman book and the Braude and Sanders articles cited in the previous chapter. The Ptolemaic framework is very present in the thinking of the North African sociologist of the fourteenth century, Ibn Khaldun, whose work is cited at the end of Chapter 2.

For the development of Orientalism, see Edward Said's *Orientalism* (New Vintage Books, 1978). The passage is from pages 3 and 4. For the development of Orientalism and African studies in Great Britain, see Colin Flight's "The Bantu expansion and the SOAS network" in *History in Africa* (volume 15, 1988). The best treatment of the emergence of African studies in France is Emmanuelle Sibeud's "La naissance de l'ethnographie africaniste en France avant 1914" in *Cahiers d'Etudes Africaines* (no. 136, 1994).

For the Ottoman Empire, consult S. J. Shaw's *History of the Ottoman Empire and Modern Turkey* (two volumes, Cambridge University Press, 1976). For a recent portrayal of how the Ottomans related to Europe, see Dan Goffman's *The Ottoman Empire and Early Modern Europe* (Cambridge University Press, 2002). For Arab intellectuals and their responses to European influence over the past two centuries, see Albert Hourani's *Arabic Thought in the Liberal Age* (Cambridge University Press, 1983); for an Algerian intellectual's reflections on the contemporary situation, see Mohammed Arkoun's *Rethinking Islam*, mentioned at the end of Chapter 1. Khaled Fahmy, in *All the Pasha's Men: Mehmed Ali, His Army and the Making of Modern Egypt* (Cambridge University Press, 1997), provides a recent study of Muhammad Ali and "modernization" in Egypt.

III

Case Studies

————————

CHAPTER 7

Morocco: Muslims in a
"Muslim Nation"

To start the case study section of this book, I begin with an area that has an ancient Islamic identity. Moroccans, in the form of Berbers who converted to the faith, participated in great numbers in the conquest of the Iberian peninsula beginning in 711 C.E. The officer who led the campaigns was Berber. At this juncture the area we now call Morocco was under limited control from the Umayyad Caliphate in Damascus and its governor in Qayrawan, the main city in Tunisia.

Morocco began to acquire a regional identity, as distinguished from Tunisia and Algeria, in the late eighth century C.E. This came when a descendant of the Prophet settled in the area, and since that time the rulers of Morocco have claimed a genealogical connection to Muhammad. They refer to their monarchy as the "Sharifian throne." But this Islamic identity at the center of Moroccan life has not always brought satisfaction or prosperity to its citizens. In this chapter we look at what it has meant, over the centuries, to be Muslim in a state with a strong Islamic identity.

The Beginnings

The name Morocco means "far west" in Arabic, because the region stood at the westernmost limits of the Islamic world. One of the early Arab generals rode his horse into the Atlantic Ocean before turning back, and shortly after that the combined Arab and Berber force crossed the straits and started the Spanish Muslim regime we call Andalusia.

In the second Muslim century illustrious refugees from the civil wars of the Middle East played a critical role in strengthening the Islamic identities of the "far west." In the 750s Abd al-Rahman, a descendant of an Umayyad caliph, escaped from the new Abbasid regime; he went on to centralize the Andalusian regime from his capital at Cordoba. Thirty years later Idriss, a great-great-grandson of Fatima and Ali, fled from the same Baghdad authorities to Morocco. A Berber group near an old Roman site gave him protection and called his settlement Mawlay Idriss, "master Idriss." A few years later Idriss died of poisoning, apparently administered by an Abbasid agent, but his servant and then his son kept the kingdom together. Later Moroccan rulers made the tomb of Idriss I into a place of pilgrimage. Today Moroccans will tell you that there are four places of pilgrimage in the Islamic world: after Mecca, Medina, and Jerusalem is Mawlay Idriss.

When the young Idriss II took over, he was able to establish the state on firmer foundations at a nearby settlement called Fez and to attract Arab populations from Tunisia and Andalusia to settle in the city. The two main quarters were called Qayrawan (cf. Kairouan on Map 2), where the Tunisians were concentrated, and Andalus. Fez has been the intellectual capital of Morocco ever since. For centuries its scholars have run a famous university, presided over courts, and issued *fatwas* or "decrees," about religious, social, and political issues.

In the early ninth century the Idrissids controlled the agricultural plain facing the Atlantic and a portion of the Mediterranean, but most of their subjects still spoke Berber languages. In fact, Idriss II was probably more at home in the Berber language of his mother than in Arabic. The dynasty had little influence in the ridges of mountains that ring the southern edge of the plain and none at all in the Sahara beyond. After the death of Idriss II the state broke into several parts around his twelve sons.

In the tenth century C.E. the Moroccan plain became the scene of conflict between competing Muslim regimes. One was the Fatimid Shia caliphate, which started in Tunisia, took control of Egypt, and ruled from Cairo. The Fatimids invaded Morocco and exacted tribute from Idrissids and the Berber chiefdoms. Their closest rival was the Andalusian regime in Cordoba, which began to call itself the Umayyad Caliphate in the early tenth century. The triangular struggle of Cordoba, Cairo, and Baghdad shattered the unified caliphate that had prevailed in most of the Islamic world.

This was one dimension of an intense struggle for theological as well as political domination. The Sunni way, the "orthodoxy" that the majority of Muslims came to embrace, was not yet dominant. Moroccan Muslims were very much a part of these conflicts and shifts in orientation. The dominant influence, in cultural terms, came from Andalusia and the cities of Cordoba and Seville.

From the eleventh century onward the relationship among the cities was reversed. It was Morocco that provided protection for Andalusia and helped slow the progress of the Christian reconquest. The Almoravids, whom we followed in Chapter 3, marched up from the Sahara into Morocco, founded Marrakesh, and moved into Spain. They slowed the momentum of the reconquest before giving way to division in their own ranks. Their successors, the Almohads, also briefly united the two areas and stemmed the tide. Over time, however, the Christians of northern Spain advanced inexorably south and drove more and more of the Andalusians out. Many of them took refuge in the "far west," bringing the artisan skills, dress, and food that still mark many aspects of Moroccan life. Scholars and artists found a ready welcome in cities like Fez and Marrakesh. In 1492 the Christian armies expelled the last of the Muslim communities from Granada and provided one final stream of refugees into Morocco.

Until this time most of Morocco, outside of the cities with considerable Arab populations, still spoke Berber languages. The arabization of the country and of much of northern Africa, as discussed in Chapter 3, came from of the pressures of nomads, Bedouin Arabs originally from the Arabian peninsula. Never popular with governments because of their constant movement, some of the Bedouin were transplanted to Upper Egypt and then pushed further west. Successive waves of them, known as the Banu Hilal, the Banu Sulaim, and the Banu Maqil, moved across the *sahil* or northern edge of the Sahara beginning in the eleventh century. From time to time they erupted across the mountain ranges and into the fertile fields and prosperous cities near the Mediterranean and Atlantic shores. Some groups became sedentary and some seized power. Most caused a great deal of destruction of settled life, in a manner that Arab and European writers sometimes depicted as locusts destroying fields or hordes destroying civilization.

To get a contemporary perspective on the way farmers, city dwellers, governments, and scholars viewed these invasions, we go to the

Tunisian sociologist who wrote syntheses of great acuity in the four-teenth century. Abd al-Rahman, or Ibn Khaldun as he is commonly known, shared the basic geographical framework of climes discussed in Chapter 6. But he was more concerned about the temperate zones of the Mediterranean and the general decline that he observed in the quality of life and government during his century. He attributed some of this decline to the nomadic invaders, who disrupted settled life throughout North Africa, but he also emphasized the growing deca-dence and corruption of the ruling classes.

Here is one portrayal he wrote of the Bedouins, whom he calls "Arabs" to evoke their lifestyle back in the Arabian peninsula:

> The inhabitants of the desert adopt the natural manner of making a living . . . . They restrict themselves to the necessary in food, clothing and mode of dwelling, and to the other necessary conditions and customs. They do not possess conveniences and luxuries . . . . They use tents of hair and wool, or houses of wood, or of clay and stone, which are not furnished [elaborately] . . . .
>
> For those who made their living through the cultivation of grain and through agriculture, it is better to be stationary than to travel around. Such, therefore, are the inhabitants of small communities, villages and mountain regions. These people make up the large mass of the Berbers and non-Arabs . . . .
>
> [The Arabs] are a savage nation, fully accustomed to savagery and the things that cause it. Savagery has become their character and na-ture. They enjoy it, because it means freedom from authority and no subservience to leadership. Such a natural disposition is the negation and antithesis of civilization . . . .
>
> It is noteworthy how civilization always collapsed in places the Arabs took over and conquered, and how such settlements were depopulated and the very earth there turned into something that was no longer earth. The Yemen where the Arabs live is in ruins, except for a few cities . . . . When the Banu Hilal and the Banu Sulaim pushed through [from their homeland] to Ifriqiya [Tunisia] and the Maghrib in [the be-ginning of] the fifth [11th century CE] and struggled there for 350 years, they attached themselves to [the country], and the flat territory in [the Maghrib] was completely ruined. Formerly the whole region between the Sudan [the Sahel] and the Mediterranean had been settled . . . .

Ibn Khaldun developed this conflict between the "desert" and the "sown" into a theory of cycles of destruction, renewal, and creation. In various forms this view has dominated the thinking of governments and students of "civilization," and their attitudes toward nomads and pastoralists, for most of world history.

The Moroccan State in Recent Centuries

The Bedouins did not indelibly mark the history of the interior plain until the sixteenth century C.E. At that time one of their lineages, the Saadians, moved north from the desert, crossed the mountains, and took control of the Moroccan heartland. They drew much of their strength, as Ibn Khaldun would have predicted, from their solidarity and spartan existence in the western Sahara. But they quickly adjusted to sedentary life, formed a dynasty, and ruled from the city of Marrakesh.

From this time onward, that is, from the middle of the sixteenth century, royal dynasties with Sharifian claims have controlled the core of the country: the farms and cities of the plain. They have often used the term *makhzen*, which literally means "storeroom," to refer both to the government and to the "useful" agricultural and urban areas under governmental control, whereas *siba*, which literally means "rebellion," was used to signify areas of mountain and desert outside their influence and often in open revolt. Often the makhzen corresponded to the areas where Arabic was dominant and the siba to zones of Berber culture. The makhzen–siba dichotomy has become a shorthand by which both Moroccan and Western writers refer to the region.

By this time Islamic orthodoxy and law had become established in the region. As in most of the Muslim world, Sunni orthodoxy prevailed in Morocco and North Africa, alongside the Sharifian claims of descent from Ali and Fatima. In legal terms the Malikite orthodox school of law was dominant. The Fez clerics played key roles in training and implementing its rather conservative interpretations. At the same time Sufi orders, as is shown in the next section, spread rapidly in Morocco and the rest of the Maghrib, including the mountains and the desert. The Malikite doctors of law looked askance at certain Sufi practices, but there was little they could do to guide the process of islamization. The Arabic language spread at a somewhat slower place, but by this time a distinct Moroccan colloquial form was emerging in the core of the country.

The Saadian rulers used their knowledge of the Sahara to extend their influence to the south. Interested in the control of salt and gold,

they mounted the only military expedition that succeeded in crossing the desert. Their army of 4,000 soldiers, equipped with muskets,
destroyed the much larger Songhay army in 1591. Substantial Moroccan colonies then settled into Timbuktu and the area of the river
called the Niger Buckle, where they eventually melded in to the local
populations. The commanding officers took the "most dangerous" elements of Timbuktu back to Morocco. Included among the hostages
was the jurist and scholar Ahmad Baba, whom we met in Chapter 5.

In the Moroccan plain the Saadians faced more urgent challenges.
The first was the expansion of Portuguese and Spanish forces, imbued
with crusading fervor, onto the Moroccan coasts. The Christians saw
this campaign as a natural extension of the reconquest of the Iberian
peninsula. The Saadian sultans mobilized their forces more successfully than the fragmented Swahili city-states facing a similar menace.
The Moroccans kept the Christians confined at the shore and sometimes drove them out of the port cities altogether (see Figure 13). The
most distinguished among the sultans received the epithet *al-Mansur*,
"the victorious," to commemorate a victory against the Portuguese in
1578. For Moroccans, their exploits were the equivalent of Saladin's
seizure of Jerusalem; they framed them in the rhetoric of reconquest,
like the Christians monarchs of Spain.

The second challenge came from a rival Muslim power. The Ottoman Empire had expanded dramatically in the sixteenth century,
taking Egypt and the North African coastal region up to the edge of
Morocco. By midcentury it was intervening actively in Moroccan politics, hoping to control the Mediterranean on three sides. The Saadians established their capital at Marrakesh, in part to escape the strong
Ottoman influence in the eastern part of the country, and made certain that Morocco stayed outside of the Turkish orbit. A certain anti-
Ottoman orientation has been a part of Moroccan state policy ever
since – even to the point of encouraging the consumption of tea, mediated by the British through their holdings in India, in preference to
the coffee usually preferred in the eastern Mediterranean.

It was under the Saadians that the Western European powers began
to appoint envoys to the Moroccan court. Al-Mansur and the other
rulers were astute in dealing with these ambassadors. They were often able to take advantage of the bitter rivalry between Spain and the
England of Queen Elizabeth, and to use both to support their independence from the Ottoman Empire. It was only in the nineteenth
century, with the impact of "modernization," that European regimes
began to exert great influence over Moroccan policy.

FIGURE 13 Defense against European intrusion. A coastal fortress at Agadir, Morocco. Photo by author, 1967.

In the middle of the seventeenth century, the Saadians yielded to another dynasty of Bedouin origin, the Alawites. Taking their name from Ali, the son-in-law of Muhammad, these Sharifian Arabs also moved across the mountains, from south to north, formed alliances, and took the makhzen plain by the middle of the seventeenth century. They have been the most successful of the Moroccan dynasties, at least in terms of longevity. They survived droughts, epidemics, and revolts in the eighteenth century; European encroachment in the nineteenth century; and French colonial rule in the first half of the twentieth century. They rule over the country today as a constitutional monarchy.

The most famous of the Alawite sultans was Mawlay Ismail (reigned from 1672 to 1727). He rivaled Louis XIV of France in longevity, splendor, and building the power of his country. He was also his equal in violence, cruelty, and cupidity. He enjoyed theological discussions with European envoys to his court. He wrote to James II, after his deposition as King of England, advising him to convert to the true religion of Islam or, at the very least, return to the better form of Christianity that was Protestantism. Ismail created a new capital at Meknes, but used Fez and Marrakesh as well. His palaces were filled with women at his beck and call, and he fathered hundreds of sons and daughters. He was probably the son of a West African concubine.

Ismail was deeply concerned about the loyalty and stability of his rule. Threats now came less from the Portuguese, Spanish, or Ottomans and more from members of his own family or Muslim leaders across the land. Ismail's solution was to create a new army of slave soldiers, drawn from West Africa. Black slave soldiers were not new in Morocco. Al-Mansur and the other Saadians had brought many slaves into their armies.

Ismail now assembled these soldiers and then issued a call for vast additional recruits directly from West Africa. He put these men and women in a special camp near the Atlantic coast and used their children to build a fighting force of 30,000 to 50,000 men. The process was described by a Moroccan historian writing in the nineteenth century as follows:

> The sultan had clothes and weapons distributed to the blacks, appointed their leaders, and gave them building materials. He ordered them to build their camp, cultivate their fields and raise their children. The sultan took personal charge of the boys and girls at the age of 10. Some of the children were placed for a year in apprenticeship to masons, carpenters or other builders, while others were employed as workers. The second year, they were trained as mule caravan leaders. The third year they learned construction. The fourth year they learned horsemanship, while the fifth year was devoted to perfecting horsemanship and firing muskets from the mounted position. At the age of 16 the young men were put in regiments under their commanders, and married to young black girls who had learned cooking, housekeeping and washing in the sovereign's palace. The prettiest girls also learned music. When their musical education was finished, they received clothes and a dowry, and were led to their husbands while their marriages were inscribed in a register.
>
> The newly wed had to give their children over: the boys to military service, the girls to service in the palace. This system of recruitment lasted until the end of the reign of Ismail. Each year the sultan went to the camp and led the appropriate children away. The military register of the black army numbered 150,000 men, of whom 70,000 were at the camp, 25,000 at another camp, and the remainder in various fortresses which the sultan had built from Oudjda to the Oued Noun [the most northeastern to the most southwestern point of the Moroccan shore]. . . . [The fortresses] numbered 76.

Ismail's system was remarkably successful in the latter portions of his reign, in reinforcing his authority against internal and external enemies. But soon the leaders of the black soldiers realized the power at their disposal and began to conspire with candidates for the throne or chiefdoms within Morocco. Ultimately they were no more loyal than the Arab and Berber soldiers upon whom the sultans had relied. During the eighteenth century the troops intervened constantly in the draining struggles for power among competing members of the Alawite dynasty.

The impact of recruitment in the West African Sahel was considerable. Moroccan forces and their local allies raided down into the Senegal and Niger river valleys, disrupted trade and production, and took away significant numbers of young men and women over several decades. In the early eighteenth century this part of the Transsaharan slave trade rivaled in intensity and impact the much better known Atlantic system.

Mawlay Ismail faced many challenges during his long reign, and none were more difficult than the call to rule with justice. This call came from learned, saintly Sufis who practiced, preached, and wrote in communities throughout the country. The most famous of these people, in the memory of Moroccans, was Abu Ali al-Yusi, or Lyusi, as he is called. His confrontations with Ismail, written and face to face, have been discussed by Moroccan and expatriate scholars for a long time.

Lyusi was almost an exact contemporary of Ismail, and he watched the Alawites consolidate power over the rivalry-ridden Saadians. His own training was in the law and Sufism, and it was from this base that he began to write and confront Ismail – after he ascended to the Sharifian throne in the 1670s. Lyusi begins one of his first epistles to the sultan in the traditional mode of great respect as follows:

> O axis and center of glory, possessor and sanctuary of glory, base and source of eminent honor [*sharaf*], locus and concentration of the highest excellence, the greatest sultan, the most majestic, the most magnificent, our Lord Ismail son of Mawlana al-Sharif, may his banners remain victorious and may his days pass in power and success.

He expresses his respect for the authority of the sultan and his descent from Ali and Fatima and then moves to the main subject of his letter – the call to God's servants to rule with justice:

> We have written this letter for at the moment this is all we can do.... Our Lord [Ismail] – may God help him – knows that the land and all that is in it belongs to God the Highest whose power is shared by no other. People are the male and female slaves of God. My Lord is one of

the slaves that God on high has made king over the others as a test. If he
rules them with justice, mercy, fairness, and righteousness, then he is
God's deputy in His land, and God's shadow over His slaves, and he will
occupy a high rank with God on high. But if he rules unjustly, violently,
arrogantly, oppressively and corruptly, then he will have become insolent
to his master [God] in his kingdom and dictatorial and arrogant in the
land without right. Then he will be subject to the terrible punishment
and wrath of God on high.

Lyusi then goes on to spell out three areas of the sultan's obligation to
God and his people: the correct collection and expenditure of taxes,
the waging of war in a holy cause, and the granting of justice to the
oppressed.

This letter is one example of the critique which Lyusi and other
"scholar-saints" brought to bear upon the sultan. The critique provided a certain check on the sultan's power. But only persons of un-
questioned spiritual and moral authority knew how to make themselves
heard in the circles of the court – and how to survive the consequences
of the sultan's wrath.

Varieties of Islamic Authority in Morocco

We have already seen the importance of one kind of holiness in Morocco: the sharifian claim, the link to "nobility" by a genealogical tie
to the Prophet. Ismail asserted this, as did Lyusi, and their contemporaries believed both of them. Holiness could also come from learning,
especially in the law. Lyusi had more of that than Ismail, whose basic
apprenticeship was in power – how to become a strong and effective
sultan. Holiness could also come from the working of miracles, and
Lyusi's abilities in this regard were confirmed by his contemporaries.
Finally, holiness could come from Sufism. Lyusi was a Sufi in the
sense of both the search for meaning and unity with God and initiation into several Sufi orders that were available in Morocco at the
time. His conviction and courage had a very firm base in the multiple
strands of Islamic distinction. He was a "marabout," dressed in the Islamic clothes of the Almoravids or *al-murabitun*; he was full of *baraka*,
"God's blessing" or endowment.

One could say that Sufism mediated all of these kinds of holiness. Morocco had been one of the main centers of Sufism since
the twelfth century. The first leaders were engaged in the search for
God, and some of them followed the guidance of the great Andalusian

Sufi who wrote extensively on the faith, Ibn al-Arabi. These men had relatively small followings. Beginning in the fifteenth century, new leaders began to form particular rituals, lodges, and levels of initiation and larger congregations – in short the orders that have characterized Sufism ever since. This phenomenon occurred in many parts of the Islamic world, but Morocco acquired a reputation within Africa as a center of Sufi creativity. A number of orders important throughout the zone, such as the Tijaniyya mentioned in Chapter 4, had their principal headquarters there. These headquarters or "mother" *zawiya*, as they were often known, could become objects of veneration and pilgrimage, especially if the tomb of the founder were located there.

By the time the Saadians and Alawites came to power in the interior plain, the Sufi orders were legion in Morocco. Some were relatively "orthodox," with their main concentrations in the cities and among members of the religious and political elites. Some were rooted in the more remote countryside and dominated by Berber communities or West Africans who had come in via the slave trade. Members of these orders professed Islam, but they often linked the profession of faith with a range of spirits, saints, and sacrifices that urban and Arab Muslims might condemn. The sultans favored the first and tried to restrain the second. In addition, they carefully monitored the stronger Sufi orders and leaders who could pose challenges to their authority.

In the early nineteenth century Mawlay Sulaiman tried to change Sufi practice and eliminate some orders altogether. He was influenced by strong currents of reform originating in the Arabian peninsula among the Wahhabite movement, whose influence remains very strong in Saudi Arabia today. In 1815 he issued an exhortation to his subjects to reject the excessive veneration of the tombs of their saints as follows:

> Know that God, in His goodness, has revealed the ways of the Sunna in order that you be able to follow them.... Turn away from the ceremonies and innovations of dress and jewelry by those who are dominated by passion and have attacked the Book, the Hadith and the Community....
>
> All of that is nothing but detestable innovation, blameworthy action, base insult, custom contrary to religious law, error and separation, the deception of the devil.... Periods have been fixed for these practices and considerable sums of money spent for the love of Satan. The people who believe in these innovations, the Aissawa, Jbala and other orders

who are partisans of innovation and error, of folly and ignorance, are
drawn to them. They wait for these times of amusement . . . .

O believers, I ask you in the sight of God did the Prophet ever consecrate such a ceremony to his uncle, the first of the martyrs? The first
caliph of our Community, Abu Bakr, did he ever consecrate such a ceremony to the Prophet? Did any of those who followed the Prophet think
of such a thing? I ask you again, in the time of the Prophet did anyone
decorate the mosques? dress up the tombs of his companions or those
of the generation which followed him?

Sulaiman tried mightily to alter the Islamic religious culture of Morocco and failed. Sufi leaders joined a Berber revolt, captured Fez,
took him prisoner, and finally forced him to abdicate in favor of his
nephew.

Sufism could not be controlled from the center. It was the major
means by which Islam was appropriated by women, who were disad-
vantaged in the schools and courts, and by Berber-speaking groups
in the rural and mountainous areas. By increasing the reputation for
holiness of the country, it attracted Muslims from other parts of North
and West Africa. Believers often coordinated their pilgrimage to Mecca
with a journey to Morocco to their favorite zawiya or the shrine of
Mawlay Idriss. Morocco's complex Islamic identity could not be easily simplified or controlled.

Moroccan Travails in the Nineteenth and Twentieth Centuries

Morocco had been involved with Europe for several centuries through
trade, diplomacy, and the gradual elimination of piracy and enslavement of Christians and Muslims discussed in Chapter 5. It signed one
of the first treaties with the fledgling United States in 1786. These relations were reciprocal compared with those of the nineteenth century.
More isolated than Istanbul or the Egypt of Muhammad Ali, Morocco
nonetheless felt the growing pressures of the European economies and
the necessity to "modernize" in Western directions. The sultans began
to depend increasingly on European military and financial advisors;
they borrowed money and mortgaged revenues to pay their debts.

For Morocco the growing influence was complicated by the Spanish
presence along its northern coast and by the French intrusion into
Algeria beginning in 1830. The sultans could hardly refuse the asylum demanded by fellow Muslims in the Maghrib or turn their backs

FIGURE 14 Muslim royalty on tour. A sketch of Mulay
Hassan, Alawite Sultan of Morocco, in the late nineteenth
century. From the Bibliotheque Nationale, Paris, late nineteenth
century collections, published in Hatier's *Histoire du Maroc*,
Casablanca, 1967, p. 314. Sheed and Ward, an imprint of the
Rowman and Littlefield Publishing Group.

on European encroachment, but successful resistance depended on
modern weapons and training, which depended on borrowing and advisors, which in turn required more compromises with the financial
integrity of the regime. The spiral was vicious and descending.

Mawlay Hassan (reigned from 1873 to 1894) (see Figure 14) is
remembered by Moroccans as the last "great" sultan who sought to

modernize the apparatus of the state and army, rule with stability and justice, and stave off the growing penetration of the European powers. At best he succeeded in slowing the pace of decline and penetration. His sons were very young and inexperienced at his death. When the regent and chief minister died in 1900, the sons struggled unsuccessfully with the conflicting interests of foreign powers, religious elites, regional barons, and the disparate people of the plains and mountains. In this context France moved slowly but inexorably to take center stage over British, German, and Spanish investments. In 1912 General Louis-Hubert Lyautey established the French protectorate over the country. Having conquered the Sharifian throne, France could now claim to be a distinguished "Muslim power" in the sense discussed in Chapter 6.

Lyautey established a dual polity and economy that endured until Morocco regained its independence in 1956. In the traditional sectors of the main cities and much of the countryside, he retained the makhzen, that is, the sultan and his court. The sultan was Yussuf (reigned from 1912 to 1927), another young son of Mawlay Hassan, and the doctrine was "indirect rule." The growing modern sector of the cities and some of the more cultivable land were under direct French control. A considerable number of French farmers, shopkeepers, and bureaucrats moved into this part of the economy. Lyautey himself, as the Resident-General, commanded both sectors. Moroccans quickly recognized that Yussuf had little power and saw that his son Muhammad V (reigned from 1927 to 1961) was in the same position.

Officially Yussuf was in charge of the traditional sector, just as sultans had been in the "precolonial" days. In fact, the French controlled that area, passed on each decision that the court might wish to take, and took some decisive initiatives of their own. One of the least popular was an effort to rule the Berber separately from the Arab populations of the country, on the grounds that Berbers did not speak Arabic (which was true only for some) and did not practice Islam very well (which was decidedly false and greatly resented). As in Algeria, the French wanted to see the Berbers as descendants of the subjects of the old Roman Empire, eager to throw off the Arab and Islamic yoke. When they sought to apply the "Berber regime" by decree in 1930, they encountered a popular revolt and quickly withdrew its implementation.

In the 1940s and 1950s Muhammad V began to assert his influence amid a growing tide of Moroccan nationalism, concentrated principally in the cities and the plain. The sultan made an effort to protect the considerable Jewish population of the country against the actions of the Vichy government, which dominated Morocco at the beginning of World War II. Muhammad developed ties with Franklin Delano Roosevelt in addition to the Free French. After the war the French tried to reassert their domination over the country and the nationalist movement. They deported Muhammad V for two years to their colony of Madagascar, but only succeeded in making him the hero of Moroccan nationalism. Forced to bring him back from exile in 1955, the French conceded independence to Morocco as a constitutional monarchy the following year.

Hassan II (reigned from 1961 to 2000) succeeded his father shortly after independence and ruled in traditional "Alawite" ways despite the modern context of the country. He muzzled the Parliament and press, diminished the freedom of dissent in the constitution, and ruled with an iron fist in a fashion reminiscent of Mawlay Ismail. He disarmed the Muslim clerics who criticized his exercise of power in the tradition of Lyusi. He used the holiness ascribed to the sultan by Moroccan tradition, and the habits of obedience of his subjects, to great advantage.

At the same time Hassan appropriated the goals of the nationalist movement, taking over the enclaves which the Spanish had held for several centuries. The most dramatic moment came in the Green March of 1975, when several hundred thousand Moroccans were mobilized to march down the coast to the Spanish Sahara to claim that territory for the Sharifian throne. By that time local and international human rights pressures had pushed Hassan II to moderate his actions. On his death his son Muhammad VI took power; he seems to be reigning in a more moderate, enlightened version of the Alawite tradition.

Further Reading

There is a large body of material in English on North Africa, including Morocco, from French, British, American, and Moroccan scholars. For two historical syntheses, see Jamil Abun-Nasr's *History of the Maghrib* (Cambridge University Press, 1975) and Charles-André Julien's *History of North Africa: From the Arab Conquest to 1830* (translated from French, Praeger, 1970). For a synthesis of what we know about Berber cultures before and after the Arab invasions, see Michael Brett and Elizabeth Fentress' *The Berbers* (Blackwell, 1996). The Moroccan intellectual and historian, Abdallah Laroui, gives his synthesis in *The History of the Maghrib: An Interpretative Essay* (Princeton University Press, 1977). A British anthropologist, Ernest Gellner, has written extensively on Morocco; see his *Saints of the Atlas* (University of Chicago Press, 1969). An excellent essay on the politics of

Morocco is Henry Munson's *Religion and Power in Morocco* (Yale University Press, 1993).

For the description of the Bedouin by Ibn Khaldun, I have excerpted from the translation of Franz Rosenthal cited in Chapter 2 (volume 1, pp. 250–1, 302–3, and 304–5). For Mawlay Ismail's black army, I have used the French translation, by Octave Houdas, of Abd l-Qasim bin Ahmad al-Ziani [Ezziani], *al-Turjiman al-Muarib an Duwal al-Mashriq wa'l-Maghrib* (Paris Ecole des Langues Orientales Vivantes, 1886), pp. 30–1. For Ismail's own correspondence, see Henry de Castries, *Moulay Ismail et Jacques II: Une apologie de l'Islam par un sultan du Maroc* (Paris E Leroux, 1903). For al-Yusi or Lyusi, see Munson's *Religion and Power*, Chapter 1. Some of the letters of Lyusi, including the one from which I quote, are found in an unusually rich source of documents for Moroccan history, in the main translations into French of Arabic material: *Archives Marocaines*, published in the early twentieth century; the quotes come from volume 9 for 1906 (pp. 110–19). For Mawlay Sulaiman's effort, I have translated from the French a passage in George Drague's *Esquisse d'histoire religieuse du Maroc* (Paris J. Peyronnet, 1951), found in Jean Brignon et al's *Histoire du Maroc* (Hatier, 1967, p. 269). For Ismail's army, see the article of Fatima Harrak in (editors) Toru and Philips' *Slave Elites*, cited at the end of Chapter 5.

For the struggles over Muslim and Christian captives in the Mediterranean area, see the Friedman book mentioned at the end of Chapter 5. For travel and pilgrimage from Morocco, see (editors) Dale Eickelman and James Piscatori's *Muslim Travels: Pilgrimage, Migration and the Religious Imagination* (Routledge, 1990).

There is some literature on the kinds of religious constructions that Moroccans have made over the centuries, within and alongside Islam. The most available work of this sort is by a British anthropologist, Edward Westermarck, *Pagan Survivals*, cited at the end of Chapter 4. Works by Moroccan authors that touch on similar subjects are Mohammed Ennaji's *Serving the Master: Slavery and Society in 19th-C Morocco* (St. Martin's Press, 1998, translated from a 1994 French edition), Vanessa Maher's *Women and Property in Morocco* (Cambridge University Press, 1974), and the works of Fatima Mernissi cited in Chapter 2.

For French colonial policy, especially toward Berbers, Arabs, and Islam, see the work of Edmund Burke III in *Prelude to Protectorate in Morocco: Precolonial Protest and Resistance, 1860–1912* (University of Chicago Press, 1976) and his article in (editors) Ernest Gellner and Charles Micaud's *Arabs and Berbers: From Tribe to Nation in North Africa* (Heath and Company, 1972).

Morocco had a very significant Jewish community (about 200,000 in the 1940s) until recent times. A few were quite wealthy and even prominent at the sultan's court. Almost all of these people have emigrated since the 1950s to Israel, where they constitute a very significant part of the Sephardic population. To explore the general subject, see Shlomo Deshen's *The Mellah Society: Jewish Community Life in Sherifian Morocco* (University of Chicago Press, 1989) and Michael Laskier's *North African Jewry in the Twentieth Century: The Jews of Morocco, Tunisia and Algeria* (NYU Press, 1994).

For Spain, Maria Rose Menocal celebrates the achievements of Andalusia in *The Ornament of the World: How Muslims, Jews, and Christians Created a Culture of Tolerance in Medieval Spain* (Little, Brown and Company, 2002). See also W. Montgomery Watt and Pierre Cachia's *A History of Islamic Spain* (Edinburgh University Press, 1965) and Titus Burckhardt's *Moorish Culture in Spain* (Allen and Unwin, 1972). On the fortunes of Jews in Andalusia, see Eliyahu Ashtor's *The Jews of Moslem Spain* (Jewish Publication Society of America, two volumes 1973–9). Andrew Hess links the Andalusian and Moroccan worlds in *The Forgotten Frontier: A History of the 16th Century Ibero-African Frontier* (University of Chicago Press, 1978).

CHAPTER 8

Ethiopia: Muslims in a "Christian Nation"

Another area of Africa with an old regional identity is Ethiopia. Not so much the Ethiopia of the twentieth century, which comprised most of the horn of Africa, but the mountainous zones of the north and west, which have high rainfall and form the main watersheds of the Nile River. This smaller zone is sometimes called Abyssinia ("Habash" for Arabic speakers living in the Middle East).

In this instance the associated religious identity is Christian, not Muslim. For centuries Middle Eastern, Mediterranean, and European people have ascribed a Christian identity to the area. Ethiopia was often associated with the Prester John of medieval legend, the Christian kingdom that lived "behind" the lands of Islam and would join with European Christians in a world crusade, as discussed in Chapter 6. This ascription was not completely erroneous, for since the fourth century some Ethiopians have been Christian, in the form of the Ethiopian Orthodox Church, and have been writing chronicles and letters to communicate that identity.

More recently the army of Ethiopia won a signal victory against European invaders and thereby guarded their independence, whereas the rest of Africa was coming under colonial rule. Emperor Menilik's triumph over the Italians at Adwa in 1896 won him undying fame in Africa and the African diaspora and helped to diffuse the association of Ethiopia and Christianity throughout the world. So we find "Ethiopian" Christian churches, usually constituted by Africans and African Americans, all over the globe today. They are rarely Ethiopian Orthodox churches, in terms of ritual or obedience, but they are testimony to the wide and deep association of the faith and the country.

So why am I dealing with Muslims in this "Christian" land? Do I want to tell you about troublesome Muslim minorities at the edges of this "nation"? No, I am writing about half of the population of the whole zone and their ancestors. I am even writing about a significant portion of the inhabitants of mountainous Abyssinia, going back many centuries, and about a very affective relationship between the early Muslims of Mecca and the Christian kingdom of Aksum, on the other side of the Red Sea. This narrative is harder to document than the Moroccan one, because of limited sources and the strong biases toward Christianity. But it is an important story and gets at the multicultural and multireligious identity at the heart of Ethiopia's history.

Christian Identity in Ethiopia

We start with the traditional story, the emergence of Christianity in the form of the Ethiopian Orthodox Church. The beginnings are well documented. Aksum was the name of the capital city and a strong kingdom. It was centered in the mountains, close to the headwaters of two big branches of the Nile River, and was one of the great Nile basin states stretching from Egypt through Sudan to the Red Sea. It begins to appear in documents in the first century C.E. as a contemporary of the Roman Empire, which dominated the whole Mediterranean zone. In the fourth century C.E., not long after Constantine adopted Christianity as the official religion of his empire, the Aksumite Emperor Ezana converted and encouraged Christian practice in his dominions. His bishop was appointed by the leaders of the Coptic church in Alexandria, and the Coptic missionary movement became the inspiration for a similar process of evangelization in the rural areas outside of the capital. To some degree the spread of Christianity followed the same path that commentators offer for Islam in Sub-Saharan Africa (see Chapter 3): from merchant minorities to ruling classes to majority affiliation in the countryside.

The adoption of Christianity as the state religion of the Roman Empire forced a series of assemblies of leaders to decide what "orthodoxy" should be – a question that Muslims confronted in their own history. Constantinople, which succeeded Rome as the effective capital of the empire, imposed its point of view in most of these assemblies in the fourth and fifth centuries C.E., but could not bring a number of eastern Christian communions to adopt some of its positions. The Ethiopian church, as well as the Coptic one in Egypt, left the majority over the issue of the nature of Christ. These eastern Orthodox communities – not to be confused with the Eastern Orthodox confessions that are tied to Constantinople – took the Monophysite position that Jesus Christ was of "one nature," not of separate divine and human natures.

The conflicts about these seemingly arcane positions were vital to the clergy and laity at the time and occasionally led to violent struggles. The main impact for our story is the relative isolation of the Ethiopian Orthodox Church from the dominant forms of Christianity around the Mediterranean, led by the Roman Catholic Pope and the Patriarch in Constantinople. Ethiopian Christianity developed mainly from internal sources, encouraged by the Aksum court, local monks, and missionaries. It became the official religion of Aksum and the states that succeeded it after the tenth century and the dominant practice of the peoples of Abyssinia.

Some of the Abyssinian states developed a new dimension of Ethiopian Christianity in their competition to be the "true" successor to Aksum. In a work composed over a considerable period of time and entitled the *Kebre Negast*, "the glory of the kings," the church asserted origins that went back to King Solomon of Israel, about 1,000 years before Jesus' birth. In essence, it claimed to be Christian before Christ by developing a story around the personage of Menilik I. He was the son of Solomon and Sheba, a wealthy and beautiful queen often identified with the Abyssinian highlands. Conceived in Ancient Israel, Menilik grew up with his mother in Ethiopia. He then went to Israel, seized the Ark of the Covenant and returned home. Since then the ark has resided in the Church of St. Mary of Zion in Aksum, while Ethiopian kings have called themselves descendants of Menilik. This is a Christian equivalent, admittedly more intense and embodied in an object, of the Sharifian descent claimed by the rulers of Morocco. The believers combined this attachment with an active pilgrimage to Jerusalem and a resident Ethiopian community in that city.

Early Relations of Muslims with Aksum

The Aksum empire was very involved on the Arabian peninsula. At times it controlled Yemen, the southwest corner, and its traders were active throughout the Red Sea area. A number of Ethiopians lived in Mecca at the time of Muhammad. Some were practicing Christians, and a few became prominent in the early Muslim community. One of the latter was Bilal, whom we encountered in Chapter 4 as a slave, then a freedman who called the faithful to prayer, and finally a military officer who helped in the conquests of Syria and Iraq. I invoked Bilal as an example of the way African Muslims attached themselves to the Islamic foundations, but he is also testimony to the cosmopolitan world that prevailed in Mecca at the time of Muhammad. Most of our information about these relations comes from the Hadith, the traditions associated with the Prophet.

Shortly after Muhammad began preaching publicly and criticizing Meccan practices, he came under pressure from the leadership of the city. He began to fear for the safety of the embryonic Muslim community. On two occasions he sent groups secretly across the Red Sea to the emperor's protection in Aksum, knowing that they would receive a good reception as fellow monotheists. A small group went in 615 C.E., and a larger group went the following year. Over 100 went in all, representing a sizable proportion of the Muslims at the time, only two to three years after the Prophet began his public preaching. Included among them were some important figures: Muhammad's daughter Ruqayya, her husband Uthman (who would become the third caliph), Muhammad's future wife Umm Habiba, and his cousin Jafar, the brother of Ali. The departures angered the Prophet's opponents, who sent a delegation of their own to persuade the emperor to force the emigrants to return. Had the emperor agreed, the fortunes of Islam might have been dramatically different.

So important were these departures, and the asylum offered by Aksum, that the Hadith often refer to these events as the "first and second *hijras* to Abyssinia," fully six years before the move to Medina in 622. After the migration to Medina Muhammad requested the return of the exiles, and the emperor complied quickly. Weighted down with gifts, the group arrived in 628 A.D. Among them was Umm Habiba, whose husband had converted to Christianity and stayed in Aksum. She had divorced him; now, supplied with a dowry by the emperor, she married the Prophet. A few years later she and another woman from the exile comforted Muhammad during his last days by recounting the wonders of the church in Aksum, particularly the murals of the saints.

Other Hadith go even further. Some traditions suggest that Muhammad accorded a special and inviolable state of neutrality, the *Dar al-Hiyad*, to Aksum. This condition existed separately from the *Dar al-Islam* and the *Dar al-Harb*, the basic dichotomy of the Islamic world, and put Aksum "off limits" for *jihad*. This tradition is also formulated in a saying attributed to Muhammad: "leave the Abyssinians alone." This was in honor of the assistance they provided to the faithful at a critical juncture in Islamic history. Another tradition maintains that Muhammad invited the emperor to convert and that he accepted and sent troops in support of the Muslim community of Medina as it struggled to take control of Mecca. The emperor hid his conversion because it was unpopular at his court.

It is impossible to appraise these less dominant strands. We can say, with some confidence, three things. First, the Aksum court provided an important refuge for the early Muslims at a critical juncture. Second, although Aksum did not lie on the main axis of Islamic expansion around the Mediterranean, it might well have been the object of Arab campaigns in the first century of Islam had Muhammad not appreciated its support in the formative years of the new religion. Finally, Muslim writers have debated the relationships between the early Islamic community and Aksum over the centuries. Those writing in a "pro-Ethiopia" vein have emphasized common Semitic identity between the Arab and northern Ethiopian peoples, the friendship of Muhammad and the Aksumite emperor, and the tolerance of the Christian court. Those writing on the opposite side have stressed the examples of Christian hostility and intolerance toward Islam dealt with later in this chapter.

Relations with Muslim Egypt

Islam spread around the Red Sea as well as the Mediterranean. Muslims – Kharijite, Shia, and Sunni – moved out along both shores and into the Horn of Africa. Many were engaged in trade, like their fellow practitioners who began to work the East Africa coast, as discussed in Chapter 3. In the Horn, however, the settlements spread more quickly into the interior, into the lowlands, and then the highlands, where the Christian state was dominant. By the sixteenth century the Muslim population of the highland areas may have constituted one third of the total population.

A number of small kingdoms, dominated by Muslims, developed in the lowlands that constitute today's Eritrea, Djibouti, and Somalia and the eastern parts of Ethiopia. The proximity of the Hijaz and Yemen, the accessibility of the Holy Cities of Mecca and Medina, and the networks of trade between Northeast Africa and Arabia made for an early and relatively peaceful process of islamization – more quickly than in the West African Sahel and the East African coast. Many of the political and religious leaders were Arab, often with prestigious connections back to the founding days of Islam. Those who became Muslim retained their local languages and constituted the vast majority of the population. Collectively they came to be know as *jabarti*, a word derived from a town near Zeila where some of the first conversions took place.

Clerics trained in law and theology helped the communities understand the heritage of Islam. Many were "missionary" minded and spread the faith in lowland and highland zones alike. Some received their training at the famous Egyptian university launched by the Fatimids in the tenth century C.E., al-Azhar. It was there that the Ethiopian Muslim community maintained a hostel, called the *riwaq al-jabartiyya*, in support of its students. Ethiopian Muslims were closely connected to the Middle East, but none of the caliphates or larger powers put a priority on supporting the faith in their area. Islamization was a local, internal process and by and large a successful one.

The development of a Muslim presence from the coast had the effect of isolating Aksum and its successor states. At the time of the Roman Empire and the birth of Islam, the highland state was closely linked to the Mediterranean world. After about 700, these networks of contact diminished. But the Christian kingdoms remained the largest and most powerful entities in the Horn and had to deal with Muslims in three principal spheres. The lowlands were dominated by a Muslim majority in close commercial relations with the mountains. In the highlands there were significant Muslim minorities who spoke the same languages and shared much of the culture of the Christian ruling classes.

Finally, the state had to work closely with the Egyptian state to sustain its relations with the Coptic Orthodox Church. The presiding bishop in Ethiopia was appointed by the Coptic patriarch in Alexandria – a practice sustained until the 1950s! Ethiopia continued to receive missionaries, theologians, jurists, artists, and advice from its sister communion. It was critical for both church and state to maintain civil relations with the Fatimids, then the Mamluk regime, and finally the Ottomans – in short with whichever authority controlled Egypt. Occasionally the Ethiopians threatened to divert the waters of

the Nile, which formed the basis of Egyptian survival, to extract con-
cessions from Cairo, but most of the time the relations were correct
and cordial.

Crusade and *Jihad*: Confrontations in Ethiopia

In the fourteenth and fifteenth centuries the Solomonic kingdom expanded into the lowlands and established control over the port of Massawa on the Red Sea, much like its predecessor Aksum. The emperors adopted a rhetoric not unlike that of the European Crusaders of
Chapter 6. They viewed the Muslims as enemies and inferiors, exacted tribute from several states, and forced some conversions. For
their part the Muslims, accustomed to independence and proud of
the achievements of Islam, sought to resist. The stage was set for the
confrontation that many historians have taken as typical of the relations
between Christianity and Islam in Ethiopia.

The Ottoman expansion into Egypt, Arabia, and the Red Sea zone
in the early sixteenth century was a precondition for the expansion of
local Muslim communities. The Turks did not, however, supply many
weapons or soldiers or sustain a great interest in establishing an Islamic
dominion in Ethiopia. The impetus to resist and exact revenge came
from local Muslim leaders and a few new arrivals from the Arabian
peninsula. One Muslim cleric, steeped in the law and able to inspire
men and women to unite and fight, was able to put together a winning
coalition.

Imam Ahmad ibn Ibrahim Gran led his followers to victory after victory in the center of "Christian" Ethiopia between 1527 and 1543. His
biographer suggests the sources of his charisma and courage as follows:

> One night while I was sleeping (said one of Ahmad's contemporaries), I
> saw the Prophet with, on his right, Abu Bakr al-Siddiq (the first caliph),
> and to his left Umar ibn al-Khattab (the second caliph), and in front
> of him Ali bin Abu Talib (the fourth caliph), may God be satisfied with
> them. In front of Ali was the Imam Ahmad ibn Ibrahim. "Prophet of
> God, I asked, who is in front of Ali ibn Abu Talib?" He answered me:
> "It is he by whom God Most High will establish order in Abyssinia."

The Muslim armies marched into Aksum and the other major capitals of the highlands. They converted churches to mosques, destroyed

some "idols" of the Christians, forced some Christians to convert to Islam, and confiscated grain, cattle, and other provisions. They did everything but capture the emperor himself. The Muslim rhetoric was equal to that used by the Christians during their expansion: their opponents were infidels, polytheists, and worshipers of Mary.

As quickly as they intruded, they left. The armies of the Solomonic regime defeated and killed the militant leader. They reestablished their domination over most of Ethiopia as Gran's coalition collapsed. Throughout the struggle the Christians kept Massawa on the Red Sea, not far from the old Aksumite port of Adulis. This permitted them to receive Portuguese aid against the Gran offensive, but then to establish diplomatic relations with Ottoman representatives in the late sixteenth century. In the seventeenth century the Ottomans even helped them get rid of the Portuguese Jesuits, who had treated Ethiopian Orthodox Christians in a very condescending manner.

The confrontations of the Solomonic dynasties and Ahmad Gran are etched into the memory of Christians and Muslims alike as the dominant metaphor of relations between the two confessions. Ahmad's campaigns did threaten the integrity of the Christian state and drove it into alliance with Portuguese missionaries and military advisors. But the Solomonic rulers then formed enduring relations with the Ottomans, who were ready to accept the religious status quo in Ethiopia and encourage the growth of trade. The fervor of both Christians and Muslims waned. "Christian" warlords fell to fighting each other. The militancy and unity of the Muslims declined, while the Oromo people migrated in large numbers into the central portions of the country. Initially the Oromo cared little about either faith.

It is tempting to see reverse parallels between the histories of Morocco and Ethiopia. In each "nation-state" one confession was dominant in the interior over long periods of time and was threatened from the coastal zone by its rival. But this analogy fails to capture the differences. In the Moroccan case Portuguese and Spanish Christians attacked the regime from outside, and the sultans were able to mobilize believers throughout the zone. The Christians had no significant support inside the kingdom. In the Ethiopian case the highland state and church had to deal with indigenous Muslim movements whose strength was inside – in the lowlands but also in Abyssinia itself. Ethiopia had a civil war, where each side evoked a militant tradition – crusade or *jihad*.

Islamization and New Confrontations

In the late eighteenth and early nineteenth centuries the fortunes of the Muslim societies of the lowlands and the center began to revive. Agricultural production prospered, and this led to increased exports to the coast. This in turn intensified the commercial networks around the Red Sea and with Egypt, the frequency of the pilgrimage, and the settlement of Arab traders and clerics near the coast. The new vehicle for islamization was Sufism, particularly in the form of orders that identified with Sunni orthodoxy and emphasized the importance of learning.

A good example of this process was Shaikh Muhammad Shafi (1743–1806). He was from the area of Wallo, in the center of Ethiopia, and began his life as a student of law, theology, and the Arabic language in one of the local schools. His teacher initiated him into the Qadiriyya Sufi order and authorized him to initiate others. Shaikh Muhammad gradually acquired a committed following and reputation for learning, saintliness, and the performance of miracles. He was on civil terms with the leaders of the small political chiefdoms of Wallo, many of whom were Muslim, but he stayed away from their courts. When he made the pilgrimage and sought authorization for waging the military *jihad*, he got little support from the Meccan authorities.

Shaikh Muhammad finally settled on a mountain ridge at a place called Jama Negus, "the community of the king," because of the size and militancy of his following. It was there that he instituted the annual celebration of the Prophet's birthday, attended by Muslims from all over Ethiopia. He also created a division of the year for his disciples: for four months they would emphasize teaching and learning; they would devote the next months to the extension of Islam by *jihad* and take the final third of the year for prayer, meditation, and Sufi devotional exercises. It was clerics in the mold of Shaikh Muhammad who anchored, revived, and spread the faith during this period.

Muslims were numerous in many parts of Ethiopia during the nineteenth century (see Figure 15). The practice of Islam was not limited to clerical or trading groups, but could also be found among ruling classes, farmers, and pastoralists. Some Muslims continued to use cults of possession and sacrifice, but leaders like Shaikh Muhammad exhorted them to change. Some of the ruling classes belonged to "mixed" families, with relatives who practiced Christianity. Clerics of both persuasions actively sought conversion to their confessions.

FIGURE 15 A painting of the diverse Muslim populations of Ethiopia in the "traditional" style by Adamu Tesfar, 2001. Collection of Al and Polly Roberts.

The Orthodox church and the highland state continued to push the connection between Christianity and Ethiopian identity.

In the late nineteenth century three talented and ambitious men succeeded in centralizing the old domains of Abyssinia and expanding into the frontiers we associate with the Ethiopia of the twentieth century (see Map 5). Tewodros II (reigned from 1855 to 1867), Yohannes IV (reigned from 1872 to 1889), and Menilik II (reigned from 1889 to 1909) brought highlands, lowlands, and other lands together at considerable cost to the Muslim communities. In an 1862 letter to Queen Victoria, Tewodros revealed his vision of himself and Ethiopia:

> My fathers, the Emperors, having forgotten the Creator, He [God] handed their kingdom to the Gallas [Oromo] and the Turks. But God created me, lifted me out of the dust, and restored the Empire to my rule. He endowed me with power, and enabled me to stand in the place of my fathers. By this power I drove away the Gallas. As for the Turks, I have told them to leave the land of my ancestors. They refuse. I am going now to wrestle with them.

The "Turks" of Tewodros were, in fact, the indigenous Muslims of the lowland and highland zones.

The three emperors, supported by the head of the Orthodox church, embarked on campaigns of expansion that often took the form of crusades. They were challenged by Egyptian expansion along the Red Sea and up the Nile, followed by the Mahdist threat (see Chapter 12). They coerced conversions, confiscated property, destroyed Muslim centers, massacred thousands of believers, and drove even more to take flight. Their rhetoric and actions equaled the Solomonic expansion of earlier centuries. Yohannes was the most active in the pursuit of Christianization (see Chapter 12 on his conflicts with the Mahdist state of the Sudan, which resulted in his death), whereas Menilik restored freedom of religious practice after seeing the devastation of the 1880s. But all three drank deeply at the well of the Christian identity of Ethiopia. Their pressures forced the Muslim leaders to concentrate more on the survival of the faith than the processes of islamization set in motion since the late eighteenth century.

Menilik developed his administration of Ethiopia in the center, in the province of Shewa just south of Wallo, and concentrated his efforts at modernization from a new capital in Addis Ababa. After he suffered a debilitating stroke in 1909, the crown council selected a regent and an heir-designate, Lij Iyasu (1896–1935, reigned from 1913 to 1916).

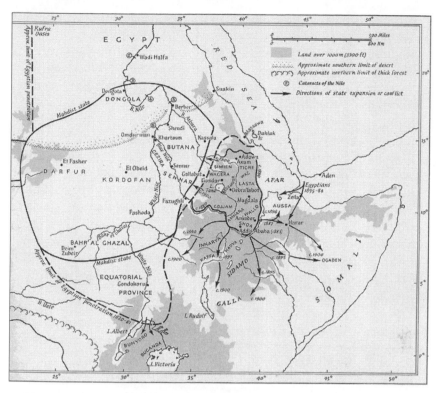

MAP 5 Muslim states and struggles in the Nile Sudan and Ethiopia. Adapted from John D. Fage and Maureen Verity, *An Atlas of African History*, New York, 1978.

He was the grandson of the emperor and the son of the governor and general Ras Mikael, whose name was Muhammad Ali before his forced conversion in the 1870s. Mikael was now the powerful governor of Wallo, with a large army to support his son's claim to the crown.

Although it is sometimes said that Lij Iyasu was a Muslim or converted to Islam, it is more likely that he envisioned a government in which Muslims and Christians would share the leadership as they often had in his home province. But Iyasu had little experience in the complex politics of Ethiopia or the processes of modernization set in motion by Menilik. He did not have the ability to run the regime, much less bring his pluralistic perspective into being.

The pressures of World War I proved his undoing. On the domestic front he integrated members of some of the Muslim dynasties into his administration. On the international front he sought alliance with

Sayyid Muhammad Abdullah, a resistor against British and Italian rule
in Somalia, and made overtures to the Central Powers. He maintained
close contacts with Mazhar Bey, the first official Ottoman envoy in
Ethiopia. Consul Mazhar worked out of Harar, the prestigious Islamic
city in the east, and encouraged Lij Iyasu to believe that an Ottoman
victory would push Italy out of its colonies and allow further Ethiopian
expansion.

Britain, France, and Italy protested to the foreign ministry of Addis
Ababa, while church and political leaders began to mobilize against
Iyasu from inside. In September 1916 a crown council excommuni-
cated him from the church and deposed him from the throne. The
next month Ras Mikael was defeated by the forces that the council
had mobilized. Ras Tafari, the future Haile Sellassie, was appointed
as heir-designate, alongside the regent and daughter of Menilik, Em-
press Zawditu. The "Christian" identity of the court was reaffirmed
and relations with the Allies were restored. Iyasu fled into exile.

Muslims and the Italian Occupation

The Italian government did not easily forget its defeat at the hands of
Menilik in 1896. It retained the two colonies adjacent to Ethiopia –
Eritrea and Somalia. Both had majority Muslim populations, and the
Italians developed their propaganda as a "Muslim power" in much the
way the French did in Morocco. When they completed their conquests
of Muslim societies in Africa by conquering Libya in 1911, they made
the following declaration to their subjects:

> Remember that God said in the Book [the Quran]: "To those who come
> in peace and do not drive you out of your country, you must work for
> the good and protect them, because God loves those who do good and
> who protect [religion]." Remember also that it is written in the Book:
> "If others are prepared to propose peace, you should accept it and have
> confidence in God."
>
> ... Italy wishes for peace. Under the protection of Italy and its king,
> may God bless your land and may it remain the Dar al-Islam over which
> the Italian flag will float as a sign of faith, love and hope.

The Italian colonial administrations were a constant irritant to the
Ethiopian regime, with its memories of access to the Red Sea in Eritrea
and influence in the Ogaden in Somalia. Ras Tafari maintained the

same opposition to the Italian presence articulated by Lij Iyasu while seeking international protection through membership in the League of Nations. But the erstwhile European allies did little to prevent Benito Mussolini and the Fascist forces from attacking Ethiopia in 1935. A modernized and efficient army "erased" the memory of the Adwa defeat. Supported by airplanes and poison gas, it moved inland from Eritrea and Somalia. By the spring of the following year it controlled the country. Ras Tafari, now Emperor Haile Sellassie, went into exile in Britain while a guerilla movement continued a futile struggle inside the country. The occupation continued into World War II, until London coordinated African and European forces of liberation and put the emperor back on the throne.

The Italian conquerors used their experience as a "Muslim power" and their sense of the "misfortunes" of Muslim Ethiopians in their brief administration of the country. Mussolini portrayed himself as the friend of Islam, much as Napoleon had done in Egypt. He built mosques, appointed Muslim judges, organized radio broadcasts in Arabic, and sponsored pilgrimages to Mecca. He coordinated efforts with campaigns against the Christian monarchy in some Arabic newspapers of the Middle East and Europe. His chief collaborator was a Lebanese journalist and author based in Geneva, Shakib Arslan (1869–1946). In 1935, just before the invasion, Arslan wrote the following:

> All those who would like to defend Ethiopia have first to read about its history and particularly regarding the Muslims living there and what they received from the Ethiopians. They will see that apart from the Muslims of Spain no other Muslim people has suffered over the centuries such atrocities as the Muslims of Ethiopia. We do not even talk about maltreatment in the early ages, of which we have historical records. We talk about events that took place in the not too distant past. It is enough to refer to what happened sixty to seventy years ago, in the time of Emperor Yohannes, and mention the number of means he used against the Muslims that were forced to become Christians.

Arslan continued his campaign, with Italian support, in the newspapers of Lebanon, Syria, and Egypt in the following years. He buttressed his case by citing the instances of hostility over the centuries. History was a battleground for perspectives on relations between Christians and Muslims, Jews and Arabs, and Europe and the Middle East.

The long-term effect of Italian practices and Arab propaganda was to intensify the ambiguous relationship that had long existed between

Muslim societies and the Abyssinian and Ethiopian states. The ambiguity continued well after the restoration of the constitutional monarchy in 1941. At his coronation in 1930 Haile Sellassie had taken on all of the trappings of the Solomonic tradition. He was the "Conquering Lion of the Tribe of Judah" in the tradition of Menilik I and Menilik II. Now he had been restored to the throne and informal leadership of the Orthodox church, with great celebration inside the country and throughout the world. He had strong ambivalence about Islam and the role that some leaders had played during the Italian occupation, although he remained pragmatic in his practices toward his Muslim subjects.

Haile Sellassie was deposed by the military in 1974. They severed the link between cross and crown, but neither Muslims nor Christians fared well under their highly centralized and secular regime. They were overthrown in 1991 and replaced by a government with a pluralistic approach to culture. Under these conditions the fortunes of Muslim communities seem to be reviving, both in Ethiopia and Eritrea, which declared its independence from the larger country in 1993. Figure 15 is a contemporary painting suggesting the great diversity of the faithful across the region.

Further Reading

The best introduction to Ethiopian history and society is the synthesis put together by Harold Marcus, *A History of Ethiopia* (University of California Press, 1994, revised edition 2002). For a look at the emergence of the Solomonic tradition and the struggles among the contenders for the Christian throne, see Taddesse Tamrat's *Church and State in Ethiopia, 1270–1527* (Oxford University Press, 1972). For later ideological struggles, see Don Crummey's "Imperial Legitimacy and the Creation of Neo-Solomonic Ideology in 19th c Ethiopia" in *Cahiers d'Etudes Africaines* (vol. 109, 1988). An older work that gives some good insight into the relations with Muhammad and his followers is Sergew Hable Sellassie's *Ancient and Medieval Ethiopian History to 1270* (Addis Ababa United Printers, 1972).

For an analysis of the "Abyssinian" tradition of early Islam, see the Sellassie reference and W. M. Watt's *Muhammad at Mecca* (Oxford Clarindon Press, 1953). Both draw heavily on the hadith (see Chapter 2) collected by Ibn Ishaq and edited by Ibn Hisham, which can be found in an English translation by A. Guillaume entitled *Life of Muhammad* (Lahore, Pakistan, 1955).

For the story of the Muslim communities of Ethiopia, a good recent introduction is the article by Lidwien Kapteijns in Levtzion and Pouwels' *The History of Islam.* A useful study of islamization in Wallo is Hussein Ahmed's *Islam in Nineteenth-Century Wallo, Ethiopia: Revival, Reform and Reaction* (Brill, 2001). Haggai Erlich gives an interesting Middle Eastern and Israeli perspective on Ethiopia, the practice of Islam, and relations with the Middle East in *Ethiopia and the Middle East* (Lynne Rienner, 1994). The citations from Tewodros' letter of 1862 and Arslan in 1935 come from Erlich.

For the centralization of Ethiopia in the late nineteenth century and the confrontations of Muslims and Christians, see the Marcus volume and three articles by Richard Caulk: "Religion and State in Nineteenth Century Ethiopia" in *Journal of Ethiopian Studies* (volume 10.1, 1972, pp. 23–41), "Yohannes IV, The Mahdists and the Partition of North-East Africa" in *Transafrican Journal of History* (volume 1.2, 1972, pp. 23–42), and "Harar Town and Its Neighbors in the 19th Century" in *Journal of African History* (volume 18.3, 1979, pp. 369–86).

CHAPTER 9

Asante and Kumasi: A Muslim Minority in a "Sea of Paganism"

I move now into case studies concentrated in shorter periods and spaces. The focus allows us to concentrate on particular persons and groups in their situations and to see the great variety of Muslim space, practice, and community across the continent. It is appropriate to begin with a "pagan" state and society, one that can in no way be called Muslim or Christian, and the situation of Muslim minorities within it. The state is the empire of Asante, singled out briefly in Chapter 4. In that chapter, I introduced the "Suwarian tradition" as a rationale developed by these Muslim communities for coping with their contexts; we may imagine similar traditions in other times and places as Islam emerged as a living faith.

The Emergence of the Asante Empire

Asante was not very old, but it came out of an old tradition. From about 1700 in the town of Kumasi, the Asante leaders built on a heritage of state formation, farming, artisan production, and long-distance trade that went back roughly 500 years. The Akan people, of whom the Asante were a part, began to create a record at the time the Empire of Mali was reaching its apogee, around 1300 C.E. Mali traders learned of gold mines in the southern forest. Encouraged by family firms and the state, they traveled south, established colonies around an Akan center called Begho, and began the export of gold to the savanna. Some of this gold reached North Africa and Europe, through the Transsaharan trade. The colonies were the first Muslim communities of the "pagan" forest zone. Over time they developed the "Suwarian" practice as a way of understanding their Islamic identity in the midst of the *Dar al-Kufr*.

Most of the early Akan states were small affairs, larger than the city-states of the Swahili coast but much smaller than the polities of the Ethiopian highlands and the Moroccan plain. Their economies were based on agriculture, fishing, mining, and trade. From time to time one of them would become dominant in the region and then decline amid the competition for resources. One constant factor was the production and trade in gold and the resulting presence of traders from the Sahel. These merchants brought cotton, leather, and other goods from the north and took back gold, kola nuts, and slaves. They established networks with local traders and producers. Typically they resided in the capitals or larger commercial centers of the states, in separate neighborhoods where they could more easily maintain their practice of Islam. Like so many Africans, they were multilingual. In addition to the Twi language of the host society, most spoke Mandinka, the language of the Mali Empire. They knew some Arabic for purposes of worship and as a product of the Quranic schools that they maintained.

Akan societies were fundamentally matrilineal, which is to say that they passed succession to office and property down through the female line. The dynasties of the small states followed this principle. Each usually had a queen mother and a king; it was the queen mother who marked the line of descent and her brothers, nephews, and sons who competed for the throne. Women as well as men participated in the councils that chose kings and queen mothers and made the major decisions of state. Over time an elaborate state craft developed among the Akan, as well as a complex aesthetic that is well known through wood sculpture (Akan fertility dolls, for example), metal sculpture (such as gold weights), and brightly colored dress (such as *kente* cloth, which is now widely imitated in scarves and doll dresses in Europe and North America).

The Asante version of this Akan tradition emerged in about 1700 in the northern part of the forest. Six matrilineages came together to form it, led by the group from Kumasi. Kumasi and the other lineages chafed at the yoke of the Akan state of Denkyera. They saw an opportunity to mobilize and won a resounding victory. Under able leadership they quickly formed a new state, conquered most of the Akan polities and formed the largest state that the region had ever seen over the course of the eighteenth century. They gave it the name of Asante, made Kumasi the capital, and established an elaborate bureaucracy, army, financial system, and diplomacy to govern their extensive dominions (see Map 6 at the end of this chapter).

The Asante built upon Akan traditions, but took them further than ever before. They also expanded on religious practice and developed a major innovation. They expressed this tradition in the form of the story of the Golden Stool, which became a way to single out the Asante state, its capital, and the obligation of its subjects to obedience. The dominant version of the story runs as follows:

> Before the reign of Osei Tutu, Kumasi was subject to the Denkyera nation and had to pay annual tribute to its king in the form of gold dust and wives. Osei Tutu was determined to put an end to this. He first set about forming a loose confederation with the nearby chiefs, through conquests, persuasion and treaties. Soon he felt he had sufficient strength to withstand the might of the Denkyeras. He therefore declared war against Denkyera by mutilating the tribute collectors and sending them back with stones. In the ensuing war, the Denkyeras were totally defeated at the famous Battle of Feyiase, near Kumasi, in 1701. Their king, Ntim Gyakari, was captured and beheaded.
>
> Osei Tutu achieved this feat with the help of his greatest friend and counselor, a man he had met in his boyhood, while he was a servant at the palace of the King of Denkyera. This is no other than the celebrated Okomfo Anokye (the Priest Anokye), the greatest and most respected priest of Ashanti. Besides his achievements as a priest, this man had such talent for directing the affairs of state that he has been described as the Cardinal Wolsey of Ashanti. Many laws and customs are referred to as Anokye's injunctions. The Union owed its secure foundation to his exceptional qualities. Tradition says Anokye had such magical powers that some of his almost miraculous deeds can be found to this day.
>
> None of the achievements of Anokye can be compared with his creation of the Golden Stool.... The day was Friday. Anokye had summoned all the chiefs of the Union to a great gathering at Kumasi. At that gathering he brought from the sky, with darkness and thunder, and in a thick cloud of white dust, a wooden stool, adorned with gold, which floated to earth and landed gently on Osei Tutu's knee. Anokye made a solemn announcement that the spirit of the whole nation, and all its strength and bravery depended on the safety of the stool. To impress this on their minds, he caused the king and the leading chiefs and queen mothers present, to give him clippings from their nails and from their hair. These were mixed into a medicine and smeared on the stool. The remainder was drunk by the contributors as a sacramental drink. Thus the sunsum (soul) of each was provided a resting or anchored place in the stool.

> Okomfo Anokye succeeded in bringing about the national conscious-
> ness that henceforth Ashanti was a nation linked by a common religious
> bond of which the Golden Stool was the visible symbol . . . .

This tradition, like the "Solomonic" genealogy of Abyssinia and the
Sharifian one of Morocco, was widely recounted and ardently believed.

The council of state kept close watch on the Golden Stool, made
of wood and highly decorated with gold. At major state ceremonies
the Asantehene would sit on a throne, and the stool – symbol of his
office and the "soul" of the Asante "nation" – sat next to him on
another throne. No one was allowed to sit upon the stool or create an
imitation. Indeed, as discussed later, Asante went to war in the early
nineteenth century when one of its subject states created a replica of
the golden stool – an act of blasphemy and rebellion. Priests in the
tradition of Anokye helped to enforce this rule and the other precepts
of Asante religion.

The queen mother and the king – called the *Asantehene* – were the
most visible figures within the Asante state. They had to negotiate
constantly with a range of people and lineages – within Kumasi, the
other Asante matrilineages and the subject provinces – to obtain and
maintain their positions. The struggle to achieve power was constant,
bitter, and often violent, but the successive generations of state leaders
were able to maintain continuity until the British conquest at the end
of the nineteenth century.

Because the core of Asante lay to the north, close to the woodland
areas and not too far from the Sahel, Muslims were present in greater
numbers than in other Akan areas. Some of those Muslims lived in
communities that challenged the Suwarian tradition of compliance;
they wanted to spread the faith and establish Muslim-majority communities. One tradition suggests that a king was deposed by the council
because he worked too closely with some of the Muslim communities –
to the point where some doubted his allegiance to Asante religious
practice.

The Muslim Community of Kumasi in the Early
Nineteenth Century

Kumasi had about 20,000 inhabitants in the early nineteenth century.
Among the most influential were about 300 Muslims who lived in one
neighborhood near the palace and worked the trade links to the north.

We are fortunate to have a contemporary firsthand source about this community, in the form of the Englishman Joseph Dupuis. In 1820 he was authorized to go to Kumasi and negotiate solutions to outstanding problems between the Asante and the British, who were active along the coast. Dupuis had spent considerable time in Morocco and spoke Arabic. This impressed the local Muslim community, most of whom knew the language of Islam mainly for purposes of prayer and reading the Quran, and led them to confide in him on a daily basis. Dupuis was thus able to gain insight into the operations of the Asante state and the lives of its influential Muslim minority. We have already met Dupuis and the leader of this community, Baba or the Bashaw, in Chapter 4.

Kumasi was at the center of trading networks linking the Sahel in the north to the coast, just as other Akan capitals had been in earlier days. Muslim merchants worked the routes heading into the capital and other market centers at the beginning of the forest zone, using beasts of burden wherever possible. Asante and other traders controlled the routes in the forest and to the coast. The Muslims, by definition, were foreigners to Kumasi. They were not Asante, not even Akan, and were not subjects of the Asantehene – at least not in the same sense as the Akan. Many of the 300 who lived in the capital came from Dagomba and other areas north of the forest – states and societies that had significant Muslim populations and were tributary to Asante. Others came from the northeast, along the routes heading to Hausaland (see Chapter 10), whereas still others came from the northwest. Most of the merchants spoke the form of Mandinka called Juula, which was also the language of trade. It was not unusual to find multilingual abilities among the Muslims: Twi, the language of the hosts, for communication with the court and their hosts in general; Juula, to communicate across the trading network; a Gur language if they hailed from Dagomba; Hausa, which was the trade language to the northeast; and Arabic, at least for purposes of prayer.

The Kumasi Muslims were wealthy and influential (see Figure 16). They lived close to the palace and thus to the deliberations of the king, queen mother, military, and civilian officials. During the delicate negotiations of 1820, they visited Dupuis' quarters almost every day to bring him the latest news. They had an enormous investment in maintaining peace throughout the full extent of the empire. Repeatedly they tried to persuade the envoy to promise the payment of tribute owed

FIGURE 16 The "Suwarian" minority in the Asante capital. A sketch of Muslims in Kumasi. From Joseph Dupuis' *Journal of a Residence in Ashanti*, London: Henry Colburn, 1824.

by the British and the coastal Akan, offering even to advance the gold themselves. Several times the Muslims urged Dupuis to use his influence to reopen the Atlantic slave trade, recently ruled illegal for British citizens. They shared the perspective of the Asantehene, who feared that the large number of slaves in the kingdom, due to recent wars and the capture of prisoners, could lead to revolt. In these and other ways, the Kumasi Muslims came close to "pushing the envelope" of the Suwarian tradition, which called for maintaining a certain distance from the ruling class.

As capital and major market, Kumasi constantly received trade caravans and visitors. The Muslim community was no exception. Visitors arrived from all areas of the north. Many of them came from families very much like that of Abu Bakr, the teenager we encountered in Chapter 5. He was an "international" with relatives from Jenne and Timbuktu in the west to Hausaland in the east and was at home in many parts of the Sahel, woodland, and forest; he just had the misfortune to get caught on the wrong side of an Asante war. Some visitors to Kumasi claimed Sharifian ancestry, which meant that they were well received at the palace as well as in the Muslim quarter. It was from such travelers to Kumasi that the community kept abreast of events in the

Sahel. News about the holy war led by Uthman dan Fodio (Chapter 10) came from such sources.

Dupuis relished his knowledge of Arabic and Islam and showed this in a very instructive encounter with the leaders of the Muslim community in March 1820 as follows:

> On the following morning . . . a deputation of the Muslims waited upon me to deliver a message of congratulation on the prospect of peace. The deputation consisted of Muhammad al-Ghamba, or Baba as he was called, Bashaw [Pasha] or chief of the Muslims, attended by Abdullah ibn Gatta Shumu, Ali ibn Muhammad, Shallom ibn Kantoma, Ibrahim al-Yandi, Abu Bakr . . . and in all nine of the principal traders, besides a proportionate number of the inferior classes, and slaves. Many of these people enjoyed rank at court, or were invested with administrative powers, entitling them even to a voice in the senate. The party having seated themselves, the chief explained the purpose of the visit, commenting at intervals upon the pacific disposition of the king towards white men, his prowess in war, the extent of his dominions, etc. Although Muslim many of these people, in common with the heathen Africans, were addicted to the use of spirituous liquors, and it was frankly insinuated by some of the bystanders that a little rum would be acceptable . . . .
>
> When they had sufficiently regaled, and as the liquor exhilarated the company, I took the opportunity to introduce a sort of satire used by the Arabs against drunkards. The astonishment . . . with which these religious men were struck at the sound of the language exceeded any conjecture I could have formed. The sentence [in Arabic] was well comprehended by the Bashaw, whose countenance betrayed a confusion that gave me pain to witness . . . . Although I satisfied their enquiries, by a confession that their religious language was known to me from a long residence among the Arabs, I found it impossible to renew the hilarity of the scene. The liquor was neglected, and an affected austerity was employed to cover the former excess. From this day forward, neither the Muslims nor any of their proselytes would indulge in the use of spirituous liquors in my presence.

Asante ceremonies were full of libations, and some of the Muslims had gotten in the habit of participating, despite clear prohibitions against the consumption of alcohol in Islamic law. They explained this to the consul by saying: "God pardon our offenses, they are manifold; drinking strong drinks we know is a relic of the days of ignorance, but it is a custom of this country which we learn from our mothers."

Dupuis appreciated the wisdom and tolerance of the Kumasi community and compared it favorably to Arab and Turkish Muslims and to the "pagans" of West Africa. His prejudices were not surprising for an educated European in the early nineteenth century. In his appendix he wrote the following:

> I should circumstantially exonerate this friendly sect [of Muslims] from ungrateful misrepresentation, by an open avowal that I found them disinterested in their proffers of friendship, liberal to an excess in courtesy, and staunch to their engagements, when their services . . . were called for. Devoid of Arabian or Turkish bigotry, they felt but a very remote interest in those anathemas of the Quran leveled against Christians and Jews as enemies of the faith: buried in the wilds of Ethiopia [in the most general sense of "dark" land], they could listen passively to the recitations of early times, when the roar of battles raged in the north, and religious frenzy desolated the Asiatic and African plains, without feeling moved otherwise than by a transient effusion of gratitude to the Almighty. . . .
>
> The Muslims of Kumasi and Salgha are nearly as jetty-complexioned as the idolators themselves; but many from the inland countries are, more or less, as fair as the northernmost desert Arabs. As another instance of deviation from the institutions of the Quran, and of which they also give their mothers the credit, their faces and bodies are cut by prolonged incisions, the object of which is to distinguish their respective tribes or nations. . . .
>
> The Muslims are the only class of subjects belonging to the kingdom who are morally scrupulous in virtues such as we prize ourselves. This the king is sensible of, and hence the attachment he evinces for the professors of that faith, is at least politically sincere; but it must be confessed also that that monarch is somewhat religiously inclined towards the followers of Muhammad from a reverential awe of the universal God, the Father, according to his imagination, of the creation, of every terrestrial deity, and of those invisible powers [who] agitate the world and inspire the hearts of men with good or evil propensities. Notwithstanding this sovereign chooses to adhere faithfully to his Pagan rites in all their manifold horrors and enormities, he does not neglect to supplicate the Muslims for their prayers, particularly when oppressed with anxiety. . . .

The king, Osei Bonsu, emerges more favorably from Dupuis' commentary than his subjects. All were eager, as discussed in Chapter 4, to obtain the power contained in the talismans made by the local Muslim community.

The Bashaw was probably the oldest member of the community as well as the most prestigious. He functioned like an elder and ward leader. As the citation in Chapter 4 indicated, he now had a white beard, traveled little, and devoted himself to a school with about 70 students. The school operated mainly at the level of the Quran. Graduates who wanted to continue their education – to become teachers, imams, or judges – probably headed to towns further north. The basic constituency consisted of the male and female children of the trading community, but among the pupils were some slaves given by the king. They were in the process of acquiring a Muslim identity and their freedom at the same time. The Bashaw was proud of his role in what he considered to be the redemption of these boys.

The Asantehene at the time was Osei Bonsu, who dominated the councils of state for over twenty years at the beginning of the nineteenth century. The Muslims usually portrayed him as a man of peace, which he was, and to some extent as a man of "faith" as the quotation above suggests. They also recognized his willingness to go to war and the pressures of some members of the council to implement a forceful policy. They realized that human sacrifice, especially at the time of the annual harvest festival, was integral to Asante religion and identity, but they thought that Osei Bonsu minimized this and saved them from having to witness the executions. Osei Bonsu often greeted them with the customary salutation or *salam*, and he asked some of the more literate Muslims to keep records in Arabic of trade goods, treaties, and a chronology of events.

More than this, the king believed in the efficacy of Islam, its book and God, and presumably associated the faith with the high god of the Asante people. He sought the power of Islam, as well as the power which the traditional priests might offer, and showed that very dramatically in his dress. On the last day of the annual festival,

> his wrists and ankles were adorned with fetish [traditional] gold weighing many pounds. A small fillet of plaited grass, interwoven with gold wire and little consecrated amulets, encircled his temples. A large white cotton cloth which partly covered his left shoulder was studded all over with Arabic writing in various coloured inks, and of a most brilliant well-formed character.

A few days later, in talking to the Muslim leaders the king posed a question:

> "What is your custom," said the king addressing himself to Kantoma and Abu Bakr, "when great men make friends?" "They swear upon the sacred book [the Quran]," was the reply. "That is good," said the king,

"because then, if they keep evil in their hearts, the book must kill them."
"True," added the Muslims, "the book contains holy words from the
great God himself. Our law is a great law; we say there is no God, but
one God, the merciful, etc." "Ah," said the king, "I like that, it is strong
sense; it is the fetish [power or baraka] of your country. Asante has no
fetish like this, but the Asante custom is good also. I know that book
[the Quran] is strong, and I like it because it is the book of the great
God; it does good for me and therefore I love all the people that read
it."

In another passage, Dupuis said that the Asante "are persuaded that
[the Quran] is a volume of divine creation, and consequently that it
contains ordinances and prohibitions which are most congenial to the
happiness of mankind in general."

Pushing the Envelope of the "Suwarian" Tradition

It was precisely the Asantehene's interest in Islam and its power that
created problems for the community. In most situations that Muslims
had faced in "pagan" societies since the days of Al-Hajj Salim Suwari,
they had been able to maintain some social distance from the ruling
class. That distance even facilitated the movement of goods and the
efficiency of markets and thus was in the interest of chiefs. These same
realities applied in Asante, but this very much more powerful state
ruled over a wide range of territories, some of which were unhappy
with the burdens of tribute. With some frequency subject communities
plotted revolt, putting the army on high alert. Coalitions of resistors
might create a real crisis.

In the early nineteenth century a significant threat arose from the
northwest, encouraged in part by the town and state of Kong, which we
encountered briefly in Chapter 5 in the story of Abu Bakr. Kong had a
large Islamic community and a long-standing hostility to Asante, which
blocked its access to gold and other trade goods to the south. It saw
Kumasi's power as an obstacle to material as well as spiritual progress.
Some of its clerics called Kumasi an affront to Islam – a "pagan"
or "fetish" power that poured libations and sacrificed human beings.
They even raised questions among Muslims in the Asante capital about
the legitimacy of their behavior and the Suwarian tradition. Kong had
helped mobilize coalitions of opposition that threatened the empire on
several occasions and pushed Kumasi to massive mobilization. Asante

usually defeated the coalitions, but only after intense conflict, great loss of life, and substantial numbers of prisoners of war – many of them Muslim. It was in one of these conflicts that Abu Bakr was captured and shipped to Jamaica. It was the potential of these conflicts, and the suspicion of some members of the palace council about Islamic conspiracies, that ostensibly led to the deposition of the king that I mentioned earlier.

The situation became very tense about 1817, when Asante intelligence reported that a subject province in the northwest had produced a Golden Stool in flagrant violation of Asante custom. The state in question was Gyaman and its capital was Bonduku, a town with a significant Muslim population of its own. Gyaman was Akan and matrilineal and had its own king and queen mother. It was also a rich area of gold production, making it essential to Asante wealth and highly coveted by rival powers. The Kong authorities encouraged the ruling class of Gyaman to join forces in a new coalition of resistance.

Kumasi issued a first ultimatum to Gyaman, whereupon the subject king destroyed his golden stool. But when the queen mother returned to her capital, she "reproached her brother severely and ordered a solid gold stool to be made to replace it," in the words of a British traveler who visited Kumasi in late 1817. The Asante army mobilized all of its resources in anticipation of an extensive, violent campaign against Gyaman and the coalition. The campaign occurred in 1819.

This meant that Kumasi was recruiting among all male subjects of the empire, including the Muslims even though they were "foreigners." This also meant harnessing the religious power of Islam – Muslim leaders would have to participate in and bless the campaign. The effect was to intensify the predicament of the faithful, well aware that they would be fighting, and bless a fight against a coalition that included Muslims; the campaign, if successful, would produce casualties and prisoners of war who were "believers." This was decidedly not a *jihad* in the tradition of the Prophet.

For a personal account of the predicament, we go to what the Bashaw and others described to Dupuis about a year after the campaign:

> In the case of the recent war of Gyaman, they informed me [Dupuis] that they accompanied the king. Subsequently I learned that the Bashaw deserted from the army, the evening after the great battle of the Tando river, and returned to Kumasi. This conduct enraged the king, who

swore that had he not been a holy man, he would have put him to death. After I became acquainted with this little history, I took a favourable opportunity to insinuate its contents to the chief [the Bashaw] who, in reply, admitted the truth; but alleged in his defense that his character as well as his life were at stake; for in regard to the former, he could not without deserving to be stigmatized as infamous, witness the horrid butcheries in the camp, so contrary to the tenets of his religion, and what would it have booted him in the world to come, had it pleased God to have destroyed him in the ranks of the infidels, when he was not fighting for the faith, but against it.

It was the bloodiest campaign they had ever witnessed, for many thousands of Muslims perished in the war, as Buna and Kong, both Muhammadan countries, had united their forces with Adinkra, king of Gyaman, who had cast off his allegiance to the king of Asante, and transferred a tribute which he formerly paid him to the Sultan of Kong. In describing some of the characteristics of the war, they declared they had actually witnessed the massacre of ten thousand old men, women and young children, besides numbers of chieftains, who were put to death by tortures the most revolting to humanity. The Asante, they affirmed, were as enemies the most terrible of mankind, and in war they were justly dreaded even by the true believers.

The Kumasi Muslim leaders survived the campaign and were able to resume their positions as confidants in the palace. There is no indication that the Bashaw, by his desertion, suffered a loss of prestige or access to the Asantehene. Osei Bonsu undoubtedly realized the predicament that he had forced on his associate and counselor of many years. He continued to use Quranic talismans, robes with Arabic writing, and the "book of the great God" (see Figures 10 and 11).

Conclusion

The Suwarian tradition introduced in Chapter 4 was designed to sustain the community of the faithful living in the *Dar al-Kufr*. It allowed them to accept the rule of non-Muslim authorities as long as they provided conditions whereby the faithful could maintain the faith. This meant places of worship, education, and adjudication, generally provided within the neighborhoods of the trading towns of the forest and woodlands. It provided for some consultation between Muslim and non-Muslim, between the trading and ruling "estates," but this was

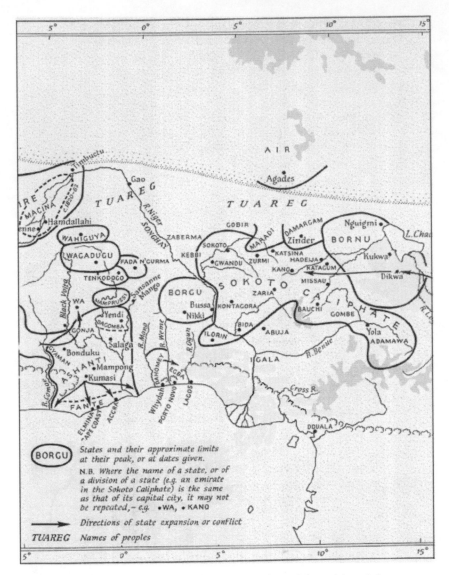

MAP 6 Muslim states and struggles in West Africa. Adapted from John
D. Frage and Maureen Verity, *An Atlas of African History*, New York, 1978.

institutionalized in and for peaceful conditions, which prevailed much
of the time. The ruling estates were modest affairs, involving perhaps
tens of thousands of people and limited jurisdiction.

But Asante was a "country for war," as its ruling class often said
in their rhetoric. It had expanded quickly and violently in the eighteenth century, without resolving a lot of internal fissures. It had a

lot of potential external enemies who knew how to exploit the fissures and create threatening coalitions. The Muslim networks inside and adjacent to the empire were inevitably implicated in the most severe threats. In those situations the faithful of Kumasi might lose their "foreignness" and become subjects of the king, who required their material and moral support. In such situations the Suwarian tradition was of little comfort, for their "character as well as life" were at stake. The Muslims endured the conflicts, about which they had little choice, and worked for the reestablishment of the comfortable conditions of peace and the Suwarian tradition.

Further Reading

The leading author of works on Asante and its Muslim community is Ivor Wilks, and his two most important books are a work of synthesis, *Asante in the Nineteenth Century: The Structure and Evolution of a Political Order* (Cambridge University Press, 1975; reissued with a new preface in 1989), and a collection of essays, *Forests of Gold*, cited at the end of Chapter 4. An exploration of the inner workings of Asante is T. C. McCaskie's *State and Society in Pre-Colonial Asante* (Cambridge University Press, 1995). Any of these works can provide ample bibliography for exploring further the dynamics of Asante and its Muslim communities.

For older and more general histories of the "Gold Coast" or Ghanaian region, see W. W. Claridge's *A History of the Gold Coast and Ashanti* (John Murray, two volumes, 1915, reprinted by Frank Cass in 1964) and W. E. F. Ward, *A History of Ghana* (London Allen and Unwin, 1967). It was Ward who introduced the new editions of Dupuis and Bowdich mentioned below.

For oral tradition of Asante recorded by an Akan clergyman in the late nineteenth century, see C. C. Reindorf, *History of the Gold Coast and Asante* (Basel Missionary Society, 1895). For the work which I have used in citations in the chapter, see Joseph Dupuis' *Journal of a Residence in Ashantee*, cited at the end of Chapter 4; my citations are found on pp. 95–6, 142, 160–1, 247n, and the appendix, pp. ix–x. The other British envoy to Kumasi, a few years earlier (1817), also published his account: Thomas E. Bowdich's *Mission from Cape Coast Castle to Ashantee* (John Murray, 1819; republished by Frank Cass in 1966). The selection from the oral tradition about the Golden Stool comes from Peter Sarpong's *The Sacred Stool of the Akan* (Tema, 1971).

For the Suwarian tradition, the authority again is Ivor Wilks. See his chapter in (editors) Levtzion and Pouwels' *History of Islam* and an article, "Consul Dupuis and Wangara: A Window on Islam in Early 19th c Asante," in *Sudanic Africa* (volume 6, 1995), as well as his older article, "The Transmission of Islamic Learning in the Western Sudan," in (editor) Jack Goody's *Literacy in Traditional Societies* (Cambridge University Press, 1968). For visual culture, see Rene Bravmann and Ray Silverman's "Painted Incantations: The Closeness of Allah and Kings in 19th Century Asante" in (editor) Enid Schildkrout's *The Golden Stool: Studies of the Asante Center and Periphery* (American Museum of Natural History, 1987).

CHAPTER 10

Sokoto and Hausaland: *Jihad* within the *Dar al-Islam*

In this book I have portrayed the West African Sahel as being part of the *Dar al-Islam* for most of the past millennium. The Almoravids claimed to create a "world of Islam" in the eleventh century, but mainly in the western region of the Sahara and then Morocco. The rulers of Mali, beginning at least from the time of the pilgrim emperor Mansa Musa, made the claim for the Sahel from the fourteenth century. Askia Muhammad made the claim for the Empire of Songhay with his accession just before 1500. His pilgrimage and consultation with al-Maghili, as discussed in Chapter 5, were testament to the Islamic identity that he envisioned for his state. Muhammad Rumfa, the sultan of Kano in Hausaland, had a similar vision, and he also consulted with al-Maghili about what constituted "Islamic government."

The movement we study in this chapter came to a different conclusion. Its members became increasingly critical of the governments they saw practicing Islam. By 1800 they were ready to draw a new line in the sand – between "ignorance" and Islam – to create a new Muslim space. They saw the *Dar al-Islam* emerging only under their leader, Uthman dan Fodio. He was a partisan of reform and then of militant revolution, not unlike movements we encounter in many African societies.

Some things had changed between 1500 and 1800: greater violence, a degradation of the environment in many parts of Hausaland, and more corruption in government. This last dimension included the complicity, from Uthman's perspective, of the ruling class and clerics of the court. The rulers called themselves emirs or sultans, which were

Islamic titles, and the ulama claimed to be offering advice in Islamic government, just as al-Maghili had done. But Uthman saw them as an exploitative class. He saved his worst invective for the Muslim advisors, whom he called "venal" *mallams*, from the Hausa word for clerics.

The conviction of Uthman is incontrovertible. But the justification for his critique required an awareness of Islam in the larger society. The consciousness of 1800 required the preparation of 1500. Uthman's movement could not have succeeded in Asante or any other society of the *Dar al-Kufr*. It could only work in an area of significant islamization, an area that was, or at one time had considered itself to be, part of the *Dar al-Islam*. Only such an area could be responsive to the critique of the reformers. Uthman got a "rise" out of the local sultan and the court clerics precisely because of their professed commitment to the faith and his charges of "apostasy" – that they had "relapsed" into "paganism" and "infidelity." He evoked strong resistance from the "establishment" in the name of traditional Islamic practice. It is to this confrontation that we now turn.

The Hausaland Setting

Hausa is one of the most widely spoken languages in Africa. Distantly related to Berber, Arabic, and the Semitic languages of Ethiopia, its original homeland is in the area that today is called northern Nigeria and Niger, where it is the first or mother language of most people as well as the lingua franca of all the inhabitants. The Hausa people have long had a reputation for agriculture and artisan production. Its best known and most widely used product, at home and abroad, is cloth. Cloth, or textile production, involved agriculture in the form of growing cotton and indigo, spinning the thread, weaving the cloth on a variety of looms, and dyeing some of the cloth with indigo in large clay pits. Textile production, from start to finish, required a number of separate skills and involved a significant proportion of the population – men, women, and children. But it was just one of the forms of production in Hausaland, alongside potting, leather working, iron working, and other trades.

These activities were at least 1,000 years old in the area. They were facilitated by the development of small states organized around markets, palaces, towns, and "closely settled zones." The closely settled zones were villages of producers – for example, of the different phases of textile manufacture. The producers brought their goods into the town market and introduced them into local, regional, and long-distance trade. The market and other aspects of the social and economic organization of town and state were supervised by rulers and bureaucracies based in the palaces. The old Hausa title for these chiefs was *sarki*, but since about 1500 most have taken Arabic and Islamic titles such as *sultan* or *emir*. The Hausa city-states were much larger than those of the Swahili coast, but they never rivaled the size of a Mali, Songhay, or Asante (see Map 5).

The most famous of these city-states were Katsina and Kano, located more or less in the middle of Hausaland. They had often been rivals for influence and wealth, including a competition to host the most important caravans of the Transsaharan trade. At the same time they occasionally came under the sway of larger political entities, such as the Empires of Songhay, to the west, or Bornu, to the east. By 1500 they made the claim of being Muslim and made some concerted effort to establish Islam as the dominant and prestigious religious practice of the land. In the case of Kano, under sultan Muhammad Rumfa, this involved bringing in al-Maghili as a consultant in Islamic practice.

The older Hausa religious practices, summarized in the word *bori*, were devalued as inferior. They were most widely followed in the countryside, beyond the purview of sultan and palace, and consisted of whole range of spirits who were consulted and appeased. Some of the spirits existed in a "Muslim" register and had names such as Mallam Alhaji (from *hajj*, the Arabic for "pilgrimage") and Mallam Alkali (from *qadi*, the Arabic for "judge"). Their presence showed how deeply Islam had taken root in the local society on Hausa terms. Muslim authorities in the cities often called the practitioners of Bori by the name for the old priestly caste of the Zoroastrians of Persia: *Maguzawa*, "Magians." By constructing an analogy to this "people of the book," the scholars transformed these "pagans" into a *dhimmi* community within the *Dar al-Islam*. This "africanization of Islam," in the terms of Chapter 4, survives to this day, well beyond the challenge mounted by Uthman dan Fodio.

These arrangements of religious practice, government, trade, and production operated throughout Hausaland during the period between 1500 and 1800. They survived across numerous conflicts within and among city-states and despite periodic crises of rainfall, the chronic environmental problem of the savanna. They were hospitable to the linguistic and ethnic diversity of the area. In addition to small isolated groups of farmers and artisans, Hausaland also hosted two larger groups of pastoral origin. One consisted of the Tuareg, a group speaking a Berber language. The Tuareg were prominent over a wide swath of the central Saharan regions, and some of them lived in the Sahel. They guided, protected, but also raided the Transsaharan caravans that crossed the desert north of Hausaland. In the language I used in Chapter 3, they were islamized but not arabized: they had overwhelmingly adopted Islam, but had kept their Berber tongue and much of the matrilineal orientation.

The other group was the Fulani, or Fulbe, who had migrated from west to east across the Sahel and constituted a large minority among the Hausa. Both groups were "classified" as Muslim in the ethnographies of commentators such as Ahmed Baba, whom we encountered in Chapter 5; each had significant numbers of Muslims.

The Emergence of Uthman dan Fodio

In northwestern Hausaland lay the sultanate of Gobir. Less prosperous and well known than its counterparts in Katsina and Kano, Gobir nonetheless had its palace, town, market, and closely settled zone. The capital was called Alkalawa. The sultan claimed to be Muslim and had learned counselors around him. More than some of the other Hausa city-states, he also gave support to Bori authorities, who formed the main health and social networks for many of the inhabitants. This was one of the dimensions of the society that attracted the ire of Uthman dan Fodio, who bore the name of the third caliph of Islam.

Uthman was born in the 1750s in an area dominated by Fulani pastoralism and not under the close control of the sultan. He came from a scholarly lineage and followed the practice of his father and uncles by going through the Islamic curriculum to become a teacher in his own right. This involved traveling to study with different scholars with different specialities, mainly in Hausaland but also on the southern fringes of the Sahara. In this peripatetic pattern Uthman broadened his perspective and gained the multilingual competence characteristic of so many Africans. He became fluent in Arabic, Hausa, and Tamacheq, the Tuareg language, as well as his native Fulfulde, the language of the Fulani. He was also initiated into the Qadiriyya order. This Sufi affiliation became an important part of his consciousness as a Muslim leader in his generation, as noted in Chapter 2. By the 1770s he was beginning to teach, preach and write, and to distinguish himself from other clerics by his vision and his charisma.

Contrary to what the interpreters of this "Islamic revolution" have maintained, Uthman did "frequent" the ruling class – specifically that of Gobir – as he acquired a reputation as a Muslim authority in northwestern Hausaland. But he was not a court cleric. When he visited the palace he was the representative of a constituency – Fulani, Hausa, and some Tuareg Muslims who lived in the countryside well away from the capital – and made strong representations for reform.

In one instance, when he was about thirty years old, he delivered a sermon to the sultan and all those who had gathered in Alkalawa for the great Muslim festival of the twelfth month of the Islamic calendar, commemorating the willingness of Ibrahim (Abraham) to sacrifice his son Ismail (Ishmael, but Isaac in the Old Testament narrative). According to the version of Uthman's younger brother, Abdullah, written about twenty years later,

> The Sultan of Gobir, who was Bawa, sent word to all the *ulama* of his country that they should gather together at his court during the Great Feast. . . . We gathered together before him, and he said what he had to say, and gave much wealth in alms to the ulama. Then Shaikh Uthman stood up before him and said to him, indeed I and my community have no need of your wealth, but I asked you this and this, and he enumerated to him all matters concerning the establishing of religion [i.e. Islam]. The Sultan replied to him: "I give you what you ask, and I consent to all that you wish to do in this our country." Then he [Uthman] praised God for that, and we returned to establish religion, and the rest of the ulama returned with their wealth.

Uthman's prestige was at a very high point at this juncture in 1787, in the capital as well as the countryside. He actually taught some members of the royal family and hoped that, if one of them took power, it would provide the chance for significant reform. One of his pupils did take power in 1801, but with the opposite effect. Sultan Yunfa feared the charisma, message, and growing following of Uthman. Like his predecessors, he tried to severely limit the ability of the group, now labeled the "reformers," to spread their influence. Conflicts multiplied until hostilities erupted in 1804.

The reform community had grown increasingly strong across the 1790s and early 1800s. Much of its leadership came from the shaikh's family: his younger brother Abdullah, his son Muhammad Bello, his

daughter Nana Asmau, and several others. The community also contained a number of Fulani, Hausa, and Tuareg students, with their
families, from all over Hausaland. As it grew in size and strength, it
became a kind of alternative society and encouraged Uthman to take
a stronger, more aggressive position. The shaikh sharpened his message. The existing regime was corrupt. It encouraged the practice of
paganism in the form of bori, imposed unlawful taxes on the peasantry
and pastoralists, and twisted the law of Islam for its own purposes. After skirmishes erupted between the two sides in this increasingly fierce
competition and the Gobir forces took some Muslims prisoner in a
military campaign and called them slaves, there was no going back.

At this point (1804) the Uthmanian community drew the line in
the sand. They migrated to another part of the countryside where
they were in greater safety and declared war against Gobir. This was
a new beginning, a new "Muslim space." Now the past of Hausaland
was classified as Jahiliyya; the true Muslim community had performed
hijra, sworn allegiance to Uthman, formed the Islamic community,
and declared the "*jihad* of the sword." In all of these acts, Uthman
and his companions consciously imitated the pattern of Muhammad
in making the *hijra* and waging the *jihad* of the sword from Medina in
the 620s C.E.

Victory over the forces of "infidelity" came, but not easily. The
Gobir army was trained and relatively strong, including cavalry and
armor. It had good defenses at the capital of Alkalawa. Uthman's forces
were much more lightly armed, but had the advantage of mobility as
well as the support of an increasingly alienated peasantry and pastoral
community. In 1808 they won a resounding victory over the sultan at
the capital and drove him into exile in the north. The following year
they established Sokoto, on the southern confines of Gobir. They were
eager to make a fresh start, with a new capital and a new pattern of
governance that was consciously Islamic.

During these same years Uthman began to hand out "flags" of authorization to some of his former students, mainly Fulani, and to encourage them to wage similar struggles against the established regimes
in their home areas. By the time Sokoto was built in 1809, most of these
students-turned-commanders had succeeded in overthrowing the core
sultanates of Hausaland, including Katsina and Kano, and forming
new dynasties. This process continued over the second decade of the
nineteenth century until new regimes, loyal to Uthman and Sokoto,
were in place throughout most of Hausaland and a considerable area
beyond – to the edges of Bornu in the east and Songhay in the west.

When Uthman died in 1817, he was replaced by his son Muhammad Bello, and Bello took the title of *khalifa* (caliph), much as the successors to the Prophet had done.

From this time on it is appropriate to speak of a Sokoto Caliphate consisting of a vast confederation of emirates that sent annual tribute to the capital as well as levies to participate in the annual jihad waged on the northern frontier against the displaced regimes. One of these perpetual enemies was the old royal family of Gobir, now installed in the area of today's Niger (see Map 6 in Chapter 9).

Uthman, his family, and his chief ministers soon began to write down their experience – how they moved from reform to revolution and the implementation of a "true" Islamic state. They wrote primarily in Arabic for scholarly consumption and primarily in the spoken languages for lay consumption. By their actions they gave a strong boost to *ajami* literature. Ajami means "non-Arabic" and refers to writing of "foreign" languages in the Arabic script. There are many *ajami* corpuses in Africa. Uthman and his entourage wrote their ajami in Fulfulde, Hausa, and Tamacheq; much of it was poetry designed for recitation, not reading. This "spoken" literature was very much like the Quran, which required recitation and was designed for the largely non-literate Arab audience of Muhammad's day, or like the early Swahili poetry and narrative – another *ajami* – discussed in Chapter 3.

One example of this ajami literature gives an excellent example of the way Uthman and his contemporaries framed the movement from reform to revolution around the heroic actions of the Prophet. It was written in Fulfulde and then translated into Hausa, not long after the declaration of war; it was designed to be read out loud in both languages. In English it is called "The attributes of the Shaikh":

> In the name of God, the Beneficent, the Merciful; may God bless the
>   noble Prophet.
> I give thanks to God for the generosity he showed me,
>   I give praise to Him, the Generous One.
> I say "Peace be upon our Prophet."
>   Know that I have [obtained] many of his characteristics . . . .
> Know that he bore with the troubles of the people,
>   Likewise am I known for this and for loving peace.
> Indeed, he never angered anyone;
>   For this too have people known me and for mercy.
> After summoning people to the religion he made the *hijra*,
>   When I made mine it cost me great effort.

At that place where the enemies came out
  As [they failed] against him so also against me did they fail.
By making the *hijra* he was indeed saved [from them],
  I did the same and the same has been repeated.
He made it at the beginning of the sixth decade [of his life],
  Of a truth, mine was indeed [made at] the same [time] . . . .
No sooner had he made the *hijra* than he waged the *jihad*;
  Likewise did I, keeping the pattern . . . .

For Uthman and his companions, it was critical to frame the gigantic step that they had taken – of reinventing the *Dar al-Islam* in the Sahel – as an "imitation of Muhammad" during the founding days of the religion. This analogy gave conviction and strength to the participants, assurance to those who were joining the new movement, and legitimacy in the estimation of scholars who could read the treatises of explanation.

The Sokoto movement did not go uncontested. The old Hausa regimes maintained a kind of guerilla warfare along the northern frontier. Yoruba and other groups to the south resisted conquest and the imposition of a new regime that they considered to be foreign and materialistic. Groups of Maguzawa inside the caliphate maintained their autonomy. The most formidable challenge, on a theological plane, came from the old West African kingdom of Bornu, to the east. Under the leadership of a learned and charismatic scholar named al-Kanemi, Bornu mobilized an effective resistance against the Fulani armies and bands that began to invade their territory in the 1810s (see Figure 17). Al-Kanemi then engaged Uthman and Bello in a debate, in a series of long letters in Arabic, about the theological justification for the *jihad*. He argued, in the first place, that the attacks were designed to extend Fulani control, and not the Islamic faith, and in the second that the religious sins of the Bornu people did not constitute unbelief and should be corrected by internal exhortation and not war.

Developing a Pedagogy of Islamization

Creating a truly "Islamic" society has always been a daunting task – just as creating a Jewish or Christian one would be. The early Arab Muslims discovered this across the two civil wars of the first Islamic century. The Almoravids created an unrealizable standard in the

FIGURE 17 An opponent of the Sokoto *jihad*. A sketch of
Shaikh al-Kanemi, a formidable Muslim cleric of Bornu. From
E. W. Bovill (editor) *Missions to the Niger*, Cambridge
University Press, 1960.

Sahara and Morocco in the eleventh century. One could say the same
of the Fatimids in Tunisia and Egypt or the contemporary regimes of
Sudan, Iran, and Afghanistan. The Taliban attracted a certain amount
of admiration from other Muslims, but more by their intensity of effort
than any economic or social accomplishments.

Uthman's movement encountered similar difficulties, but it would
be hard to find a more intelligent and thoroughgoing effort to establish

a new kind of Muslim space. The formative places were Degel, where the community spent most of its time before the *hijra* of 1804, and then Sokoto, which the community envisioned as a very different kind of Muslim capital. All of the members of Uthman's family, his principal advisors, and a number of former students participated in this task. After the founder's death his son Bello reigned as caliph for twenty years (1817–37), established the fundamental practices of the regime, and pushed hard for the transformation of the society.

In many ways the key figure for islamization was Uthman's daughter and Bello's sister, Nana Asmau (1793–1864). Named for a woman who brought food to the Prophet when he was in hiding, Nana was a teenager when she provided sustenance for the soldiers during the critical years of fighting. At about the same time she married Gidado, one of the leaders of the fighting who soon became the Wazir or chief minister of Muhammad Bello. This strengthened her role within the caliphal court and particularly the pedagogical functions that her father, brother, and husband encouraged.

Nana neither competed with these prominent male figures, nor aspired to political leadership within the Sokoto regime. She fulfilled all of the responsibilities of wife and mother ascribed to her by a patriarchal society. At the same time she developed a second vocation as student, scholar, Sufi, and pedagogue. In so doing she strengthened the strong tradition of women's education in Uthman's family and opened the way for women to exercise intellectual and spiritual leadership in the larger society. As a participant in the *jihad*, as well as member of the caliphal family, she was accorded the greatest attention.

The tasks of education, nurture, and the elevation of Islamic practice in Gobir was formidable. Among the women, children, and slaves, who were the least literate but most critical members of the society for spreading the faith, the task was awesome. Nana Asmau saw the Bori system, which provided a great deal of meaning, socialization, and healing in Hausa society, as not only her enemy but also the example of the way to structure her mission. She recruited a number of agents, primarily women of her age or younger, to be her teachers and provided them with training. She then sent them back to their home villages in a kind of "extension" service. She communicated with them on a regular basis, often by personal visits. Nana had the wisdom to recognize the old patterns of islamization and africanization of Islam. She saw the incorporation of Islamic themes into Bori, and the value of Bori practices for solving the problems of everyday life. She affirmed the value of talismans, as long as they contained Quranic verses, that is, as long as they were "Islamic" (see Figures 10 and 11). She then integrated these insights in her mission to transform the society.

Nana Asmau wrote extensively in the languages that were widely used in Hausaland. She made a special point of writing Fulani and Hausa ajami poetry for recitation to her teachers, families, and whoever would listen to her. A huge corpus of her writings has now been collected and published so that students and scholars can see the writings in the original Arabic script, Roman script, and English translation. She attacked some of the most difficult problems of establishing a new Islamic society.

One of these was to try to encourage healing and counseling, "Islamic" style, over against the older, time-tested Bori practices. She wrote, for example, about the "medicine of the Prophet," an old tradition within Islam designed for spiritual, material, and physical healing by the recitation of particular Quranic verses. Here are excerpts from one of her efforts, written for recitation in 1840. In this case she composed in Arabic to provide a kind of primer for other instructors to use:

> In the name of God, the Beneficent, the Merciful. God bless and protect the noble Prophet and his Family, Companions and since supporters.
>
> Asmau, daughter of the Shehu, the Commander of the Faithful, the light of the Age, Uthman ibn Fudi (May God be pleased with him and pour blessings upon him), said:
>
> Now we proceed. This is a book which we have named, "Glad tidings to Brethren on using the *suras* from the Quran of the Generous Creator." God is the one who leads us in the right direction and unto Him we return. Success is due to God.

SURAT AL FATH (no. 48)

> It was related by one of the pious men [of old] that whoever reads it three times when he sees the crescent moon on the first night of *Ramadan* will have God increase his income until the end of that year.

SURAT AL-NAJM (no. 53)

> Whoever writes it on a clean piece of gazelle-leather and wears it will increase his power and will defeat anyone who disputes him . . . .

SURAT AL-WAQIAH (no. 56)

> . . . One of the pious men said: "If it is read for a dead person, he will be relieved of his sins; if read for a sick person, he will be made comfortable. If written and worn by a woman undergoing child-birth, she will deliver the

child by the grace of God the Exalted One. It is effective on everything to which it is attached."

SURAT AL-HASHR (no. 59)

Some experts say that the end of al-Hashr is a remedy for every form of sickness except death itself....

SURAT AL JUMA (no. 62)

It was reported by the Prophet: "Whoever reads Surat al-Jum'a will be granted forgiveness for sins up to the number of those who attend the Friday congregational prayer. Anyone who persists in reading it shall be safe from the whispers of Satan....

SURAT AL-HAQQA (no. 69)

He said: "Whoever reads Surat al-Haqqa will be judged leniently by God. If it is worn by a pregnant woman, then she will be protected from all ailments."

SURAT AL-JINN (no. 72)

It was related by the Prophet: "Whoever reads Surat al-Jinn and then frees a slave will be rewarded according to the number of jinns who believed Muhammad and the number of jinns who did not believe him...."

SURAT AL-BURUJ (no. 85)

It was related by the Prophet (may God bless and protect Him): "Whoever reads Surat al-Buruj will be given the reward of one who stands on Arafat [a mountain outside of Mecca]. Its special characteristic: when hung on a weaned child, it makes the weaning process easier to bear."

Nana was not always successful in her preaching and teaching. But she certainly made inroads into traditional practices and created communities of Islamic practice in the rural areas where few had existed before. She is greatly revered in northern Nigeria today. It is in no small part because of her efforts that Islam has become so deeply embedded in the culture of Hausaland.

Conclusion

The *jihad* of Uthman, the Sokoto Caliphate, and the efforts of leaders like Nana Asmau have had a profound impact on northern Nigerian society. The "Uthmanians" would not have welcomed the violent conflicts among Muslims and Christians today, and they would be

concerned about the poverty and inequalities faced by Nigerians, problems they addressed in the early nineteenth century. But the serious-
ness of their reform and their attention to implementation through
attentive administration, annual jihadic campaigns, elaborate pedagogies, and extensive interpretation have helped embed Islam in the
culture of Hausaland today. They inscribed the region "permanently"
into the *Dar al-Islam*. It is their effort around 1800, much more than
the attempt of sultans like Muhammad al-Rumfa in 1500, that forms
the historical social charter of today's northern Nigeria – and the basis
for establishing Sharia law in a number of states within the region.

Further Reading

For understanding Uthman and the Sokoto Caliphate, we are blessed with
an abundant literature, although disproportionately from the founders and
defenders of the regime. The best general treatment, including an introduction to the works produced by the founding family, is D. Murray Last's
The Sokoto Caliphate (Longman, 1967). An excellent biography of Uthman
is Mervyn Hiskett's *The Sword of Truth* (Oxford University Press, 1973).
For a treatment of how the heritage of Uthman is used in recent Nigerian
history, see Jonathan Reynolds' *The Time of Politics (Zamanin Siyasa): Islam
and the Politics of Legitimacy in Northern Nigeria, 1950–66* (University Press
of America, 1999).

Some of the rich internal literature is contained in translations of works by
Uthman, his brother Abdullah, and his son Bello. See, for example, Abdullah
dan Fodio's *Tazyin al-Waraqat* (Ibadan University Press, 1963, translated
and edited by M. Hiskett), the source of the first citation in the chapter; and
Uthman dan Fodio's *Sifofin Shehu* (translated and edited by R. A. Adeleye
and I. Mukoshy in the *Research Bulletin*, Center of Arabic Documentation at
Ibadan, vol 1.2 for 1966), the source of the second selection. Both selections
can be found in a text I prepared with Douglas Smith, *Sources of the African
Past* (Africana Press and Heinemann, 1979; reprinted by iUniverse 1999).
For external impressions of the Sokoto Caliphate, see Samuel Johnson's *A
History of the Yoruba* (Routledge, 1921) and Hugh Clapperton's *Journal of a
Second Expedition into the Interior of Africa* (John Murray, 1829, reprinted by
Cass, 1966). For al-Kanemi's debate with the leaders of Sokoto, see Louis
Brenner's "The *jihad* Debate between Sokoto and Borno: An Historical
Analysis of Islamic Political Discourse in Nigeria" in (editors) J. F. Ade
Ajayi and J. D. Y. Peel's *Peoples and Empires in African History: Essays in
Memory of Michael Crowder* (Longman, 1992).

For the pedagogy of the regime and the career of Nana Asmau, see Jean
Boyd and Beverly Mack's *One Woman's Jihad: Nana Asma'u, Scholar and*

Scribe (Indiana University Press, 2000). Boyd has also written a biography of Nana Asmau entitled *The Caliph's Sister* (Cass, 1989), and she and Mack have collaborated on a monumental collection of Nana's writings, in Arabic, Hausa, and the Fulani language, including English translations: *The Collected Works of Nana Asma'u, 1793–1864* (Michigan State University Press, 1997). This is the source of the "medicine of the Prophet" citation at the end of the chapter. For insight into Bori practice, see Michael Onwuejeogwu's "The Cult of the Bori Spirits among the Hausa" in (editors) Mary Douglas and Phyllis Kaberry's *Man in Africa* (Tavistock, 1969).

CHAPTER 11

Buganda: Religious Competition for the Kingdom

The East African kingdom of Buganda offers another variation on islamization, beginning in the precolonial period and extending to the regime established at the end of the nineteenth century by the British – who made Buganda the core of their larger colonial territory Uganda. Muslims had not been present in this state, set on the northern shores of Lake Victoria, neither as merchants, as we have seen in Asante, nor as part of the ruling in class, as we saw in Hausaland or Mali. The young Muslims we encounter in Buganda in the late nineteenth century were first-generation practitioners. They were interested in trade to be sure, but especially in power. In their heady, rapidly changing society it was possible to imagine going from no Islamic identity to a Muslim state in one generation.

These local Muslims had considerable encouragement in their ambition: the Swahili and Omani merchants operating out of Zanzibar (see Chapter 3) in the late nineteenth century. These traders, unlike those of the Suwarian tradition we saw in Asante, were often active missionaries for the faith, not unlike the European Christian missionaries who were spreading throughout Africa in the same period. Indeed, the Zanzibaris often saw themselves in religious as well as commercial competition with the Europeans. Momentum was increasingly in the hands of Western entrepreneurs and governments, and Africa was on the verge of falling under European control. In this context Islam had an additional appeal that we saw in the Moroccan and Ethiopian chapters, and will see again in Chapters 12 and 13, as an alternative to European, colonial, and Christian identity.

The Structures of Buganda Society

Buganda was precisely the kind of place where rapid change could happen. It was a society based on about twenty clans, "super lineages," with strong identities maintained by particular religious cults and shrines. Collectively the gods and shrines were known as the Lubare. Most clans lived by agriculture, based on cereals and tree crops like the banana, grown in the rich soils and tended by the women, and pastoralism, built around cattle and the men. Those who resided on the northern and western shores of the lake often gained their livelihood from fishing. In the sixteenth century these clans developed a state structure to defend themselves against the more powerful kingdom to the northwest, Bunyoro. By the nineteenth century Buganda developed a strong army and a fleet that operated on the lake and with these instruments expanded to the west, north, and east. The society also developed several institutions that fed the ambition of insiders and outsiders alike.

One was the royal lineage, which combined patrilineal and matrilineal dimensions within a fundamentally patriarchal framework. The kings or Kabakas came from one line, defined patrilineally; sons usually succeeded their fathers. On their mothers' side, however, they might be descended from any of the clans; they were always buried on the clan land of their mother. Polygyny was practiced. A new Kabaka brought his existing wives to the palace and was encouraged to take new ones as a way of cementing his authority. Sons of any of these wives might accede to the throne through the influence of the king and his counselors, female as well as male. This situation led to intense competition and infighting among candidates, mothers, and clans whenever a Kabaka died or seemed to be in poor health.

Another institution was the movable palace. Using the traditional architecture of timber and thatch, the kings built palaces in different parts of the kingdom, usually close to the northern shores of the lake and Kampala, the capital of today's Uganda. It was not unusual for a king to move his capital every few years. The move might relate to strategic options, the ability to supply the food and other material requirements of the bureaucracy, or questions of loyalty and support, which were typically tied to influential clan leaders and their locations and constituencies. Each capital had a name and became attached to particular memories and traditions in the fortunes of the state and the monarch.

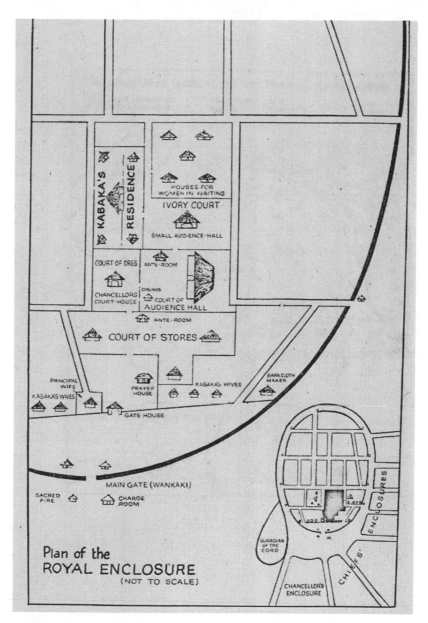

FIGURE 18 The focus of intense competition. A sketch of the Buganda palace in the late nineteenth century. From J. P. Thoonen, *Black Martyrs*, New York: Sheed and Ward, 1941.

Inside of the palace (see Figure 18) was another institution that intensified the competition for political and religious allegiance: the school for pages. Clans and influential people put forward young male candidates, usually in their teen years but sometimes even younger, to apprentice at the court. Those who were accepted and moved to the palace as "boarders" were soon caught up not just in their duties but also in the drive for power and position within the institutions of Buganda – especially when a new Kabaka came to power. The pages watched the Zanzibari and European explorers, traders, and missionaries who came to the kingdom in increasing numbers in the late nineteenth century. If they received encouragement from the king and his counselors, they might well learn a new language, such as Swahili, and a new religion, such as Islam. This is what happened to some pages under Kabakas Suna and Mutesa in the middle of the nineteenth century.

Buganda is often compared with Asante as a very strong kingdom that survived into the twentieth century and the colonial period. That much is certainly true, but Asante was a more cohesive and conservative state in which the king was charged with maintaining the national identity and key religious practices. The Kabaka, in contrast, was the subject of a number of tensions rooted in the clan structure. He might pay particular attention to gods who had acquired special prestige: Mukasa, a "high" god concerned with health and prosperity, or Kabuka and Nende, two competing gods of war. But these gods, together with their shrines and priests, were rooted in particular clans that were competing for influence, especially by offering wives to the king, in the hopes that "their wife" would father the next Kabaka. Buganda did not have, in other words, a clearly identified national priesthood. This unusual religious structure, combined with the moving palace, changing bureaucracy, and school for young pages, gave Buganda a capacity for rapid change – as well as the potential for violence and disintegration. It gave the Kabaka more latitude for innovation than his counterpart in Asante.

The Spread of Islam in Buganda

As indicated in Chapter 3, Swahili culture developed in East Africa not long after the foundation of Islam. It was cosmopolitan, in its orientation to the Indian Ocean trade, and local, in its attachment to coastal custom and agricultural production. The Swahili were Muslim

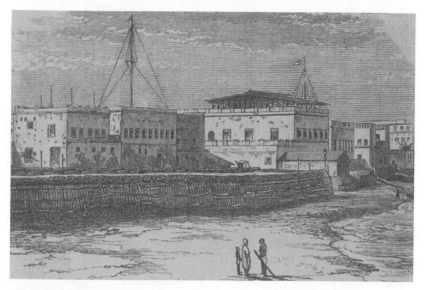

FIGURE 19 The headquarters of Omani and Swahili expansion in nineteenth-century East Africa. An engraving of Zanzibar. From Henry M. Stanley, *Through the Dark Continent*, New York: Harper and Brothers, 1878, volume 1.

and had incorporated Islamic folklore into the traditions, as the story of Muhammad's ascension reveals. The culture and language were largely confined to the coast, however, and Islam was scarcely practiced in the interior.

Until the nineteenth century, that is. That was when the Omani Arabs invested in the East African trade (see Map 3). They moved their main base from Oman, on the southeastern end of the Arabian peninsula, to Zanzibar Island (see Figure 19). Under their leader, the sultan, they established a certain hegemony over the Swahili settlements on the mainland, in what today is Kenya and Tanzania. They began to organize caravans of traders to make regular forays into the interior. The caravans brought back ivory to meet growing Asian and European demand. They brought back slaves for export or to work plantations of grain and cloves at the coast. In the process they enlarged the East African slave trade discussed in Chapter 5 and began to spread Islam through the vehicle of Swahili culture, in places such as Tabora and Ujiji in today's Tanzania. In the atmosphere of a growing European presence, including Christian missionaries, and a growing Islamic consciousness, the merchants and caravan leaders became increasingly committed to the expansion of their faith.

Buganda was one of the "prizes" of Zanzibari extension. Known from the outside as an area rich in crops, cattle, and fish; strong militarily through an army and fleet; and strategically located at the headwaters of the Nile, Buganda attracted its share of attention. The first Swahili arrived at the Buganda capital in the 1840s, during the reign of Kabaka Suna (ca. 1830–56). They were interested particularly in the acquisition of ivory from the elephant hunters working in the service of the state. Not unlike the northern Muslims at the court of Asante, the Swahili traders – usually called Arabs by the indigenous sources – were frequent visitors at the palace. They were allowed to establish close relations with the local population and in particular with the pages. Soon a few learned Muslims took up residence in or near the palace, began to teach classes, and read the Quran to the king.

The Development of Islam under Kabaka Mutesa

Mutesa took over in the late 1850s upon his father's death (see Figure 20). Ambitious to encourage Buganda expansion, in military and commercial terms, and curious about the wider world of East Africa, he saw Muslim identity as a crucial ingredient of his strategy. He not only accepted the presence of traders and teachers at his capital and the maintenance of trading relations but also actively encouraged his officials and pages to read the Quran and practice Islam. He learned the prayers himself and celebrated the main Muslim festivals. Because Buganda did not have a clearly defined national priesthood that could marshal opposition to outside influences, it was possible for Mutesa to promote a new faith in an open way.

The first Buganda Muslims were associated with the most significant new fact of religious practice: reading. The "Readers" were the younger officials and pages who gathered around their Swahili teachers to recite the Quran and say the prayers. For the vast majority of the local people, who were not literate, this was a conspicuous act. In traditions recorded in subsequent decades, this is the way that the "advent" of Islam was presented:

> King Mutesa asked [his Swahili counselor] what it was his father (Suna) used to talk to them about, when they visited him, and he replied that they used to talk about God.... So King Mutesa said: "Well then, come and teach me to read," and he brought a Swahili called Makwega, who taught the king every day, and he learned Mohammedanism very

FIGURE 20 The king courted by Muslims, Christians, and traditional authorities. A photo of Kabaka Mutesa and his chiefs. From Stanley.

quickly. Others learned with him . . . . When the king changed capitals he persevered in his reading and fasted during the first fast, and he then ordered all his subjects to read Mohammedanism. He also learned to write in Arabic.

Mutesa was sympathetic to Islam and undoubtedly considered himself to be a Muslim by the late 1860s, when he was about thirty years old. He built a large mosque in his capital, assigned several pages to guard it, and came there to the Friday prayer with a large group of his chiefs. He urged chiefs and subjects to perform the Muslim prayers, introduced "Muslim" cotton attire in place of the traditional bark cloth, and observed the month of fasting. He changed royal burial practices, disinterring a number of previous kabakas, reuniting the jawbone with the skeleton and reburying them close to his capital; this was probably related to the teaching of his Swahili mentors about the necessity for the body to be "united" in order to be resurrected. It would not be too much to say that in this period he saw Islam as a kind of "state" religion similar to the "phase 2" that I discussed in Chapter 3. With the Kabaka's encouragement a small but significant minority of Ganda, at the capital and to some extent in the hinterland, adopted the practice of Islam.

But Mutesa was also the focus of clan competition and the influence of the Lubare. He was an autocrat who expected loyalty from his subjects – and particularly the pages boarding at his palace. By the mid-1870s these pressures came to a head, and some of the older counselors gained the ear of Mutesa:

> Then the chiefs [of the older generation], when they understood . . . how displeased the Kabaka had become with the readers putting on airs . . . , they [the chiefs] bore witness to the following crimes . . . . First, they [the readers] abuse the Kabaka for non-circumcision, saying he is a *kafir* [unbeliever, infidel] and not able to lead them in prayer in the mosque . . . . They abuse the Kabaka because he eats *kafir* meat, which is not slaughtered by Muslims, and he eats pig . . . . And they slandered the mosques, saying that they were built badly in an unholy way . . . . So the Kabaka ordered all those pages of the palace to be seized, and all those chiefs of the mosque who were reading, and commanded the executioner Mukajanga to take them . . . to be burned by fire for their crimes . . . . Thus religion was hated, as he favored the *kafir*, for now the *kafir* had obtained power over the Readers.

In this instance Mutesa opted not for Muslim practice but for Buganda custom that the king's body should neither be cut nor his blood shed. But in fact the conflict had its roots less in custom than in the intense competition, the "lobby" of the chiefs and Lubare, and the king's reaction to the growing assertion of his young Muslim officials. The result was the execution of about seventy leading Muslims in 1876.

The Islamic community at the court nonetheless remained strong. Consisting of local Ganda and Swahili, who often served as teachers and leaders in prayer, it was important for maintaining trade relations with Zanzibar. By the late 1870s these Muslims watched with some concern as Mutesa welcomed new outsiders to his court: travelers like Henry Stanley and missionaries from Great Britain (Anglican) and France (Roman Catholic). Stanley was born in Wales and spent his formative years in England and the United States. He established a reputation as one of the leading European explorers of central Africa and assisted the ruler of Belgium in carving out the empire that became King Leopold's Congo in the late nineteenth century. In the 1870s he visited Buganda, where he viewed Mutesa immediately as an object in the emerging competition between Islam and Christianity:

> My impression of him [Mutesa] was that he and I would become better acquainted, that I should make a convert of him, and make him useful

to Africa . . . . Mutesa has impressed me as being an intelligent and distinguished prince . . . . I saw over 3,000 soldiers of Mutesa nearly half
civilized. I saw about a hundred chiefs who might be classed in the same
scale as the men of Zanzibar and Oman, clad in as rich robes, and armed
in the same fashion, and have witnessed with astonishment such order
and law as is obtainable in semi-civilized countries. All this is the result
of a poor Muslim's labor: his name is Muley bin Salim. He it was who
first began teaching here the doctrines of Islam. False and contemptible
as these doctrines are, they are preferable to the ruthless instincts of a
savage despot . . . .

Stanley reveals all of the prejudices of race, ethnicity, and religion
that characterized Europeans in the late nineteenth century. At the
same time he points to the competition for land and people of the imperial era, especially for a polity located at the headwaters of the Nile
River. Zanzibar and to some extent Islam would eventually lose out
to Britain and Christianity, in great part because of the superiority
of European technology of all kinds and over all competitors. Stanley
also shows a grudging admiration for the intelligence of Mutesa, the
power of his state, and the achievements of Buganda and Islam. His
"Muley bin Salim" was a prominent Zanzibari trader and teacher who
had begun his missionary labors in Buganda several decades before.

The Intensification of Religious Competition under Mutesa

By the late 1870s Mutesa was in poor health, probably from syphilis,
and no longer able to maintain steady control of the competing forces
inside and outside of his realm. He had periods of great energy, however, and remained interested in Buganda's power, the competing external forces, and even the competition among religious forces – both
external and internal. The religious competition now escalated considerably, with the arrival of Anglican missionaries from Britain and
Catholic missionaries from France. Mutesa allowed the missionaries to
create stations in or near his capital and to attract pages to their schools
and workshops. Some of these young men became Readers, literate in
reading in English or Luganda, the local language that the missionaries
quickly transcribed in Roman characters. The transcription enabled
them to translate the Bible and create a competition with the readers
of the Quran. The Ganda people of the capital soon began to refer to
the new groups by national and religious names. The "Protestant"

party were Bangereza ("English") or "People of the Book," the Catholics were Bafransa ("French"), and the Muslims were Baarabu ("Arabs"), all distinguished from the Lubare or practitioners of "traditional" religion. The first three groups were Readers, compared with the nonliterates, who lived mainly outside of the capital, in the rural areas, and belonged more to the older generation.

To get a glimpse of the religious competition, we go to the story of a Ganda man who came to the court as a child and passed through the various "stages" of religious adherence at the court. The following account of Kalemba is a baptism or conversion narrative, recorded by Catholic missionaries in 1882:

> My father had always believed that the Baganda did not have the truth. He sought it in his heart. He had often said so to me, and before dying he told me that one day men would come to teach the good way. This statement made a profound impression on me, and every time the arrival of some foreigner was announced, I would watch him and try to make contact with him, telling myself that perhaps he was the one prophesied by my father. That was how I began frequenting the Arabs who came for the first time under the reign of Suna. Their beliefs seemed to me superior to our superstitions. I received instruction and embraced their religion with a number of other Baganda. Mutesa himself, to please the Sultan of Zanzibar, whose power and wealth had been exaggerated to him, declared that he also wished to be Muslim. The order was given to build mosques in the provinces. For a moment it seemed that the whole country would embrace the religion of the false Prophet. But Mutesa had an extreme repugnance for circumcision. . . . I succeeded, with a few others, in hiding my conversion and in passing for a friend of our gods; in secret, however, I was still faithful to the practice of Islam.
>
> So there I was when the Protestants came. Mutesa gave them a good welcome. He had their book read at court and seemed inclined towards their religion, which he called much superior to that of the Arabs . . . . Several months went by and then Mapera [*mon père*, "my father," a reference to Father Lourdel of the White Fathers order] arrived. Mackay, my teacher, was careful to explain that the whites who had just arrived [i.e. the French] did not know the truth. Their religion was the "religion of the woman." They adored the Virgin Mary . . . . But God was gracious in making me understand that you teach the truth and that you are truly the men of God my father spoke about.

Kalemba gives us insight into how the religious competition felt from below and inside, in the heady and dangerous atmosphere of the court. From above and the court, the perspective that dominates most of the sources, we know that Mutesa, despite his infirmities, was able to evaluate the competence of the competing groups of foreigners in their midst. He felt that European technology and organization were superior to that of the Swahilis.

Mutesa also thought that an alliance with Europeans might assist him in defending his kingdom from another threat, coming not from the east but the north. Just as Egyptian expansion down the Red Sea worried Emperors Tewodros and Yohannes, the Egyptian drive up the Nile valley worried Kabaka Mutesa – and may have colored his hesitation about Islam, even though the adventurers who spearheaded the move were anything but pious men. By the 1870s groups of Egyptians, Turks, Sudanese, and others were exploring, trading, and raiding in the areas just north of his kingdom, a phenomenon that we will be exploring in the next chapter. Mutesa assumed that European technology and support might be a good antidote for this menace as well.

Struggles for Power and Religion after Mutesa

Mutesa became increasingly ill in the last years of his reign and sought healing and solace from every source. He was less able to control the competition between the different religious factions, who soon acquired arms and military experience in anticipation of a succession struggle. In 1884 Mutesa passed away and his young son Mwanga, with little experience in palace intrigue or foreign policy, took over the post of Kabaka. Protestant, Catholic, Muslim, and Lubare factions had been poised for this moment and intensified their competition in the new situation. European and Swahili missionaries were part of that competition, but the leadership now came almost entirely from the Ganda, who had been living at the court under Mutesa and had moved into positions of authority in the military, the state bureaucracy, and the clans. Mwanga, less than twenty years old, tried to preside over the competition. Like his father Mutesa, he depended on older counselors for advice at the beginning of his reign. Unfortunately for him, the advice in the early 1880s came in very divided form.

The result was that Mwanga went back and forth in his loyalties for the next four years, favoring now one faction, now another. In 1886 he did what Mutesa had done ten years before, executing a number of devout Readers, in this case Christian and especially Catholic. Many of these men have since been declared martyrs by Rome. By 1888 Mwanga's inconsistent practices and changing alliances produced a brief surge of unity across Christian and Muslim lines, resulting in his overthrow. The factions soon fell to fighting each other, each with its own standard bearer from among Mutesa's sons.

The Muslim party was the largest and best armed, and by the end of 1888 had succeeded in driving out the Protestants and Catholics. But the conflict continued, now between Buganda custom and Muslim zeal. In the words of a very opinionated observer, the British missionary Robert Ashe,

> Having thus got rid of their Christian rivals, the Muhammedans now determined that the whole of Uganda should profess Islam; and in order to accomplish this resolve, they realised that it was necessary to begin by converting the king.... Kiwewa [a son of Mutesa] now saw that he was in the hands of fanatics of the worst type, and began bitterly to regret that he had suffered these Muhammedan bigots to drive from the kingdom his Christian chiefs, who, at any rate, had not proposed baptism to him, as the Muhammedans were urging upon him the initiatory rite of their religion [circumcision].
>
> Kiwewa declared point blank that he would never consent to the rite.... The Muhammedans brought Kiwewa's younger brother, Kalema, who, to gain the kingdom, willingly embraced Islam [and circumcision].

Religious identity was now more clearly than ever attached to the state, the identity of its king, and particular customs, such as circumcision or baptism. Candidates for the kingship, all of them sons of Mutesa, were now willing to identify openly with the religious parties. The Protestants and Catholics, with their respective missionaries, now regrouped in the western regions of the kingdom, persuaded young Mwanga to become their standard bearer and recaptured the capital in 1890 with superior weaponry. The Muslim party was then driven from the central region and regrouped to the west under another son of Mutesa, "Prince" Mbogo. Kalema in the interim had succumbed to smallpox.

By this time the British dominated the area over against other contenders: Sudanese in the north, Germans in what became Tanganyika to the south, and Zanzibaris at the coast – themselves increasingly under British control as well. The principal British leader in the early

1890s was Frederick Lugard, who helped the Christian parties – and especially the Bangereza or Protestants – to consolidate their control of the kingdom by allocating positions in the bureaucracy and the provinces to particular leaders. Competition between Protestant and Catholic was now translated back to the local, social, and religious level, as Buganda was incorporated into the much larger colonial entity called Uganda.

The Muslim party did not fare well in the new arrangement; their old sponsor, Zanzibar, was now under British control. But they did not immediately lose their capacity to contend for power. Their standard-bearer was still Mbogo. They had strong representation in the leading clans. Other leadership came from the Zanzibari and a group of people called the Nubians. The Nubians were Sudanese who had enlisted with the Turko-Egyptian military forces and then evacuated their country during the days of Mahdist domination described in Chapter 12. Some Nubians were employed by the British as they established their control over Buganda and Uganda.

All of these Muslims were expected to show loyalty to the new colonial regime and its protege, Kabaka Mwanga. In 1892–3 the Muslims sought to reassert their control. Armed with guns they confronted the colonial forces in the Kampala area, but were forced to back down in the face of British cannon. The colonial and Ganda armies, under Christian leaders, defeated the Muslims and captured Mbogo. In the words of one of the young Protestant writers of the time:

> When they had been defeated the Muzungu ["white man," in this case the governor who succeeded Lugard] said to the Kabaka [Mwanga] that he had seen it was not good to keep Mbogo in Buganda because he was going to spoil people's hearts. He said that when his soldiers [many of them Sudanese] saw Mbogo they regarded him as the Kabaka because he was of their religion. He said they were with Selim Bey [the Sudanese soldier and leader] . . . . For this reason, he [the governor] said Mbogo had to be taken to Zanzibar and in addition he was old. If he were a young man he would have been taken to a far island.

The British and other European imperial powers often deported strong leaders to far away destinations, such as the Asantehene Prempeh, who was forced to live on the Seychelles Islands for twenty-four years. Mbogo was older and less "dangerous," so he spent only three years in Zanzibar, now a British territory. Then he returned home to preside over the bitter but resigned Muslim community of his homeland. The

SLIM SOCIETIES IN AFRICAN HISTORY

ivors expressed their bitterness in a song that captured the recent experience of a cattle plague:

> We shall be wiped out for our religion,
> As the buffalos have been wiped out by rinderpest.

Conclusion: Muslim Fortunes in "Christian" Buganda

Uganda and its southern core of Buganda are rarely thought of as "Muslim" countries. The time of Muslim supremacy at the court, from the late 1860s to the early 1890s, is usually forgotten. One reason has to do with sources. The Muslim Ganda were much less literate than their Christian competitors, and they usually expressed that literacy in Arabic – or Swahili in Arabic characters. They were less prone to write histories and ethnographies of Buganda. As a consequence it is harder to discern this community and personalize its membership, even during the period when it was dominant. Another reason is the need for a longer period of gestation to create an "Islamic state," as we saw in Hausaland: Uthman dan Fodio built on a long tradition of Islamic practice, even though he questioned the sincerity and judgment of the courts and clerics of his time. Buganda and the East African interior did not have old Islamic traditions, but the Muslim party did have older roots in the palace culture than the Christians – back to the time of Suna and Mutesa.

Still another reason for the stereotype is the assumption that "Swahili Islam" was never missionary in intent. As discussed in Chapter 3, this reluctance to proselytize was typical of most of the history of the coastal peoples, just as the "Suwarian Islam" of Chapter 4 was characteristic of the commercially oriented communities of the forest zones of West Africa. But things could change, as they did in the nineteenth century. Expansionist impulses, whether the smaller ones of the Omani Arabs or the stronger ones of the British and Germans, produced religious as well as political competition. When that was joined to a powerful but fragile regime, with a ruler who was not hemmed in by a national priesthood, Buganda could become a "Muslim state" in one generation. Or at least move considerably in that direction under the leadership of the king. The local forces of resistance then emerged. They combined with the aggressiveness of the Christian missionaries, the debilitating illness of the sovereign, and the increasingly intense "scramble" for Africa to interrupt the trajectory of islamization.

The period from the 1890s to the present was difficult for the Muslims. The Islamic community and tradition did survive in Buganda and Uganda as a whole. Ganda Muslims moved into the northern part of the colonial territory, along with some of the Sudanese, and formed Islamic traditions which are still vibrant today. Some of them were employed by the British as agents, interpreters, and chiefs. But for the most part they felt, not without justification, that Buganda and Uganda had become "Christian" country in which they would always be marginal. At first blush one might compare their experience with that of Muslims of Ethiopia, who at various times were killed, forced to convert, or subordinated as second-class citizens by strong "Christian" regimes. But the Muslim population of Ethiopia, and today's Eritrea, is much larger and more deeply entrenched than the descendants of the Readers of Buganda.

Further Reading

For a good general account of Islam in Buganda in the nineteenth century, see David Sperling's chapter in (editors) Levtzion and Pouwels' *History of Islam*. A larger study is Arye Oded's *Islam in Uganda: Islamization through a Centralized State in Pre-Colonial Africa* (Wiley, 1974) and his earlier work, *Islam in Uganda* (Halsted Press, 1947). A good recent study of Buganda is Christopher Wrigley's *Kingship and State: The Buganda Dynasty* (Cambridge University Press, 1996). The Uganda historian Semakula Kiwanuka has provided a rich account in *A History of Buganda: From the Foundation of the Kingdom to 1900* (Africana, 1972), whereas Michael Wright has interesting sections on the Muslim party in the late nineteenth century in *Buganda in the Heroic Age* (Oxford University Press, 1971); the couplet on Muslim resignation comes from his p. 133. For a fascinating biography on the bewildering transformations in and around Buganda, see Michael Twaddle's *Kakungulu and the Creation of Uganda, 1868–1928* (Ohio University Press and James Currey, 1993).

The best anthropological account from the time is John Roscoe's *The Baganda* (Macmillan, 1911). A recent one, with an emphasis on religious and symbolic meaning, is Benjamin Ray's *Myth, Ritual and Kingship in Buganda* (Oxford University Press, 1991); he provides description and commentary on the changes in custom under Mutesa. The most important contemporary accounts by European travels and missionaries are J. H. Speke's *Journal of the Discovery of the Nile* (J. M. Dent and E. P. Dutton, 1863), H. M. Stanley's *Through the Dark Continent* (Harper and Brothers, 1878, two volumes), and Robert Ashe's *Chronicles of Uganda* (London, Hodder and Stoughton,

1894, reprinted by Cass, 1971). These have been reprinted and are generally available.

The sources quoted here come from a range of places, but they can all be found in Chapter 3 of my book with Douglas Smith *Sources of the African Past*, cited at the end of Chapter 10. A number of rich sources come from the *Uganda Journal* published from the 1930s, including an article in 1947 under the title "How Religion Came to Uganda" and John Rowe's 1969 analysis of sources, "Myth, Memoir and Moral Admonition: Luganda Historical Writing, 1893–1969" in the *Uganda Journal* (1969).

CHAPTER 12

The Sudan: The Mahdi and Khalifa amid Competing Imperialisms

Muhammad Ahmad, the Mahdi of the Sudan, was the African Muslim best known to the outside world in the nineteenth century. Preacher, teacher, and writer, he lived just over forty years (1844–85) but left an indelible imprint on his native region. He drew on his understanding of Islam to mobilize a major portion of the Muslim population against foreign intrusion and economic decline. He understood that God was calling him to be the Mahdi, the rightly guided one who comes during the troubled times at the end of the world.

The imperialism he faced goes by the name of the Turko-Egyptian regime or Turkiyya. The Sudanese, over the course of the nineteenth century, came to use the expression "Turk" to refer to all of the people of Turkic, Slavic, Arab, or European origin associated with the regime and its exploitation. Egypt, still officially part of the Ottoman Empire, began to expand in the early nineteenth century after Napoleon's invasion and under the direction of Muhammad Ali (see Chapter 6). From Cairo and a southern base in Khartoum, Muhammad Ali commissioned traders to find sources of slaves and ivory in the upper reaches of the Nile and support the dramatic modernization process of Egypt. Beginning in the 1820s these entrepreneurs explored, traded, and raided in the vast marshes of the Upper Nile. They set up villages and factories in the northern or Arabic-speaking areas of the Sudan and preyed upon the small-scale societies to the south (see Map 5).

By the early 1880s the British superimposed themselves on the Turko-Egyptian network. Eager to strengthen their huge investment in India, they developed connections throughout the Middle East,

FIGURE 21 Arousing opposition to the "Turks" in the Sudan. A sketch of a Muslim preacher of *jihad* in the Sudan in the early 1880s. From Normal Daniel, *Islam, Europe and Empire*, Edinburgh University Press, 1966.

culminating in the opening of the Suez Canal in 1869. European and American soldiers, explorers, and adventurers enlisted with the Turko-Egyptian regime, which was increasingly under British influence, and some found their way into the Sudan. Some of them even found their way to the sources of the White Nile and aroused the anxiety of Kabaka Mutesa, as discussed in Chapter 11. In 1882 the British actually occupied Egypt to protect their interests and became even more closely associated with the regime in the south. Their presence provided even more proof for many Sudanese Muslims that Turko-Egyptian rule was exploitative and not Muslim.

Muhammad Ahmad took the title of Mahdi in 1881 and began to mobilize his following against this combined Turko-Egyptian-European intrusion. He called all of the intruders, and their Sudanese allies, "Turks." For him this expression meant infidels who, in many cases, came from Muslim backgrounds and had become apostates to the faith. They were worse, in his eyes, than the "pagan" small-scale societies in the southern part of the region. The Mahdi tapped into a wellspring of resentment at the outsiders and drove them out of the Sudan altogether (see Figure 21). In the process he laid siege to Khartoum and killed Charles Gordon, the general sent to command the surviving imperial forces.

Shortly after the death of "Gordon of Khartoum" in 1885 the Mahdi himself passed away and was replaced by the *khalifa* Abdullahi. It was the Khalifa's regime that clashed with King Yohannes of Ethiopia, mentioned in Chapter 8 (see Figure 22 later in this chapter). The British, again from their Egyptian base, defeated the *khalifa* in 1898, under a general as well known as Gordon: Horatio Herbert Kitchener. They then dominated the region, under the name of the Anglo-Egyptian Condominium, until the independence of the Sudan in 1956. One of the principal groups that the British had to deal with was the Mahdiya, the descendants of the Mahdi and his followers. The prestige of the group was, and still is, enormous. The history of the Mahdi, the Khalifa, and the Mahdiya had enormous influence on British and Western perceptions of Islam as well as upon the Sudan itself.

The Sudan as the Nile Corridor to the Interior

The Nile is the main avenue connecting North and Sub-Saharan Africa. The river, in contrast to the desert, allows constant communication between north and south. For this reason various groups that we can call "Egyptian" and "Sudanese" have interacted, dominated each other, and exchanged cultures over the last 6,000 years. The Nile has been the lifeblood of Egypt, making it possible over the millennia for large numbers of people to live together in an area that otherwise would be desert. Egypt and its many rulers have always been concerned to influence, if not control, their neighbors to the south.

The Arab Muslim conquerors of the seventh century quickly took Egypt but not the Sudan. They worked out trade and tribute relations with the south that endured for centuries. Gradually Islam and the Arabic language spread upriver, weakening Christian and other ruling classes, isolating the Nubian languages, and creating the cultural and linguistic map of today's Sudan: an arabophone and Muslim North, sometimes unified around a state or states, and a South of small-scale societies speaking a number of languages and practicing a variety of religions. Since the late nineteenth century small communities of Christians have emerged in the south, thanks to European missionary initiatives. Their presence has given a sharper edge to the conflict of North and South over the entire twentieth century, across the decades of civil war between and within the two regions.

The Sudan region was also the location of an important west–east movement. Pilgrims from West and Central Africa, particularly the regions that we call today Chad, Niger, and Nigeria, moved overland to fulfill a fundamental obligation of Islam. Typically they went through the central portions of the Sudan to the Red Sea, crossed to Jeddah, and made their way to Mecca. Many financed the voyage by working along the way, and some of them settled permanently in the Nile valley on their way to or from the Holy Lands. In the late nineteenth century they became an important source of followers of the Mahdi, whereas in the twentieth they constituted a kind of labor pool in the Anglo-Egyptian Sudan. A significant number of these pilgrims came from the Sokoto Caliphate at the time of the British conquest of the early twentieth century (see Chapter 10); they combined the traditional obligation to go to Mecca with the act of *hijra* from infidel rule.

Most of the people of northern and central Sudan, what I call the North, belonged to Sufi orders. Sufism had been present in the Sudan for some time, but in the nineteenth century it spread much more widely, under the impulse of new orders, many of them centered in nearby Mecca and Medina. Most of the West Africans who settled in the central Sudan were Sufi, often with the same Qadiriyya allegiance as Uthman and his family (Chapter 10). Muhammad Ahmad combined his learning with affiliation and then became a leader in the order called the Sammaniyya. Most of these movements developed local roots and grievances, over against the "official" Islam of Egypt, symbolized often by the venerable Cairene university al-Azhar.

The Turkiyya

After the British drove Napoleon out of Egypt in 1801, a military man of Albanian origin took over the reins of power in Egypt. Nominally under the control of the Ottoman Empire, Muhammad Ali quickly established his autonomy, dramatically modernized the economy, and extended his control in many directions. Beginning in 1821 he established the Turko-Egyptian regime of the Sudan to obtain gold, ivory, and slaves, who would be used for military service, agricultural labor, and domestic work in his modernizing economy. He established the base of operations in Khartoum at the junction of the White and Blue Nile rivers; he recruited Arabic-speaking Sudanese employees from the river valley and placed the whole operation under a governor-general.

The governor-general, responsible to a ministry for the Sudan in Cairo, presided over a large bureaucracy and army spread across the northern and central portions of the Sudan. Officials and soldiers supervised a taxation system as well as the flow of ivory and slaves from the southern areas. The administration gradually spread south and west over the course of the nineteenth century, but the governor-general had increasing difficulty in controlling the raiding, trading, and taxation that characterized the system. By the latter decades of the century, most Sudanese saw the system as violent and exploitative and called it the Turkiyya, the regime of the "Turks."

Ismail (1863–79) renewed the modernization impulse of his grandfather Muhammad Ali and tried to combine the old operations with fitful attempts to suppress the slave trade. His efforts, and those of his Egyptian and European agents, were perceived in the same pattern of exploitation, corruption, and "infidel" rule by many Sudanese. Ismail pushed the exploitation further, however, to finance expeditions in other areas, particularly Ethiopia (see Chapter 8) and toward Buganda (Chapter 11). By seeking to obtain more ivory and taxes, he pushed the Sudanese farmers and pastoralists, their tribal leaders and even some officials of the Turkiyya itself, to the brink of revolt. It was in these circumstances that Ismail appointed Charles Gordon to be the first European governor-general of the Sudan and gave him the unenviable – and contradictory – mission of restoring order and extracting more resources.

The Reign of the Mahdi

I have not yet discussed the Muslim view of the end of time. In many ways it is comparable to Christian views, as expressed in the Book of Revelation. No one obviously can know about the end and the Day of Judgment, but this has not prevented leaders of various religions from trying to envision the end of time and using it to exhort their listeners in the present (see Figure 21). Difficult times, of poverty and oppression, often evoke these views; occasionally a charismatic figure also invokes measures to save the faithful – usually conceived as a relatively small number who will be preserved while the rest perish. Muhammad Ahmad came to understand that he was called by God for this mission and took the title of Mahdi. In his case, he felt compelled to attack the forces that he identified as oppressive.

Muhammad Ahmad grew up in the Nile valley not far from Khartoum. The son of a boat builder, he pursued a standard peripatetic education, learning the Quran and then a series of works with different teachers of law, theology, and Sufism. He showed an aptitude for scholarship, teaching, and preaching, and he became an active member of the Sammaniyya Sufi order. In the 1870s Muhammad established his own reputation as an ascetic and rigorous partisan of reform. His base was Aba, an island in the White Nile, but he traveled up and down the river and to Kordofan, a large savanna region to the west. His personal interactions confirmed his sense of mission, amid the growing disorder of the central Sudan. He studied the traditional teachings about the Mahdi, sensed that they applied to him, and communicated this awareness to his disciples. Abdullahi, one of the leading disciples who came from the Kordofan region and became his successor, strongly encouraged his master. In 1881 Muhammad Ahmad took the title of Mahdi. He began to accept oaths of allegiance and accumulate a large following.

Soon the Mahdi came into open conflict with the Turkiyya. Adopting the language of the Prophet, he led Abdullahi and his other followers on a *hijra* to the west and called them *Ansar*, "helpers," the name given to Muhammad's supporters in Medina. Over the next four years the Mahdi gained support and won most of his encounters with the armies of the "Turks." An 1882 letter to the Khartoum regime expresses his fervor and suggests the attraction which his preaching had for the exploited Sudanese:

> You say that Our only followers are the ignorant Baqqara [a pastoral group of the Kordofan] and the idolaters. Know then that the followers of the apostles before Us and of our Prophet Muhammad were the weak and the ignorant and the nomads, who worshipped rocks and trees. As for the *ulama* and the rich and the people of power and luxury, they did not follow them until they had ruined their places, killed their nobles and ruled them by force.... And whereas you say, 'Arise and come to us, that you may go to the place of guidance, Mecca,' know that Our going is only by the command of the Apostle of God, in the time that God wills. We are not under your command, but you and your superiors are under Our command..., for there is nothing between Us and you save the sword....

The Mahdi reminds us of Uthman and the community that he fashioned in Gobir, as discussed in Chapter 10. Both leaders framed their actions in the language of early Islam and the Prophet, who was always the model to follow. But there are three significant differences between the Sudan of the late nineteenth century and the Hausaland of the late eighteenth century. First, Muhammad Ahmad moved much more quickly to challenge the power structure. Second, the power structure was primarily external and imperial, the Turko-Egyptian regime. Uthman had to gradually make the case that the indigenous Hausa rulers were not really good Muslims or Muslim at all. Finally, Muhammad Ahmad took the title of Mahdi, the person who would come in the last days, suggesting a level of disruption and trauma that we have not encountered before.

By 1882 the Khartoum regime recognized the military and ideological challenge that the Mahdi posed. They mobilized their defense, in letters to the Mahdists and the Muslim community at large, often written by people with diplomas from the prestigious Al-Azhar University in Cairo. They did not deny the doctrine of the "Rightly-Guided One" who would come at the end of time, but rather the authenticity of Muhammad Ahmad's claims. They rejected the assertion of Sharifian descent, which was so important to the rulers of Morocco (Chapter 7), and the claims of exploitation and disruption. In one statement, written by one of the learned *ulama* who worked for the regime, they said:

> For it is not hidden from you that the harsh trials by the political authority and the lack of a place of refuge do not exist. For you and I live in comfort, safety and quiet. Our refuge, the refuge of all, does exist: it is His Highness the Khedive [the ruler in Cairo] and His Excellency the Governor-General of the Sudanese provinces..., and the district officers of their administration, to whom you have recourse in your affairs, who grasp the oppressed by the hand and take vengeance upon the oppressor.

These claims to oppose oppression and provide security rang hollow for most Sudanese.

By 1884 the Mahdist forces controlled most of the central and northern Sudan and had the Khartoum regime on the defensive. From Egypt the British sent Gordon back to evacuate the surviving forces from Khartoum and other garrisons. Gordon had established his reputation in China and other parts of the world as a devout and incorruptible Christian, a "crusader" against the slave trade. He had little knowledge of Arabic or Islam. He thought to evacuate the "Turks" by his personal magnetism and the impression he would make on the Sudanese. Instead, he received rejection after rejection from the Mahdi, such as the following:

> Know that I am the Expected Mahdi, the Successor of the Apostle
> of God. Thus I have no need of the sultanate, nor of the kingdom of
> Kordofan or elsewhere, nor of the wealth of this world and its vanity. I
> am but the slave of God, guiding unto God and to what is with Him . . . ,
> and God has succored me with the prophets and the apostles and the
> angels and all the saints and pious men to revive His Faith . . . .

In late January 1885, before a relief column could arrive from the
north, the Mahdists invaded the city, destroyed its defenders, and de-
capitated General Gordon.

The Reign of Khalifa Abdullahi

The Mahdi gave serious attention to the administration of his new
territories during his short reign, but he died abruptly – perhaps of
typhus – in June 1885. Abdullahi, designated as the principal *khalifa*
during the Mahdi's lifetime, took the reins of power and received oaths
of loyalty in his capital of Omdurman, next to Khartoum, over the rest
of the year. But he faced serious internal opposition until the early
1890s, especially from the family of the Mahdi, who went by the name
of Ashraf, the "descendants of the Prophet." The Mahdi's sons in
particular claimed that they were the rightful successors. Abdullahi also
had to deal with a serious famine across most of northern and central
Sudan as well as external opposition, especially from Egyptian and
British forces to the north and along the Red Sea. His biggest problem
was one of scale: how to restore order in an enormous region the size
of the United States east of the Mississippi. In times of prosperity this
would be a formidable task. In a time of famine, and after decades of
raids and wars, it was impossible.

The Khalifa focused much of his energy on the eastern frontiers of
the Sudan, where he had to deal with Turko-Egyptian-British initiatives along the Red Sea coast, an emerging Italian presence that would
result in the colony of Eritrea, and a resurgence of the Christian monar-
chies of the Abyssinian highlands (see Chapter 8). The Mahdi had
taken a conciliatory line toward the Abyssinians, evoking the old tradition of friendship between the Prophet and the Emperor of Aksum.
In the late 1880s the Khalifa became particularly concerned about the

expansion of Yohannes to the northwest, as well as his forced conversions of Muslims. One of the members of his inner circle recorded
these deliberations about the situation as follows:

> They [the Abyssinians] were reputed for [bravery] among the nations
> for generations until God brought the light of our master Muham-
> mad . . . , who told [his people] to "leave the Abyssinians alone as long as
> they leave you alone . . . . Later the kings of our time and especially the
> kings of the Turks, because of their weak belief . . . and their negligence
> of Islamic commands, and their abandoning of the jihad, . . . enabled the
> infidels to enter the land of Islam and take control over portions of it
> and build churches with bells . . . .
>
> When Yohannes established himself on the Abyssinian throne he
> became arrogant . . . and he invaded Islamic territory . . . . And Yohannes
> is the most hateful of the Abyssinians towards Islam. Someone who knew
> him told me that if he saw a Muslim in the morning it would depress
> him so that he would immediately take the cross which he worships and
> put it over his face.
>
> And when God sent the Mahdi he wrote to Yohannes calling him to
> join God, but he answered in an ugly way and sent his armies to fight.
> From this it is clear to anyone who has the fire of God in him that fighting
> the Abyssinians today is not only a legal option but a very emphasized
> duty for the Islamic nation . . . .

The hostilities continued for several years along the frontiers between "Muslim" Sudan and "Christian" Ethiopia. The Khalifa's forces
sacked Gondar, the Solomonic capital, in 1888. The decisive battle
came in 1889, when Yohannes attacked the Mahdist fortress of al-
Qallabat (or Metemma in the Ethiopian versions; see Figure 22). He
was on the verge of winning when he was wounded and died. His death
led to the rout of the Christian armies and rejoicing in Omdurman.
The temporary collapse of Ethiopian expansion had the ironic effect of
allowing the Italians to expand in Eritrea and develop an even stronger
threat to Islamic interests.

The end of the Mahdist state came less from internal dissension than
from outside powers. The British had never abandoned the intention
of recovering the Sudan and this critical part of the Nile corridor. As
the European scramble for Africa intensified, as the Italians, Belgians,
and especially the French threatened to move into the Sudan, the
British and their Egyptian subjects moved up the Nile. Under the
leadership of Horatio Herbert Kitchener, they advanced slowly, from

FIGURE 22 Conflict between Christian and Muslim at Metemma (al-Qallabat) in 1889. A painting by an unknown Ethiopian artist, ca. 1930. Collection of Suzanne Miers.

1896 to 1898, building a railway as they went. They won each of the major battles against the Khalifa's forces, taking advantage of superior fire power as well as dissensions among the Sudanese. In September 1898, they triumphed in the climactic battle for Omdurman, defeating a considerable portion of the Ansar army. One of Kitchener's first actions was to destroy the tomb and exhume the body of the Mahdi; he threw the bones into the river and allegedly drank from the skull. The new governor-general, avenger of Gordon, would not leave a shrine by which Sudanese might rally against the Anglo-Egyptian Condominium. As for the Khalifa, he died trying to mount a counterattack against his old capital the following year.

British Colonialism and the Mahdi's Family

Soon the British faced the complex problems of ruling over the largest of the African colonies created by the European scramble for Africa, an area exhausted by decades of war, starvation, and disease. The Sudan included then all of the North, with some heritage of unity in earlier kingdoms and the Turko-Egyptian regime, and the diverse agricultural and pastoral societies of the South, where people coped with the marshy environments around the meandering White Nile. The North was Muslim and arabophone, for the most part; the South was "pagan" and "idolatrous" and could receive Christian missionaries. The name given for this complex entity was the Anglo-Egyptian Condominium.

The authorities in the Sudan were British, without question. They were partially subordinated to the British authorities in Egypt, and they used Egyptians and Egyptian institutions, including such venerable ones as the University of Al-Azhar, to administer their new dominions. Indeed, the colonial masters encouraged an Islam dominated by orthodox Sunni forms, whereas Sufi lodges, tombs, and celebrations were actively discouraged. They created Gordon Memorial College to train the Sudanese elites.

Many Sudanese called the new government the Second Turkiyya. It was not very popular, and the British felt an increasing need to cultivate local support. During World War I they began to reach out to the son of the Mahdi, Abd al-Rahman al-Mahdi, and to exploit his anti-Turkish and pro-Arab sentiments in the struggle against what remained of the Ottoman Empire. Sayyid Abd al-Rahman was born just after his father died and had been kept under surveillance in the early years of the twentieth century. He had a large following in Omdurman and along the White Nile. Over the course of the war he became a close ally who could reassure Sudanese about the justice of the Allied cause, sign the Sudan Book of Loyalty, and provide intelligence about any revolts.

After the war the British expanded the alliance on a number of fronts. In particular, they discovered the Sayyid's ability to mobilize land and labor in the Gezira, the peninsula of land between the White and Blue Niles. The land, much of which his family owned, was well suited for growing cotton, which the British sought for their textile mills at home. The labor included many Sudanese and West African Sufis who had settled over the course of the nineteenth century and responded to the call of Abd al-Rahman. In the 1920s and 1930s the collaboration between colonial authorities and the Mahdiyya, who went by the names of Ansar and *Umma*, "the community," continued to grow. After World War II the British allowed Abd al-Rahman to rebuild the tomb of his father as a place of pilgrimage just outside the capital. The Umma then became a powerful political force in independent Sudanese politics.

The descendants of Khalifa Abdullahi, on the other hand, enjoyed no such good fortune. He came from the west, from the "tribal" areas as opposed to the more sedentary and urban river valley. He was blamed for the divisions and exhaustion of the land. He had actually ruled, or tried to rule, over the vast expanse of the Sudan, and its enemies within and without, for a much longer period than his predecessor. The Mahdi died at the height of his prestige, before the very limited cohesion of his movement was evident. He could be lionized by Muslim Sudanese as a devout but rigorous Sufi and even by secular Europeans as a nationalist mobilizing opposition to the "Turks." His credentials as a resistance hero, on religious and nationalist grounds, were impeccable, and his descendants and members of the Umma party have capitalized on that throughout the twentieth century. We will see a similar combination, of resistance tradition and colonial collaboration, in the case of the Muridiyya in the next chapter.

Further Reading

The English literature on the Mahdi, the Mahdiyya, and the Sudan is voluminous, including firsthand accounts by European explorers, soldiers, and officials; novels depicting the conflicts; and secondary accounts of what the sequences meant for British imperialism. There is also a considerable literature from the Sudanese perspective, including abundant translations of the Arabic letters and treatises that reflect the Mahdist point of view. Some of the impressions of the Mahdiyya in European writings, particular those of the British, can be found in Chapter 15 of Norman Daniel's *Islam, Europe and Empire* (Edinburgh University Press, 1966), which was used for Figure 21.

The most complete treatment of the Mahdi is still P. M. Holt's *The Mahdist State in the Sudan 1881–1898* (Oxford University Press, 1970, second edition). His bibliographical section discusses the sources on the Mahdist state, many of which are widely available. An older work is A. B. Theobald's *The Mahdiya: A History of the Anglo-Egyptian Sudan, 1881–1899* (Longman, 1951). Some very useful sections on Mahdist relations with Ethiopia can be found in Haggai Erlich's *Ethiopia and the Middle East* (Lynne Rienner, 1994) and Richard Caulk's "Yohannes IV, the Mahdists and the Partition of North-East Africa" in *Transafrican Journal of History* (volume 1.2, 1972, pp. 23–42). See also Chapter 8 of this volume. The citations in this chapter come from Holt and Erlich.

The best treatment of the colonial period and the emergence of the Umma under Abd al-Rahman's leadership is Martin Daly's *Empire on the Nile: The Anglo-Egyptian Sudan 1898–1934* (Cambridge University Press, 1986). For articles see Hassan Ahmed Ibrahim's "Imperialism and neo-Mahdism in the Sudan" in *International Journal of African Historical Studies* (1980) and two pieces by Gabriel Warburg, "Religious Policy in the Northern Sudan: Ulama and Sufism, 1899–1918" in *Asian and African Studies* (1971) and "British Rule in the Nile Valley, 1882–1956, and Robinson's Theory of Collaboration" in *Asian and African Studies* (1981).

CHAPTER 13

Senegal: Bamba and the Murids under French Colonial Rule

The Buganda of Chapter 11 was just coming under British rule at the end of the nineteenth century. The Mahdist forces of Chapter 12 resisted the colonial rule of the Turko-Egyptians and then confronted the hostility of their European conquerors in the twentieth century. Only over time did they find formulas for establishing their autonomy in religious, social, and economic matters. The Sufi order that we now examine faced similar challenges: conquest by the French, in this case, followed by colonial rule in the framework called French West Africa.

Here the leaders never took any military action against the invaders and never invoked the language of the end of times. Instead, under the designation Murids, "novices" or learners in faith, they sought to create an autonomous sphere, a new intellectual and social framework for the spread and practice of Sufi Islam. When they understood the determination of the French to dominate the area with a more pervasive government than the region had known before, they accommodated in the same ways as the Mahdiya.

In the process, their founder, Amadu Bamba Mbacke, suffered three periods of exile (1895–1912) at the hands of the French (see Figure 23). At the same time he forged a framework of Islamic practice that has given his descendants and followers cohesion for over a century, not just in Senegal but across many parts of the world. The case of Bamba and the Murid order he created provide the opportunity to see the changes in the colonial order and in its "Muslim policy" and the adaptation of a community of Sufi Muslims to a modern, Western-dominated world.

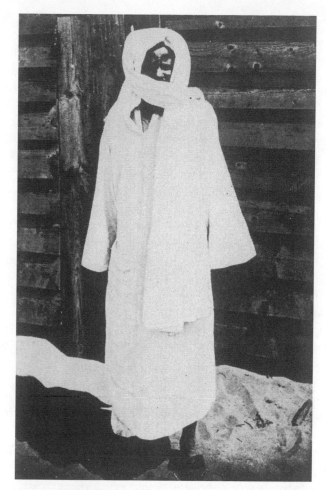

FIGURE 23 A Sufi saint in Senegal. The 1913 photograph of Amadu Bamba Mbacke, founder of the Murid brotherhood. From Paul Marty, *Etudes sur l'Islam au Sénégal* (two volumes, Paris, 1917; volume 1, facing p. 222). This copy came from the Fowler Museum of Cultural History at UCLA.

Senegal in the Late Nineteenth Century

Senegal was a much smaller and more cohesive region than the Sudan, long before it became a French colony and independent country. It was set between rivers, the Senegal in the north, marking the gateway to regions that the Almoravids once controlled and to the Sahara desert,

and the Gambia and Casamance to the south, marking the entrance
to the smaller-scale societies that dominate the coastal regions. The
practice of Islam goes back a thousand years, in the form of merchant
minorities and ruling classes. Among the largest groups, the faith has
been dominant for about 500 years. These groups include the Fulbe
or Fulani, distant cousins of the people of Uthman dan Fodio, and the
Wolof, who occupy the western, coastal regions of the country. Since
the 1900s Wolof has become the dominant language and culture of
the country, alongside a marked French influence.

The dominance of Islamic practice did not correlate, however, with
Islamic states, or at least not very successful ones. Reform movements
similar to that of Uthman dan Fodio occurred in various parts of Fulbe
and Wolof Senegal from the seventeenth through the nineteenth centuries, but they never had the impact, in breadth or depth, or the staying
power of the Sokoto Caliphate of Chapter 10. Most of the traditional
aristocracies survived, in weakened form, until the French conquest.
Their rulers were Muslim, their courts contained clerics who served
as counselors, and their practice was probably similar to the court of
Gobir that came under the criticism of Uthman. They were not able to
maintain order, secure prosperity, or resist the steady encroachments
of the French.

The focus of attention in the late nineteenth century was the Wolof
kingdom of Kajoor, which controlled the coast and a considerable
hinterland between Saint-Louis, the older French staging area at the
mouth of the Senegal, and Dakar, the emerging center and eventual
capital of French West Africa, to the south. The king or Dammel
sought to rule over this area and divergent constituency with great difficulty. He faced competition from other royal lineages, the power of
his own "crown" soldiers, conflicting Muslim opinions about what he
should do, and constant French intervention.

This situation came to a head in the 1870s and 1880s under
Dammel Lat Joor Joop, a man who is often considered the "national"
or "resistance" hero of Senegal. Lat Joor was, in fact, a very complex
figure in a complex situation. He spent some of his early years with
a reformist Muslim in the south, swore allegiance to the faith, and
probably tried to rule in accordance with Islamic law more than his
predecessors. At the same time he had to satisfy his crown soldiers,
accustomed to raiding and exploiting the peasantry, and maintain a
system of slavery upon which the more powerful had come to depend
over centuries of involvement in the Atlantic slave trade. By the 1880s

he also faced a concerted French effort to control his kingdom in the interests of the rapidly developing cultivation of peanuts.

In the 1880s French imperialism took the form of a railway linking Saint-Louis and Dakar and cutting across the heartland of Kajoor, which was also the major peanut producing region. Lat Joor gave grudging consent to the project initially, but withdrew his cooperation as he saw how the rail would end his independence. The French completed the project and opened the line in 1885; a small platoon killed Lat Joor in a shootout the following year. His death can be taken as the beginning of colonial rule in Senegal.

The Emergence of Amadu Bamba and His Followers

One of the Muslim scholars and Sufis who lived through the fortunes of Kajoor was Amadu Bamba Mbacke (ca.1853–1927). He was born to a family of clerics or marabouts in local parlance – a word deriving from the Almoravids examined in Chapter 3. Bamba grew up in Bawol, the Wolof kingdom south and east of Kajoor. In the 1860s he spent some of his youth with the same Muslim reformer as Lat Joor and then joined the king after he moved back to Kajoor. At this juncture Bamba was still a student. He sat at the feet of a number of clerics, including his father, who became an important counselor to the king. From this perspective he witnessed the great difficulties involved in ensuring order, prosperity, and the practice of Islam. He came to believe that it was impossible to combine the pursuit of power and the pursuit of piety and opted for the latter.

Bamba persuaded his father to reduce his involvement at the Kajoor court. The father, just before he died in 1883, entrusted his pedagogical vocation to his son:

> Continue to learn the Quran and the sacred texts, without forgetting grammar and jurisprudence. It is only in this way that you will be able truly to understand religion and serve God and His Prophet. The country at this moment is in a very confused state. The only way in which you can aid others and yourself is to flee from the things of this world. Watch over your brothers; I entrust them to you, because it is in you that I have the greatest confidence. Help them to acquire the qualities that you have already.

Soon after this Bamba took his following back to Bawol, to the village of Mbacke where he was born.

Senegalese nationalist historiography has invented an encounter between Bamba and Lat Joor in 1886, on the eve of the Dammel's death.
In this meeting the king asked for advice and support, whereas the
marabout supplied a blessing for the soul of the ruler but no aid for
his cause. The tradition has the effect of transferring the king's military resistance, however limited it may have been, into the marabout's
spiritual resistance to French colonial rule.

In fact, the evidence is overwhelming that Bamba was back in Bawol in 1886, building his following, developing his Sufi teaching, and
reflecting on how a Muslim community should live in the troubled
conditions of the late nineteenth century. It was during the late 1880s
and early 1890s that he wrote a great deal of poetry; read extensively
in the Quran, the *hadith*, and other Muslim sources; and began to
shape his community. Early on he recognized the need for a range of
options. Some of his followers had no previous experience of Islam
and were oriented toward work and obedience. Others were already
knowledgeable about the faith and could aspire to "maraboutic" leadership. Among the leaders of the community were two of his brothers,
Ibra Fati and Shaikh Anta, and one of his earliest disciples, Shaikh
Ibra Faal. Bamba's mother, Mame Diarra Bousso, was also a very
inspirational figure.

Most of Bamba's reflection took place in the context of Sufism. Like
many Sufis, he evoked a Hadith in which the Prophet, after his victory
against the Meccans at the battle of Badr, exhorted his followers to
return to the greater *jihad* of the soul. He affiliated with Sufi orders
in his search for meaning. He associated with the Qadiriyya tradition
that Uthman dan Fodio celebrated; he affiliated especially through the
Sidiyya, clerics of southwestern Mauritania. At one time he linked up
with the Tijaniyya order that we saw in Chapter 4; in West Africa in
the late nineteenth century it connoted resistance to colonial rule, at
least in the minds of the French. Bamba was not satisfied with either
order and increasingly felt that he was called to inaugurate a new way
and a new teaching appropriated to the conditions of Wolof Senegal
and its disrupted state. He felt this call frequently, for example, when
he established a new village with the name Touba, "conversion," not
far from his home town in 1887, or in dreams and revelations around
his fortieth birthday, in 1893 – at the same time that the Prophet
began to sense his call. Finally, during his second exile in southwestern
Mauritania in 1904 he received a revelation and founded his own order.
He called it by the name which had been used for some years, the
Muridiyya, those who are "novices" seeking the Lord.

Conflict and Collaboration with French Authorities

The French did not adjust easily to ruling over societies of Muslims. In Algeria, their first "laboratory," they had innumerable conflicts with their constituents and over the years learned how to co-opt some of them and to rule in ways that would not overly alienate the rest. In Senegal, as they established the institutions of colonial rule at the end of the nineteenth century, they followed somewhat similar practices of trial and error. Some form of "indirect rule" was obviously necessary to keep down the costs of administration and enlist the local population to grow peanuts, pay taxes, and maintain order. In the 1890s the French sought to generate indirect rule through members of the local aristocracy, including a son of Lat Joor and some members of the old crown soldiers. By the early 1900s the limitations of this practice had become evident: many of the subjects resented these colonial chiefs and gravitated into the orbit of marabouts who renounced political power while ensuring a certain religious, social, and economic stability for their disciples. By World War I the French realized that their principal allies in maintaining order and exploiting peanuts would be not the chiefs but the Sufi marabouts with large constituences. Foremost among these was Bamba, his family, and the Muridiyya.

But the French and the Murids did not come to this mutual accommodation easily. In 1895, at a time when the colonial authorities were quite anxious about their new system of chiefs, they arrested Bamba, subjected him to a "kangaroo" court in Saint-Louis, and exiled him to Central Africa on charges of sedition. They accused him of plotting to wage the military *jihad* – a tradition which Bamba never embraced. The director of political affairs put it this way in his brief to the colonial authorities:

> Amadu Bamba, pupil of Shaikh Sidiyya, Moorish marabout of the Qadiriyya sect, had professed in the last few years the Tijani doctrine which involves preaching holy war. Anyone with experience in the country and with the preachers of holy war will immediately understand that Amadu Bamba, without seeming to, was preparing very adroitly to act in the near future, almost surely during the next dry season.

Local colonial officials knew how to impress the imperial circles in Paris about the dangers posed by Bamba.

They were not as successful in impressing Bamba himself. In fact, the marabout not only survived seven years of exile. He deepened his

FIGURE 24 Bamba's miraculous prayer on the ocean
waves. Photograph of a glass painting of Amadu Bamba
praying on the water as he is taken into exile by the French,
by Daouda M'Ballo, ca. 1998, Dakar, Senegal. From the
collection of Al and Polly Roberts. Fowler Museum of Cultural
History at UCLA, X97.14.33.

faith and understanding of his calling in troubled times. He wrote
poetry and corresponded with family and disciples back in Senegal.
Upon his return he testified to miracles and other signs of God's protection of his person. Foremost among these signs, and the one most
remembered by subsequent generations of followers, was his prayer
on the waves of the ocean. Denied the freedom to pray on board the
ship taking him into exile, Bamba unfurled his mat on the water and

prayed before the amazed captain, administrator, and priest at the rail of the ship (see Figure 24).

Working out the Patterns of Accommodation

By the early 1900s the French realized that the system of colonial chiefs was not working effectively. The chiefs had mixed loyalties. They profited from their connections to the colonial bureaucracy and their salaries. At the same time they expected to continue the practices of precolonial chiefs, which included considerable extraction of the re-sources of peasants and pastoralists as well as participation in slavery. Some of their subjects expected a certain amount of largesse, in keep-ing with traditional practices. Most resented the new source of author-ity: the chiefs received their positions from the colonial officials, not through traditional councils.

In this context, the Murids became quite popular. Their marabouts had little connection to the colonial order. They encouraged their fol-lowers to work, particularly in growing the food crop of millet and the cash crop of peanuts, and to pay tithes or contributions, but they did not extract excessive payments. They provided education, welfare, and reassurance in turbulent times. In the early twentieth century a French administrator expressed admiration for Murid industry as follows:

> At this moment they [the Murid farmers] concentrate only on their fields which are immense and magnificent. These natives do not work the soil in the same way as other cultivators. For example, working by the light of the moon, they stay in their fields until eleven o'clock in the evening, then go to pray at the mosque, and only then eat their meals.

It was in this context, in 1902, that the French brought Amadu Bamba back from his first exile in hopes of stabilizing the colonial econ-omy and political order. They saw their action as one of generosity, whereas the Murids interpreted the return as a triumph over the impe-rial authority. Very soon the colonial chiefs, and particularly Mbakhane Joop, the son of Dammel Lat Joor, protested that they could not main-tain control over their subjects. By June of 1903 the French arrested the Sufi leader and exiled him again, this time to southern Mauritania. They entrusted Bamba to their Moorish ally, Shaikh Sidiyya, with the following instructions:

> You will give him counsel drawing on your deep religious commitment and experience. You will prevent him from communicating with the

people of Bawol and Senegal who could trouble his time of reflection and inspire him with the same ideas that have led to his exile before. You will remind him that it is because of you especially that I have shown mercy and generosity towards him.

Bamba did not take easily to the tutelage of Sidiyya. He accepted neither the assumptions of racial superiority of the Moors and the French, nor the nomadic lifestyle. He developed his pedagogy further, did some writing, and kept his own counsel and contacts with his Wolof following. After about a year of exile he had a revelation that led him to declare that the Muridiyya was now a separate Sufi order with its own rituals. At the same time he certainly realized, more fully than before, that European control of Senegal and Mauritania would endure and that he had no choice but to accommodate to that reality.

The French, for their part, realized that Shaikh Sidiyya could not control Bamba and that they had little to gain by keeping him in Mauritania. In 1907 they allowed him to return to northern Senegal and in 1912 to a closely monitored life in Diourbel, a town in Bawol. It was shortly after his return to Diourbel that he was photographed, perhaps for the only time in his life, probably by the local French administrator (see Figure 23). It is this picture that has been copied and reproduced in a variety of ways by the Murid faithful and artists.

By this time Bamba was ready to make public statements about the acceptability of French rule. In 1910 he made the first such declaration, which the colonial authorities circulated as an indication of Murid accommodation with the colonial regime, as follows:

> The French Government, thanks to God, has not opposed the profession of faith but on the contrary has been friendly towards Muslims and encouraged them to practice (their religion). We have noted that in many of the lands of the blacks that, thanks to French occupation, the inhabitants who, far from being Muslim were pillagers, living at the expense of travelers and the weak, have changed to become calm and peaceful and that now, among them, the sheep and the jackals march together.

The Murids affirmed these ties during World War I, when the French were put on the defensive at home. The marabout declared his support for the Allied cause, against Ottoman Muslim soldiers as well as Germans. More importantly, he encouraged his followers to enlist. One example of their loyalty and courage came amid the terrible losses in the Dardanelles campaign of 1915, when French commanders heard Murid soldiers singing the poems of Bamba to maintain their morale.

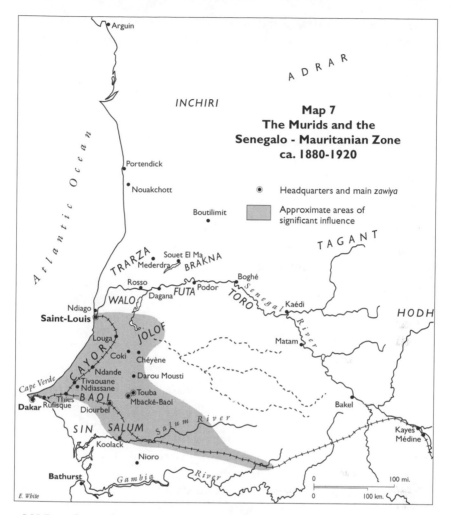

Map 7
The Murids and the
Senegalo - Mauritanian Zone
ca. 1880-1920

⊙   Headquarters and main *zawiya*

      Approximate areas of
      significant influence

MAP 7 The implantation of the Murids in Senegal. Adapted from David Robinson, *Paths of Accommodation: Muslim Societies and French Colonial Authorities in Senegal and Mauritania, 1880 to 1920* (Ohio University Press, 2000).

Just as the Murids had come to accept a system of secular rule in Senegal, they accommodated to a war in which some of their opponents were Muslim.

At the same time the founder kept his distance from the centers of colonial power, consistent with his lifelong position. He banned the building of Western schools in eastern Bawol. He controlled many appointments in the area and preserved the autonomy of his religious capital, Touba. Even amid the surveillance in Diourbel he followed his own routines of meditation, reading, and writing, rarely seeing the administrators who were posted there. He developed his own space far from the commercial or "modern" sector of the town.

Succession and Closer Relationships

Bamba died in 1927. He was quickly replaced by his oldest son, Mustapha, who took the title of *khalifa* or *khalife général* – a combination of Arabic and French terms reflecting the colonial Islamic culture that had developed in Senegal. The French monitored the succession carefully. They even deported Bamba's younger brother, Shaikh Anta, who was the most entrepreneurial and least submissive member of the family, for several years. Over the ensuing decades the relationship between colonial authorities and the Murid leadership – first Mustapha, then his younger brother Falilu – grew closer. The image of Bamba's "spiritual resistance," his ability to survive his exiles, provided a certain cover to cooperation for his sons.

The Murids became the dominant social and economic force in the peanut basin, with the support of the administration (see Map 7). Officials and even governors attended annual festivals to commemorate the events of Bamba's life and death; they accepted patterns of "indirect rule" in the Bawol area, consulting with the order about the location of the rail lines, cooperatives, and other institutions. They allowed the order to construct an enormous mosque in Touba, a project dear to Bamba but realized after his death. The Murid leadership learned how to intervene in the elections of officials in the coastal communes and then in the country as a whole. They came to play a decisive role in the choice of candidates, and this continued after Senegalese independence in 1960. Leopold Sedar Senghor, poet, philosopher, and first President of Senegal (1960–80), enjoyed strong support from *khalife général* Falilu, even though he was a practicing Catholic.

Between the 1930s and independence the Murids expanded throughout the peanut zone. Most of the rural expansion was to the east, along the Dakar-Bamako railway and the frontier of peanut cultivation that the French encouraged. The expansion often occurred at the expense of Fulbe pastoralists, whose claims to the land seemed less compelling to the colonial authorities. Murid farmers cultivated less and less millet in favor of peanuts, at least until the colonial subsidies disappeared after independence. The decline in price did not encourage a return to food crops but rather a movement to the cities, and the pedagogy that Bamba created became critical to the identity that the urban Murid communities forged.

Expansion in Time, Space, and Art

Beginning in the years following World War II significant numbers of Murids began to migrate to the coastal cities of Senegal and to other parts of Africa. After independence the migration continued and extended to Paris, Turin, and other European centers. By the 1980s these currents reached New York and other cities of the United States. "Amadu Bamba Day" has been celebrated in New York since 1989, when it was first declared by Mayor David Dinkins and Congressman Charles Rangel.

Typically these Murids in Europe and North America started as street vendors. The communities were entirely male, and they shared rooms in hotels and rooming houses. They furnished their rooms in very rudimentary ways, but "created Murid space" by pictures of the founder, the mosque in Touba, and other marabouts. Over time they opened shops, invested in real estate, and brought their wives and children to live with them. On a regular basis they sent contributions back to Touba and "went home" to visit, joining perhaps a million of the faithful for the annual festival commemorating Bamba's return from exile.

A marabout of the Mbacke family who frequently travels to Italy to minister to the needs of Murids there captures the relations across the network. In an interview he had this to say:

> Economic difficulties are difficult for everyone, and I and my family are no exception. As a marabout, and since all of my work involves religious teaching, I have no contributions other than those from my disciples, many of whom were in Italy. Consequently I travel there to help them with their problems and receive their aid in return.... They often asked me to pray for them and help them obtain papers to prevent police intervention, as well as aid their families in Senegal. They had great respect for the social charter of the founder and for the rules laid down, and aided one another in all situations. They worked hard and saved their money. In exchange they hoped for the benediction of their marabouts and improvement in their material situations.

This testimony comes from a relatively minor figure in the order. The youngest of Bamba's sons, Shaikh Murtada, has also been visiting the Murid communities around the world on a regular basis, for several decades, reinforcing the ties and bringing substantial contributions back to eastern Bawol.

One key to the success of the order in sustaining its cohesion across time and space is the pedagogy developed in the early decades by Bamba. The founder contributed a vast corpus of poetry and prose, of instruction for reading and recitation. Much of this material took the form of homilies about the life of the Prophet and exegesis of passages from the Quran. Bamba also encouraged a division of labor and learning and a form of apprenticeship to prepare the next generation of leaders. He encouraged the development of cells of worship and solidarity that functioned in the new villages of Murid expansion and then in the urban environment. The structures have been reestablished time and time again; Murid space has been created and re-created in new settings.

Another important ingredient has been the ability to accept a variety of situations in which non-Muslims were controlling the levers of political and economic power. This ability began with the adaptation to French colonial rule, which was graphically forced on Bamba but which he came to accept, because of the opportunities which it could offer for islamization and the extension of the order. The support of the Allied cause during World War I, and again in World War II, are cases in point. This quality served the Murids well as they moved into the lowest echelons of the economic and social structures of Europe and North America in the late twentieth century.

In addition to the verbal commemoration and recitation of Bamba's writings and the use of photographs, the faithful in the cities of Senegal and across the world "created Murid space" in a variety of other ways. In Dakar, the capital of Senegal and home to hundreds of thousands of Murids, this includes pamphlets in comic book format, with illustrations, designed for instruction, healing, and a variety of needs. The writing is often in Arabic script but in the Wolof language, and many of the faithful can read or recite it – not unlike the *ajami* literature of Uthman's community in Chapter 10, the Swahili discussed in Chapter 3, or indeed the Quran itself. The visual art includes urban wall murals, devotional designs on canvas, and reverse-glass paintings (see Figure 24). These paintings are typically done on the backs of window or plate glass and then viewed from the other side. The viewing adds a mirrorlike impression that enhances the mystical or Sufi impact. Favorite images are reinventions of the Diourbel photograph of the founder, constructed in a variety of ways; the enormous mosque in Touba; and images produced out of the exile. The pamphlets and visual artifacts are now available throughout the far-flung network, reminding Murid faithful of their origins and spiritual home.

Further Reading

The major works in English on the Murids come from the pen of the British sociologist Donal Cruise O'Brien: *The Mourides of Senegal* (Oxford University Press, 1971) and a collection of essays, *Saints and Politicians* (Cambridge University Press, 1975). He has also edited a volume dealing with Sufi orders in West Africa in general, with Christian Coulon, entitled *Charisma and Brotherhood in African Islam* (Oxford, 1988). For a treatment of the evolution of Murid relations with the French colonial authorities, see my work *Paths of Accommodation: Muslim Societies and French Colonial Authorities in Senegal and Mauritania, 1880 to 1920* (Ohio University Press and James Currey, 2000), Chapter 11. Most of the quotations in the chapter come from *Paths*.

The most extensive work on Bamba and the founding of the order is a dissertation defended in 2002 at Michigan State University by Cheikh Anta Babou and entitled "Amadu Bamba and the Foundation of the Muridiyya: The History and Development of a Muslim Brotherhood in Senegal, 1853–1927." A recent effort to capture the early decades of Murid history is James Searing's *"God Alone Is King": Islam and Emancipation in Senegal. The Wolof Kingdoms of Kajoor and Bawol, 1859–1914* (Heinemann and James Currey, 2002).

For the extension of the order around the world, the most accessible accounts are by Victoria Ebin in Barbara Metcalf's *Making Muslim Space in North America and Europe* (University of California Press, 1996) and Donald Carter in *States of Grace: Senegalese in Italy and the New European Immigration* (University of Minnesota Press, 1997). See also Sylviane Diouf-Camara's "Senegalese in New York: A Model Minority?" in *Black Renaissance* (volume 1.2, 1997). For the community in New York, see Cheikh Anta Babou's "Brotherhood Solidarity, Education and Migration: The Role of the *Dahiras* among the Muslim Community of New York" in *African Affairs* (volume 101, April 2002). To put this networking in a larger context, see Robert Hefner's "Multiple Modernities: Christianity, Islam and Hinduism in a Globalizing Age" in *Annual Review of Anthropology* (volume 27, 1998).

The leading interpreters of Murid art are Allen F. Roberts and Mary Nooter Roberts; see their article, "'Painting Like Prayers': The Hidden Side of Senegalese Reverse-Glass 'Image/Texts'" in *Research in African Literatures* (Indiana) (volume 31, no. 4, 2000). For an online version of the exhibit that the Roberts put together, see www.aodl.org. A variation on Figure 24 can be found in this collection.

For the Tijaniyya, another order of African origins that has spread very widely and was mentioned in Chapter 4, see (editors) Jean-Louis Triaud and David Robinson's *La Tijaniyya: une confrérie islamique à la conquête de l'Afrique* (Karthala, 2000). It contains articles in English as well as French.

Conclusion

In this book I have examined a range of Muslim societies in African history, from large to small scale, over the long and short term, and in general and very specific ways. Throughout I have sought to show the variety and originality in Islamic practice in Africa. This does not mean that there are "Islams" in Africa in the plural any more than there are "Islams" or "Christianities" in the world. The common core of Islamic belief and practice remains. Millions of Muslims make the pilgrimage to Mecca to express this unity. Millions more in their homelands celebrate the "birthday" of the Prophet every year.

But there are certainly different Islamic religious cultures in Africa. Uthman dan Fodio, discussed in Chapter 10, would have been critical of the "fatal compromises" of the Suwarian tradition of Chapter 9. The Mahdi of the Sudan would have rejected them even more quickly. But they were working from an assumption that they lived in the *Dar al-Islam*, at least in areas that had been part of the *Dar al-Islam*. This sense of "Islamic country" might come from the affirmations of sultans that they were ruling in the name of the faith. It might come from speaking or learning Arabic, the language of the Quran and Muslim origins, or even from speaking Swahili, Hausa, or Fulfulde, languages with strong infusions of Arabic words – especially for religious practice. Uthman and the Mahdi were successful in building movements precisely because of the Islamic traditions, however corrupted, in their areas. It is hard to imagine that they would have succeeded, or perhaps even tried to reform practices in the forests of Asante, where the Suwarian tradition held sway, or that the Ganda Muslim party would have been able to impose its creed in the countryside, even without British intervention. The tradition of Islamic practice was simply not present.

This is a book about how Islam has "become indigenous" to Africa. In a superficial sense, that is absurd. Islam obviously began in the Arabian peninsula in the seventh century C.E. It is older there and where the Arab Muslims spread the new faith in the first centuries of its existence. Using those criteria only Morocco might qualify as "indigenously Muslim."

But this is to miss the point. Arabic-speaking Muslims constitute less than 20 percent of the Muslims in the world today and only half of those living on the African continent. Islam has taken root not only from the "far west" of Morocco to the "east" of Iran, and not only in the "core" languages of Arabic, Persian, and Turkish, but also in an amazing variety of cultures from Senegal to Indonesia and increasingly in Europe and North America. French is the language of Islam in France, just as English is in the United States. Practitioners of the faith have crossed boundaries of all kinds.

Although the Quran and the prayers of Muslims will always be principally in Arabic, the inspiration of Islam can be appreciated only by seeing how the Swahili, Hausa, and Fulbe people have incorporated and transformed Arabic vocabulary in their own languages. Or by how they have adapted the Arabic script to writing their own languages in a phenomenon we call *ajami* or "foreign writing." Or by how they have embraced the Abrahamic tradition and made it their own, as in the Swahili account of the ascension of Muhammad. "Becoming indigenous" in my lexicon means taking root, taking hold, being appropriated, being transformed without losing the tie to the origins of the faith.

Processes of Islamization, Arabization, and Africanization

I have used the terms *islamization* and *africanization* to refer to this phenomenon of taking hold. Islamization may include the process of conversion, individual or social. As discussed in Chapter 3, we might say that the Lamtuna as a "tribe" converted to Islam in the eleventh century or went from a very limited understanding of the faith to a much deeper and more radical one under the leadership of Ibn Yasin. In Chapter 11 we can sense the excitement of young pages in Buganda about becoming Muslim and the possibility of "converting" the country to Islam under the leadership of Kabaka Mutesa before the reality of royal power and court conflicts took hold. But it is difficult with the sources we have to get close to the individual or collective experiences of religious and social change. We are more likely to get the results of the change after they have happened and from the outside.

But islamization is much more than conversion. It is the process of creating a Muslim time and space, of going from the time of "ignorance" to the time of Islam, from the space of "unbelief" to the space of "belief." Theologically that might be communicated as changing from *Dar al-Kufr* to *Dar al-Islam* or expanding the *Dar al-Islam* to encompass the rest of the world, but this doesn't begin to capture the complexity of islamization. I prefer to think of "making Muslim space," to borrow from the title of the book edited by Barbara Metcalf, *Making Muslim Space in North America and Europe*. This is what Africans did and have been doing over the fourteen centuries of Islam: making Muslim space and then remaking it in successive generations.

The task was made easier by the "portability" of Islam, in the Quran, books of law, common obligations, and recognizable institutions such as the mosque, the court, and the school. But creating Muslim space required much more. It meant absorbing Arabic vocabulary; developing pedagogies in local languages for teaching Arabic, the Quran, and Islamic law; and creating concrete places for practice, such as the city of Mawlay Idriss in Morocco or Touba in Senegal, and concrete protections such as talismans. It meant creating specific times for practice and observance of such events as the birth date of the Prophet, the sacrifice that Ibrahim was ready to make of his son, or the exile of Amadu Bamba. It meant creating literacies, pedagogies, and patterns for transmitting the faith down the generations, for both laity and clergy, women and men, and the lower as well as the upper ranks of society.

Then, of course, subsequent generations of Muslims might recreate Islamic space and time. This was the conclusion that Uthman dan Fodio came to. For more than a decade he preached reform to the sultans and clerics of Gobir, not unlike the call to justice that Lyusi made to Mawlay Ismail, as discussed in Chapter 7. Gradually Uthman adopted a more militant position, in cadence with the growing community around him. In 1804 the momentum shifted decisively to revolution, and that required a new *hijra*, *jihad*, and capital. In all of this change Uthman imitated the pattern of Muhammad in the seventh century C.E. The resemblance was real. Both men faced growing opposition, growing danger, and in some sense were driven to take up the sword. The Mahdi and Khalifa pursued a similar path in the Sudan. Bamba sought to create new Muslim space in a different, more interior way, in the changed circumstances of French colonial Senegal.

Islamization is very different from arabization. The two processes could go together, as they did gradually up the Nile into the Sudan, or abruptly across North Africa in the first century A.H. But arabization got its big boost when the Banu Hilal, Banu Sulaim, and Banu Maqil (see Chapter 7) moved across North Africa and the Sahara beginning in the eleventh century. These Bedouin did a lot for the language but little for spreading the faith. As Ibn Khaldun portrayed them, they were the "desert" opposed to the "sown," and sometimes they destroyed the fabric of Islamic civilization that had been built in the cities and agricultural plains. In another twist it was the descendants of the Bedouins, the Saadians and Alawites of Morocco, who realized the importance of capturing, using, and transmitting that civilization as part of their heritage for posterity.

I have been more interested in the pioneers of islamization than the practitioners of arabization. But there is an Arabic core that is involved in all islamization. God spoke to Muhammad in Arabic through the agency of Jibril. The early Muslims, under the leadership of Caliph Uthman, put these verses together in Suras or chapters. This became the canon, the Quran, designed for recitation, and it has been recited for hundreds of millions of children and adults down the ages. The prayers were spoken in Arabic. Not as many Muslims were able to fulfill the obligation of pilgrimage to the Arabic-speaking Holy Cities, but those that did were marked for life. In various ways Muslims in Africa and the world over acknowledged the precedence of Arabic in the practice of the faith, over Turkish, Persian, Urdu, Swahili, and all of the other "Muslim tongues" of the earth.

Lamin Sanneh, a professor of religion at Yale University, has elaborated on this theme in a challenging work, *Translating the Message: The Missionary Impact on Culture*. He suggests, not incorrectly, that Christianity has been more open to translation than Islam. Whether from Aramaic, Hebrew, Greek, or Latin, Christians have put their scripture and rituals into the "vernaculars" that people spoke and were learning to write. Christians can practice and learn from an English Bible or a Russian or Amharic or indeed an Arabic one and have a full sense of understanding and participating in their faith.

But Muslims have also translated their message. They have taken Arabic vocabulary into their languages and transformed the words according to local linguistic patterns. They have developed pedagogies and literatures for teaching the Quran and Arabic in Swahili, Tamasheq, and Hausa and even theological rationales, such as the Suwarian one described in Chapter 4, for understanding the practice of Islam in "pagan" lands. This rationale drew on writings in Arabic, but it was transmitted from generation to generation orally, in Juula. The amulets I have mentioned contained verses from the Quran, but they were enveloped in leather; worn around the neck, waist, or arm; and then understood as a protection for the person. The robes worn by the Asante or Senegalese kings displayed Arabic writing or were studded with talismans; they were objects of power. At this point we mix the processes of islamization and africanization or – to put it another way – the processes of making the faith universal and local at the same time. This is, after all, the essence of a faith that spreads and endures. It is expressed locally, concretely, and it unites the believer to many other people across the face of the earth.

Making Muslim Space

But let us return to the metaphor of creating Muslim space and how ancient and specific this is on the African continent. Idriss the First brought it in his person to Morocco in the late eighth century, through his descent from the Prophet. His successors on the "Sharifian throne" expanded this space as they developed their own genealogies and made his tomb into the fourth holy site of Islam – from their point of view, of course. They came to define their *Dar al-Islam* in very geographical terms in the northwestern corner of the continent. This was especially true along the coast, where they had to defend Morocco against Portuguese and Spanish Christians determined to extend the reconquest of Iberia. Challenge created response and very specific boundaries. The Sokoto Caliphate gave a strong geographical meaning to Muslim space and kept it alive in the annual *jihads* waged on the northern "frontier." The Mahdi and the Khalifa had a sense of what constituted the *Dar al-Islam* in the Sudan, and they moved quickly to take control of it. The "Solomonic" monarchs of Ethiopia in the late nineteenth century had an equal conviction about what constituted "Christian" territory. The struggles of the Khalifa and Yohannes in the late 1880s were about defending the borders of those competing conceptions of space.

There were other ways to define Muslim space. The emigrants from Mecca in 615–6 created a refuge before the *hijra* of 622, and they did this inside of Christian Aksum, where the emperor gave them reception and protection. This tradition, taken from the Hadith, has survived to this day in the expression, "leave the Abyssinians alone"; at times it has encouraged tolerance and respect between Ethiopian Muslims and Christians. The Mahdists had to overcome this memory when they resisted the encroachments of Emperor Yohannes into the *Dar al-Islam* of the Sudan.

Far away in West Africa the Muslims of Kumasi created space in their neighborhoods, schools, and mosques in the interests of sustaining Islam in the midst of what was obviously a *Dar al-Kufr*. Abu Bakr carried his Muslim identity with him to Jamaica, as surely as Idriss brought his from the Middle East to Morocco; somehow he managed to keep it alive across several decades in a hostile environment. Amadu Bamba created an "interior" Islamic space for himself, in the Sufi tradition, and it enabled him to survive the exile to central Africa and return with enhanced credentials of Muslim leadership. Ahmed Baba survived his exile to Morocco, as discussed in Chapter 5. Unlike Abu Bakr, he was an adult and an established scholar; his hosts could not keep such a prestigious figure in slavery. Indeed, Baba helped to reinforce the bases of the Transsaharan slave trade by articulating the "ethnicities" that were Muslim – and those that were not.

In Hausaland before Uthman's reform Muslims worked in a different way. They institutionalized the status of *dhimmi*, "protected community," for non-Muslim groups who adhered to Bori traditions; these Maguzawa or "Magians" were not literate in any language, but by analogy with the "People of the Book" they were drawn under the umbrella of Islam and given protection from war and enslavement. In various ways African Muslims, and Muslims the world over, have imaginatively and pragmatically redrawn the boundaries between the world of unbelief and the world of Islam, between the time of "ignorance" and the time of Islam. The boundaries are always there, between alcohol and abstinence, scarification and veil, or Bori and Islamic medicine, but talismans, miracles, dances, libations, and lived experience blur the lines.

Colonial rule created new challenges. Amadu Bamba and the Murids set about creating new Muslim space and "visual culture" in secular Senegal: a home, a place of meditation, a mosque, a photograph, a painting of a miracle – all could serve the purposes of worship and practice. For the Murids as for the Suwarians it did not matter that the ruling authorities were not Muslim. Nor was it important whether the majority was Muslim. No polls were taken, no votes counted. Local communities created, transformed, and transmitted cultures in their own space and time.

What is still very difficult to discern in the sources is the situation of Muslim women in African history. How did they go about creating "female space" amid strongly patriarchal societies? How did the models of Khadija, Fatima, and Aisha, as well as the efforts of the Prophet to improve the situation of women, inspire generations of Africans? We are beginning to learn about situations in the twentieth century through research into figures such as Mame Diarra Bousso, the mother of Bamba. But we have little to illuminate earlier periods beyond stereotypes about harems of women who remain faceless and nameless.

Nana Asmau is an exception to this generalization. She emerges because of her lineage, education, and calling to write and teach. She has been an inspiration to women, and men, for almost 200 years. She created female space within a self-consciously Islamic and patriarchal society by developing a pedagogical vocation alongside the expected roles of wife and mother. She did not challenge the fundamental hierarchies of Sokoto, but she did encourage the education, intelligent practice, and well-being of women and the lower ranks of the social hierarchy.

Crossing Boundaries and Stages

Another way of thinking about islamization is crossing boundaries and breaking frontiers. We might say that the initial boundaries were "ethnic," between Arabs and Berbers or Arabs and Swahili, to adopt the formulas I used in Chapter 3. But even though these ethnic identities have a reality, they are not partitions or compartments. Very early in the history of Islam non-Arabs began to make the pilgrimage, learn the Quran, and teach the Islamic sciences. Ibn Yasin was a Berber who became an Arab and then a missionary to the Lamtuna Berbers. He felt the same conviction about applying the Prophetic model in the western extremities of the Sahara as did Uthman in Hausaland or the Mahdi in the Sudan. The same examples are found with Ahmad ibn Ibrahim and other Swahili missionaries who sought to convert Mutesa and "capture" the kingdom of Buganda, and Ahmad Gran and Shaikh Muhammad Shafi in Ethiopia.

But to stress missionary and reform movements as the main way to cross boundaries is to impoverish the story. We should appreciate the gradual appropriation and assimilation of Islam into Swahili culture, vocabulary, architecture, and folklore. This is islamization too, a slower process, perhaps one less recognizable as "Muslim" by an Ibn Battuta. But we must remember the ethnocentricity of our otherwise invaluable observer. The Moroccan traveler liked neither the nudity that he saw in the Empire of Mali nor the "breaches of orthodoxy" along the Indian Ocean. But he is not the only authority about what is or is not Islam. Indeed a strong case could be made to listen primarily to the voices of the Swahili theologians and poets over the centuries about what Islam means in East Africa.

So the boundaries between what is Muslim and what is not remain, but they are better understood in particular contexts and relations and not by orientalists, professors in Al-Azhar, or Islamists. We could choose a person from Kilwa island, for example, over against someone from the East African interior. A person from Zanzibar, vis-à-vis a practitioner of "Lubare religion" in Buganda; the Mahdi in relation to an apologist for the Turko-Egyptian regime; Amadu Bamba in conjunction with a court cleric from Kajoor; and Ahmad Baba and Abu Bakr, with their decidedly different experiences of slave trade and slavery. These advocates for particular kinds of practice reveal the drama of religious and social competition.

The most dramatic instance of crossing boundaries was discussed in Chapter 9 in the story of Baba, the Muslim leader in Kumasi, as he was mobilized to accompany Osei Bonsu's campaign of retribution against Gyaman in 1817. The king did not need Baba's military prowess, which was nonexistent at his advanced age. He wanted his religious authority, as the head of the Islamic community, a man of learning and prayer. That mobilization created an intolerable burden for Baba. He was raised to live in a Muslim minority and serve a pagan king, but not to kill or be associated with the killing of his "fellow" Muslims. With "his character as well as his life" at stake, he deserted. The king, once vengeance was exacted from those who made the Golden Stool and a more normal routine resumed in Kumasi, recognized the dilemma and decided that it was more important to retain Baba's "holiness" than to get rid of him. The "Muslim space" of Kumasi was challenged but then restored. Presumably both king and Baba learned important lessons about the boundaries of faith and practice, and different faiths and practices, in the process.

The Suwarian tradition of integration and cooperation could be challenged, and was challenged, by West African reformers. Some of them emerged in Kong, the center of many of the "plots" on the northwest frontiers of Asante. It was reformers who helped mobilize the "Kong coalition" that threatened Kumasi around 1800 and resulted in the capture and deportation of Abu Bakr to Jamaica. It was Kong that mounted a second coalition fifteen years later, persuading Gyaman to fabricate a second Golden Stool. Kumasi responded by an even greater mobilization and victory. In the process the Asantehene put Baba's "character and life . . . at stake," and Asante identity as well. In both instances Kong failed to shake Asante's links to "fetish" statecraft and religion.

The confinement of Swahili Islam to the coast could also be challenged, as it was under the impulse of Omani and Zanzibar ambition, in the larger context of European expansion. "Arab" missionaries created a strong following among Ganda Muslims. Together they dominated Buganda for much of Mutesa's reign and were the largest "party" in the capital for several decades. "English" Protestants and "French" Catholics gave them serious competition, but let us not forget the Buganda contribution to the competition – a highly centralized capital, ambitious generations of pages, a king freer than most to innovate in religious practice, and Lubare practitioners throughout the realm. Buganda changed dramatically in the late nineteenth century. It did not become "Islamic country," and in some respects it finally became "Christian country" – but not without outside help and not down to its roots.

All of these sequences, rendered in as much detail as the sources permit, are more real than the formula presented in Chapter 3 of minority, court, and majority Islam. That scheme can still be useful in some respects, if it is applied with nuance and discretion. It may, for example, help us to appreciate the situation of the Juula of Chapters 4 and 9, who remain in the "minority position" for centuries and develop a rationale for its long duration. It certainly helps us understand the Islamic "preconditioning" that Uthman dan Fodio built upon, as well as the intensity of his anger at the old Hausa regimes. The absence of an earlier Islamic presence in Buganda helps explain the difficulties encountered by the fervent Readers of the capital in the late nineteenth century. The presence of an earlier *Dar al-Islam* allows us to comprehend the charges of "apostasy" that the Mahdi directed against the "Turks," those who once had led the Islamic world through the Ottoman Empire.

But the formula is not helpful for understanding the colonial period, when African Muslims lived under secular European regimes, regimes they often called Christian. Bamba, by his ability to create new Muslim space and pedagogy in Senegal, helped to speed an unusually wide and deep process of islamization, when the faith became really dominant for the majority. And a "majority" stage, in the form of the success of the Sokoto revolution, doesn't begin to capture the difficulty of Nana Asmau's task – to fashion a new Islamic space among the women, children, and slaves. Asmau pushed radical islamization to the limit in the villages of Hausaland. We might say that ultimately she failed, but in the same way that creating a complete Muslim community anywhere in the world – including Mecca – eludes human capacity.

Imperialism and Resistance

Islam and Islamic religious cultures became the vehicles of resistance to imperialism. The imperialism itself could be quite complex. In the case of the Sudan, it was Ottoman, Turkish, and Egyptian, as well as European. In the case of Morocco, it was Ottoman as well as Portuguese, Spanish, and finally French. Ethiopia successfully resisted imperialism the first time around. But Middle Eastern intellectuals like Shakib Arslan could point to the atrocities perpetrated against Muslims by the imperial Ethiopian state and make the dramatic comparison to the "Christian" reconquest of Andalusia. The numerous references to Turks in this volume attest to the enduring influence of the Ottoman Empire as well as the persistence of stereotypes about it.

It is nonetheless overwhelmingly true that the principal imperialism over Islamic and African lands has been European. A "coastal" imperialism in the past 500 years, a "cultural" imperialism in the past 200 years, and a "landed" imperialism in the past 100, resulting in the geographical boundaries and basic institutions which affect the lives of most African Muslims today. The "coastal" was marked by Crusader-like attacks on Moroccan and Swahili installations and an arrogant attempt to convert and control the Abyssinian Christians. Then it took on the mantle of the Atlantic slave trade that took millions of Africans, including some Muslims like Abu Bakr, to the Americas.

The Ottoman Empire limited European encroachment in some areas and exerted an imperial dominion of its own in northern Africa.
Its decline was obvious in Napoleon's invasion in 1798. This intrusion, with the effort to appropriate the heritage of Ancient and Islamic Egypt, is the conventional marker for the beginning of "cultural"
domination. Europeans were persuaded of their superiority and urged
strategies of modernization on the now "backward" lands of Islam and
Africa. They applied the old stereotype of Ham, invented Hamitic languages and lineages, and sought to distinguish the "blue-eyed" Berbers
from the "swarthy" Arabs of Morocco. At the same time they were curious about the Other and others around the world they were taking
over. Thus they created Orientalism and Africanism, two overlapping
frameworks in which much of the knowledge of African societies is
contained. Cultural domination reinforced the control of coasts and
seas in increasingly strong doses over the nineteenth century.

The "landed" imperialism starts with the scramble for Africa in the
late nineteenth century, the sequence that we can see behind the people and events in Buganda, the Sudan, and Senegal. The irony of the
years since 1900, of the period of European colonialism and "postcolo-
nialism," is how widely Islam has spread during that time. Sufi orders
continued to be important vehicles under colonial rule and demonstrated that islamization did not depend on *jihad* or an Islamic state.
The *hijra*, interpreted to mean getting away from European or infidel
rule, was heroic, as in the case of those who fled the British conquest of
the Sokoto Caliphate and settled in the Sudan. But it wasn't practical
for most people. Nor was it successful, because European influence
was everywhere, even in Mecca and Medina. Nor was it necessary:
Islam could survive and flourish, as it always has, in many conditions.

Indeed, I would argue along with some Sufis that islamization might
go further, in terms of numbers of practitioners and quality of practice,
if the government were not in Muslim hands. Leaders such as Amadu
Bamba of Senegal and Shaikh Muhammad Shafi of Ethiopia knew that
power corrupts. They recognized that the conditions recommended for
waging *jihad* did not exist and that the results of militant *jihad* could
be catastrophic. Relieved of the burden of ruling, Sufi leaders could
concentrate more effectively on improving faith and practice and the
conditions of the people they served. Muslim space did not require
Muslim rule.

World War I produced some accommodation between imperial powers and Muslim subjects. The Pan-Islamic campaigns, the

Ottoman alliance with the Central Powers and its call for *jihad* against European rule, aroused the anxiety of France, Britain, and Russia. Bamba and other marabouts were ready to endorse the French cause and send their followers to the battle front. The British overcame their enmity toward the family of the Mahdi in order to forge a new alliance against the Turks. Mussolini then used the frustrations of Muslims in the Horn of Africa to sustain his brief regime in Ethiopia. Like Napoleon, he was the "friend" of Islam. But all of the imperial powers sought to contain and quarantine their subjects, as Senegalese, Sudanese, or Ethiopian, rather than members of the universal Muslim community.

Sufi accommodation, secular regimes, and colonial containment have been intensively challenged by radical Muslim thinkers and doers, inside and outside the continent. We can call them Islamists, those who see Islam as a comprehensive way of life and wish to establish – or reestablish – the Sharia as the law of the land. The early radicals challenged Sufism, or at least the Sufi orders that seemed to wander most from Sunni orthodoxy. They had considerable influence on rulers such as Mawlay Sulaiman of Morocco. Their successors protested against imperialism, colonialism, and the quarantines of Muslims and searched for alternative ways to be "modern," to appropriate the heritage of the West.

More recently the challenge has moved further, against the ruling classes who took over when colonial authorities left, as well as the West, in the form of its leader, the United States, and its ostensible lackey, Israel. This strand of Islamism recasts again the boundaries of Islamic space and time: the Jahiliyya may be everywhere, and any means justified to express the rage and commitment of the new righteous community. The events of September 11, 2001, have demonstrated the culmination of one strand of this radical interpretation. Osama bin Laden and the al-Qaida network have targeted not only America and Israel, Christians and Jews, but also the ruling elites of Saudi Arabia – custodians of the Holy Cities who portray themselves as the paragons and interpreters of Islamic orthodoxy. The events have also energized those who would demonize Islam in the terms of the old Western tradition discussed in Chapter 6.

The Islamist construction of Islam is an African as well as a Middle Eastern or South Asian phenomenon. Like all of the interpretations discussed in this book, it builds its case around Muhammad and the early struggles in Islam. It claims to be interpretation, *ijtihad*, not innovation, *bida*, in the vocabulary introduced in Chapter 2. It selects certain events, certain passages from the Quran and Hadith, certain commentaries. The reconstruction is intensely believed, but never entirely new.

As a process it is reminiscent of how Uthman dan Fodio patterned his life around the Prophet's or how the Mahdi called his followers the Ansar. Bamba used a tradition associated with Muhammad after the battle of Badr to make his case for the "greater" internal *jihad*. Others, such as the Swahili with their stories taken from the Biblical tradition or the Mali rulers with their descent from Bilal, tied themselves in more nuanced, less assertive ways to the Islamic tradition. African Muslim societies will survive Islamism and transform their complex heritage again and again, without losing the originality of their contributions to the faith.

Further Reading

I have borrowed the term *Islamic religious cultures* from Louis Brenner, Professor of Religion and History at the School of Oriental and African Studies, University of London, in his 1999 inaugural lecture, "Histories of Religion in Africa," published in 2000 by SOAS. Brenner also has a very useful book describing the "alternative modernity" that some dedicated Muslims have tried to introduce into today's Mali: *Controlling Knowledge: Religion, Power and Schooling in a West African Muslim Society* (Hurst, 2000). An earlier volume that he edited is also very useful: *Muslim Identity and Social Change in Sub-Saharan Africa* (Indiana University Press, 1993). The Metcalf book was published by California Press in 1996.

For Islamism in Africa and more contemporary themes that I have not emphasized, see David Westerlund and Eva Evers Rosander's (editors) *African Islam and Islam in Africa: Encounters between Sufis and Islamists* (Ohio University Press, 1997), as well as the Levtzion and Pouwels volume mentioned throughout this work.

The full reference to Sanneh's work is *Translating the Message: The Missionary Impact on Culture* (Orbis Books, 1989). For discussions of conversion, including processes of islamization, consult a discussion engaged by Robin Horton and Allen Fisher: Horton's "African Conversion" in *Africa* (1971), Fisher's "Conversion Reconsidered: Some Historical Aspects of Religious Conversion in Black Africa" in *Africa* (1973), and Horton's rejoinder, "On the Rationality of Conversion, I and II" in *Africa* (1975). For Web images sympathetic to al-Qaida, see www.azzam.com. For a site that demonizes Islam, see www.islamexposed.com.

Glossary

ajami: "Non-Arab," the writing of a non-Arabic language in the Arabic script; in Africa, Swahili, Hausa, Fulfulde, and many other languages were written in ajami.

Ansar: "The helpers," applied to the people of Medina who supported Muhammad after the hijra of 622 C.E.; also used for the Mahdi's supporters and other core Muslim groups.

Asantehene: The ruler of the Asante Empire.

baraka: Blessing or charisma.

bida: "Innovation" in Arabic, condemned by Muslim theologians and lawyers.

bori: A set of customary practices among the Hausa, labeled as "pagan" by Uthman dan Fodio.

caliph: "Successor," title applied to the successors of the Prophet and later regimes; sometimes applied to successors to the founders of Sufi orders.

Dar al-Harb: "The world of war," the areas and peoples which Muslims are supposed to combat.

Dar al-Hiyad: "The world of neutrality," sometimes applied to Abyssinia.

Dar al-Islam: "The world of Islam," the areas and peoples occupied by Muslims.

Dar al-Kufr: "The world of unbelief," a synonym of the Dar al-Harb.

Dar al-Sulh: "The world of truce," between the Dar al-Islam and the Dar al-Kufr.

dhimmi: "Protected," referring to the "People of the Book" (typically Jews, Christians, and Zoroastrians) who are allowed to continue practicing their faiths in the Dar al-Islam.

emir: "Commander," ruler.

fetish: Material object associated with magic, from a Portuguese word, and used to refer to "pagan" religion.

fitna: "Discord," civil war.

Gezira: "Island" or *jazira* in Arabic; used for the land between the White and Blue Niles.

Hadith: Traditions about the Prophet collected over the early centuries of Islam.

hajj: The pilgrimage to Mecca performed in the twelfth month of the Muslim calendar; one of the five pillars of Islam.

hijra: "Emigration," ascribed to the movement of Muhammad from Mecca to Medina in 622, and marking the year 1 in the Muslim calendar (A.H.).

ijtihad: "Interpretation," acceptable to Muslims in ways that bida is not.

imam: "In front of," the person who leads in prayer at the mosque.

Islam: "Submission," understood as submission to God and the root meaning of the faith; can refer to the time of faith (as opposed to Jahiliyya) or the world of faith (as in Dar al-Islam).

Islamicists: Word applied to those who specialize in the study of Islam.

Islamists: Word usually applied to those who, since the 1950s, have called for the restoration of the Sharia and Islam as the basic framework for society.

jabarti: Name often applied to Ethiopian Muslims.

Jahiliyya: "Ignorance," the state in which the world was before the revelation of Islam.

jihad: "Effort," often described as the effort of the heart, hand, tongue, and sword; today often treated as synonymous with the jihad of the sword.

kafir: "Unbeliever."

khalifa: "Successor" to Muhammad or to a subsequent "founder" of an Islamic regime; applied to Uthman's and the Mahdi's successors; also used in "French" form of khalife or "khalife général" in Senegal; see also caliph.

kharaj: A land tax.

Kharijites: "The seceders," those who believed the caliph should be chosen on the basis of merit, not descent or power.

Lubare: The "traditional" gods of Buganda, embedded in the clan structure.

madrasa: A school at a level beyond instruction in the Quran.

Maguzawa: "Magians" or Zoroastrians; a term applied to non-Muslim Hausa.

makhzen: "Storehouse," by extension the government, usually applied in Morocco.

mallam: Hausa word for Islamic cleric, derived from the Arabic *mu'allim*, "teacher."

marabout: Cleric, derived from al-murabit or Almoravid.

Mawlay: "Master," usually applied to the rulers of Morocco.

Monophysite: "One nature" of Christ, the doctrinal position of several eastern churches, including the Ethiopian Orthodox Church.

muezzin: "One who calls to prayer" at the mosque (*mu'adhdhin*).

mujahidun: "Those who wage the jihad."

murid: "Novice," used as name for the Sufi order (Muridiyya) founded by Amadu Bamba.

qadi: "Judge" trained in the law.

Qadiriyya: One of the older Sufi movements, named after Abd al-Qadir al-Jilani (twelfth century).

Ramadan: The ninth month of the Muslim calendar, devoted to the fast, one of the five pillars of Islam.

sahil: "Coast," by extension used for dry savanna borders of the desert.

salam: "Peace," and a shorthand for the most typical Muslim greeting, *salam alaykum*, "peace be upon you."

salat: Prayer, one of the five pillars of Islam, performed at five intervals during the day.

Sammaniyya: A Sufi movement in the Sudan to which Muhammad Ahmad, the Mahdi, belonged.

sarki: Hausa word for ruler.

Sharia: The divinely ordained law of Islam, developed in the early centuries of the faith.

Sharif: "Noble," usually with the meaning of descent from the Prophet by Fatima and Ali.

Shia: "Followers," those who believe that descendants of Muhammad by Fatima and Ali should serve as caliph (or imam) and lead the Muslim community.

siba: "Dissidence," referring to areas not under government control, particularly in Morocco.

Sufism: Islamic mysticism, emphasizing the internal dimensions of the faith.

sultan: "Authority," a ruler in a Muslim state with a more secular connotation than caliph.

Sunni: "The way," referring to the "mainstream" or majority of Muslims, often equated erroneously with "orthodoxy."

tamasheq: The Berber language spoken by the Tuareg.

tifinagh: The script used for the Tamasheq language.

Tijaniyya: One of the newer Sufi movements, named after Ahmad al-Tijani (eighteenth century).

Touba: The Murid capital built by Bamba, from the Arabic *tuba*, "conversion."

umma: "Community," used to refer to the whole Islamic community.

zakat: Alms-giving, one of the five pillars of Islam.

zawiya: "Lodge" or headquarters, usually of a Sufi order.

Index

Abbasid, 8, 9
Abd al-Qadir al-Jilani, 19, 20, see also
    Qadiriyya Sufi order
Abdullah dan Fodio, 143
Abdullahi, the Khalifa of the Sudan, 171,
    176, 179, 180
Abraham (Ibrahim), Abrahamic tradition,
    xv, 9, 12, 35, 44, 143
Abu Bakr, Abubacar, 7
    Abu Bakr, the juula and slave, 61–63,
        129, 134, 202
Abu Talib, 5
Abyssinia, 5, 54, 108–109, see also Ethiopia
    "leave the Abyssinians alone," 112, 177,
        202
Adam, 35
Adwa, 108, 121
aesthetic and aesthetics, 125
Africa, Africans, Sub-Saharan Africa, xvii,
    xviii
    conquest and rule of, 84–85, 207
    stereotypes of, 42, 54, 69, 76–77,
        207
    the study of Africa, 87, 207
africanization of Islam, 27, 32, 42–58, 198,
    201
Ahmad Baba, 67–68, 96, 202
Ahmad Gran, 114–115
Aisha, 6, 7, 21
Akan, 55, 124
Aksum, 5, 109, 110, 111, 114
al-Azhar, 17, 113, 179, 204
Al-Kanemi of Bornu, 146, 147
al-Maghili, 66–67, 139, 141

Alawite dynasty of Morocco, 97–105
alcohol, 130
Algeria, 20, 187
    French imperialism in, 102
Ali, 7, 21, 49, 50
Almoravids, 39, 93, 139
alms, alms-giving, 15
Amadu Bamba Mbacke, 182, 185–195,
    202, 206, see also Murids
    arrest and deportation, 187, 189–190
    creating Murid space, 192, see also
        Muslim space
    images of, 183, 188, 190
    public statements of, 190–191
amulets, 45, 52, 53, 56, 57, 132, 149, 201
analogy, 14
Andalusia, Andalusian, xvi, 91, 92, 93, 121,
    206, see also Spain
ansar, 6, 7, 174, 180
Arab, Arabs, 32, 51, 94, 130
Arabic, Arabic language, Arabic script, 5, 9,
    27, 45, 53, 61, 87, 125, 128, 198, see
    also literature
    Moroccan form, 95
arabization, 8–9, 27, 40, 93–95, 142,
    200
architecture, 33, see also mosque, visual art
    and culture
artisan production, 125, 140
Asante, 45, 52, 57, 62, 124–127, 137, 156
    Muslim community in, 124, 133,
        134–135, 137, 202
Askia Muhammad, 66
Ayatollah Khomeini, 8

215

Made in the USA
San Bernardino, CA
25 January 2014